The Tiger Leading
the Dragon

The Tiger Leading the Dragon

How Taiwan Propelled China's Economic Rise

SHELLEY RIGGER

ROWMAN & LITTLEFIELD
Lanham • Boulder • New York • London

Published by Rowman & Littlefield
An imprint of The Rowman & Littlefield Publishing Group, Inc.
4501 Forbes Boulevard, Suite 200, Lanham, Maryland 20706
www.rowman.com

6 Tinworth Street, London SE11 5AL, United Kingdom

British Library Cataloguing in Publication Information Available

Library of Congress Cataloging-in-Publication Data

Names: Rigger, Shelley, 1962– author.
Title: The tiger leading the dragon : how Taiwan propelled China's economic rise /
 Shelley Rigger.
Description: Lanham : Rowman & Littlefield, [2021] | Includes bibliographical references
 and index.
Identifiers: LCCN 2021005855 (print) | LCCN 2021005856 (ebook) | ISBN
 9781442219588 (cloth) | ISBN 9781442219595 (paperback) | ISBN 9781442219601
 (epub)
Subjects: LCSH: Taiwan—Foreign economic relations—China. | China—Foreign
 economic relations—Taiwan. | China—Commerce—Taiwan. | Taiwan—
 Commerce—China. | Taiwan—Economic conditions—1975- | China—Economic
 conditions—1949-
Classification: LCC HF1606.Z4 C6825 2021 (print) | LCC HF1606.Z4 (ebook) | DDC
 337.51249051—dc23
LC record available at https://lccn.loc.gov/2021005855
LC ebook record available at https://lccn.loc.gov/2021005856

♾™ The paper used in this publication meets the minimum requirements of
American National Standard for Information Sciences—Permanence of Paper
for Printed Library Materials, ANSI/NISO Z39.48-1992.

This book is dedicated to the memory of

Kelly Ann Chaston-Ameri, 1961–2010
Nancy Bernkopf Tucker, 1948–2012
Alan M. Wachman, 1958–2012
and
Rebecca R. Rigger, 1927–2013

Contents

Preface

The Umbrella King

You probably know that your iPhone, notebook computer, and running shoes were most likely manufactured by companies headquartered in Taiwan. If you follow international business news, you may even have heard of the companies that make those products, companies like Foxconn, Quanta, and Yue Yuen. But unless you've spent your life in the desert, you've almost certainly owned a product made by a company you've almost certainly never heard of: the Fu Tai Umbrella Group. Fu Tai doesn't have the name recognition or glamor of a high-tech company, but the humble umbrella is something almost everyone needs, and Fu Tai makes *a lot* of umbrellas—more than any other company in the world.

Fu Tai founder Chen Tian-fu was born on a farm in 1926 when Taiwan was part of the Japanese empire. The story of his life is both extraordinary and ordinary. His achievements are exceptional, but at the same time, his personal trajectory mirrors the path his country took over decades. Telling his story allows us to trace the narrative of Taiwan's economic development from agriculture to industry, from export manufacturing to overseas investment, mostly in mainland China. Chen grew his business by grasping opportunities made possible by a succession of state policies and market trends, so his story also tells us much about Taiwan's policy makers as well as the global economy in which it developed.

Chen began his business career just after World War II, as the export manager for a fruit company. The business was simple: Taiwanese farmers grew bananas and pineapples for consumers in Japan. The hardest part of the industry was canning the pineapples and making sure the bananas got where they were going before they rotted. But it was a golden age for Taiwan's fruit growers; the island was known, in the 1950s, as the Banana Kingdom. There was even a Banana King, a businessman named Chen Cha-mou. Taiwan's government encouraged the trade. Agriculture was Taiwan's comparative advantage, and exports brought in much-needed foreign exchange.

Even as a young man, however, Chen Tian-fu believed in two maxims: "Stay a step ahead" and "Make long-term money, not opportunity money." According to a profile in Taiwan's *Business Weekly* magazine, Chen saw that the banana market would soon be saturated, and by 1951 he was already looking for a line of business that would lift him out of the hypercompetitive, low-margin Banana Kingdom.

In 1953, Chen took his savings of 1,300 US dollars and opened a shop in Taipei to make umbrellas. At first he traded bananas for umbrella frames manufactured in Japan, which was at that time a leading umbrella exporter. In 1953, Chen and nine employees labored together to assemble Japanese-made frames and fabric into six thousand umbrellas per month. In the *Business Weekly* profile, Chen reminisced about being teased by the Banana King: "Everybody's making money selling bananas so they can spend it to buy umbrellas. Now you want to go start an umbrella factory?"

Moving into manufacturing in the early 1950s was risky. Taiwan's government closely managed Taiwan's industrial transition, imposing a high tariff on imported components like the umbrella frames Chen needed. But Chen recognized that all that banana selling (and rice selling and sugar selling) was creating a demand for consumer goods, so rather than waiting for the market to mature, he decided to stay a step ahead. Nylon and steel umbrellas were a big improvement over the paper umbrellas Taiwanese had been carrying for centuries. Paper umbrellas are lovely, but their bamboo-and-string workings and oiled-paper canopies make them expensive, heavy, and not terribly reliable in a downpour. Given Taiwan's tropical climate—it rains more than a hundred eighty days each year in Taipei—reliable, affordable, lightweight nylon umbrellas were a welcome innovation.

Fu Tai's early history is a classic import substitution story. Abundant cheap labor—including Chen's own—compensated for the company's low level of technology and investment capital. With only the most rudimentary technology and imported components, Chen managed to make mass-produced umbrellas available to Taiwanese consumers at a price they could afford—and that allowed him to accumulate capital to reinvest in his business.

And reinvest he did. Within a few years he was fabricating his own components from imported unprocessed steel, which raised his company's value-added and technology levels and also won him a lower tariff rate because he was no longer importing industrial components. Over time, Fu Tai moved from simple assembly to tackle far more diverse and complex manufacturing processes, including steel fabrication and galvanizing, plastic molding for handles, nylon fabric printing, and design.

As Chen's theory of business would predict, it didn't take long for others to see the potential in umbrella manufacturing, and new suppliers soon entered the market. As the government began supporting manufacturing, first for domestic consumption, then later for export, small shops sprouted up across the island. At the height of Taiwan's export-manufacturing boom, Chen Tian-fu recalls, the slogan on everyone's lips was "Turn living rooms into factories." Farmers used the slow season to become the downstream base of operations for manufacturing all manner of consumer goods, including umbrellas.

With Taiwan's transformation from Banana Kingdom to Umbrella Kingdom (and toy kingdom, flip-flop kingdom, plastic doodad kingdom, etc.), Chen Tian-fu's investments paid off. Fu Tai's operation blossomed into a complex of factories clustered in the Taipei suburb of Wuku that transformed raw materials into more than three million completed umbrellas each year— while also producing frames for another six and half million units, which Fu Tai sold to other assembly operations in Taiwan and abroad. Fu Tai maintained its lead in the industry because it was established and had an advantage in technology. By becoming a supplier of parts to the smaller outfits, *Business Weekly* observed, Chen turned competitors into customers.

At its peak, Taiwan's umbrella industry dominated the world market. More than three hundred factories operated by eighty different firms supplied two-thirds of the umbrellas imported by the US and Western Europe. By the mid-1970s, few mass-market suppliers remained outside of Taiwan; even

Japan, which only two decades earlier had supplied components to Taiwan's nascent industry, was making almost exclusively high-end products.

Fu Tai participated in import-substitution industrialization, making umbrellas for the local market, and export-oriented industrialization. The company also took part in contract manufacturing, another critical element of Taiwan's economic development path: in the mid-1970s, about a quarter of Fu Tai's total output went to an American company, Totes Inc., headquartered in Loveland, Ohio.

The prospect of establishing a brand and marketing it in the US was a daunting one, but selling under the Totes brand enabled Fu Tai to concentrate on product development and quality manufacturing—the things it was best at—instead of brand development and marketing. Contract manufacturing was and remains a common strategy for Taiwan's manufacturing companies. Fu Tai was unusual, though, in the amount of resources it dedicated to research and development. The company holds hundreds of patents for new umbrella technologies; it developed the first automatic open-and-close umbrellas and many other innovations. Chen Tian-fu's son told *Business Weekly*, "What I most admire about my father is his spirit of constant R&D."

Contract manufacturing has its advantages, but it generates low profits. Most of the brand-related value in a product accrues to the brand holder, while contract manufacturers can seem almost interchangeable, leaving them in a weak position to bargain for higher prices. For Taiwanese (and other successful contract manufacturers, including many in Japan), quality and reliability—attributes that rely heavily on trusting relationships and steady management—are what keep their customers coming back. While contract manufacturing remains important to its business model, Fu Tai eventually established foreign subsidiaries to sell under its own brands. The first Fu Tai brands were introduced in the US in 1991. Fu Tai has sold in the US under the Rainkist, Leighton, and Tina T labels as well as through private label production.

Taiwan's export manufacturing boom was made possible by low labor costs, but rapid growth drove up wages. Per capita income in Taiwan more than doubled between 1961 and 1971; then in just three years it doubled again. In a single year, 1973, labor rates increased by 50 percent. Chen—ever a step ahead—anticipated this development and began diversifying his business early on to ensure Fu Tai would have business units in emerging industries as well as the more vulnerable consumer manufacturing.

To that end, Fu Tai spun off companies—including some joint ventures with Japanese firms—specializing in many aspects of the production process. Those affiliates then branched out into other lines of business, ranging from chains for motor scooters to heating pipes to aluminum capacitor covers. In each of these industries, Fu Tai's related companies attained significant market share, putting them at or near the top of their industry. They also fed technology back into Fu Tai—for example, helping Fu Tai incorporate aluminum into umbrella designs.

Taiwan's reign as the umbrella kingdom ended in the early 1980s when rising wage bills forced Fu Tai to look beyond the island for manufacturing opportunities. In 1982, Fu Tai opened factories in Costa Rica and India. In 1990, it joined the trend that is the topic of this book: it opened manufacturing operations in mainland China. Today, Fu Tai and its subsidiaries make umbrellas, metal goods, and wood and plastic components in Xiamen and Suzhou. The corporate family is held together and supported by a sales office in Taipei and an investment group located in Hong Kong. Said the head of Taiwan's umbrella manufacturing trade group in 2008, "Fu Tai's position is unassailable; it is the industry leader, including on the mainland."

From agriculture, to manufacturing for domestic consumption, to export manufacturing, to diversification, to foreign direct investment, Fu Tai has passed through all of the stations on Taiwan's economic development journey. In the 1990s, the Umbrella King gave his company a new lease on life when he moved labor-intensive production to mainland China where costs were low, all the while building his customer base and innovating new products. By staying a step ahead and focusing on the long term, the company Chen Tian-fu founded in 1953 has held its lead over competitors, and, as *Business Weekly* wrote of Chen, "Rain or shine, he is always holding an umbrella for Taiwan's umbrella manufacturing industry." Actually, Chen Tian-fu didn't just build Taiwan's umbrella industry. He was also part of an even bigger, more consequential trend: mainland China's emergence as the Factory to the World. That trend is what this book is about: how thousands of Taiwanese entrepreneurs built their businesses and in the process transformed China's economy—and the world's.

Acknowledgments

Although dragons have been an important motif in Chinese culture for centuries, the idea that the dragon symbolizes China itself is relatively new. It got a big boost in 1980 when a Taiwanese pop musician named Hou Dejian released the hit song "Descendants of the Dragon" with the refrain "In the ancient East there was a dragon and its name was China." Hou blazed a path that many other Taiwanese followed a few years later: in 1983 he moved to mainland China, where his song was again a hit. When Hou joined student protesters in Tiananmen Square in 1989, the People's Republic of China (PRC) expelled him, but it kept "Descendants of the Dragon," rebranding Hou's protest song as a nationalistic anthem.

At the same time the dragon was being appropriated as a symbol of the PRC nation-state, Hou's homeland, Taiwan, was gaining a spirit animal of its own: the tiger. While the world was transfixed by Japan's vertiginous ascent (it became the world's second-largest economy in 1968), its smaller capitalist neighbors—Taiwan, South Korea, Hong Kong, and Singapore—were busy scrambling up behind it to become global players in their own right. Analysts took to calling them the "Four Asian Tigers," high-growth economies that clawed their way from agricultural backwaters to industrial powerhouses in less than forty years.

By the mid-1980s, Taiwan's economy was hitting a wall. Wage hikes, new regulations, and exchange rates were driving up the cost of manufacturing.

In 1987, Taiwan's government lifted restrictions on travel to the PRC, and Taiwanese entrepreneurs immediately recognized the mainland's potential as a low-cost manufacturing platform. The PRC was still early in its economic opening; few Chinese had the capital, know-how, or connections to supply goods for international companies. The Taiwanese Tigers had all three, and they used the assets they had built in Taiwan to lead the Dragon into the global economy.

Writing this book took much longer than I expected. On the way to completion, I've had help from tycoons and taxi drivers; intellectuals and influencers; entrepreneurs and entertainers; politicians, party members, and philanthropists. Naming every one of them would be impossible, but I am deeply thankful for each one's willingness to share their story.

I'm especially grateful to my academic colleagues who have labored long and hard to understand and explain the economic transformations in Taiwan and the People's Republic of China. Many of those scholars became good friends over the years, including Chen Chih-jou, Chen Ming-chi, T. J. Cheng, Douglas Fuller, Tom Gold, Chun-Yi Lee, Lin Gang, Syaru Shirley Lin, Gunter Schubert, Tao Yi-feng, and Wu Jieh-min. Other colleagues/friends who have influenced this work (whether they know it or not) include Nathan Batto, Richard Bush, Larry Diamond, Dafydd Fell, Sara Friedman, Bonnie Glaser, Nancy Guy, William Kirby, Murray Rubenstein, Hans Stockton, Kharis Templeman, Steve Tsang, Robert Weller, and Joe Wong.

While naming everyone who helped me is impossible, there are a few individuals who contributed in ways that mustn't be overlooked. Parts of the book borrow from papers I coauthored, one with Toy Reid and one with Gunter Schubert. I had invaluable assistance from two tenacious researchers, Rose Vassel and Shelly Lu. My students Lincoln Davidson, Alex Gittin, and Alana N. helped in myriad ways, as did my teacher/friend Fan Meeiyuan. My family—David, Jamie, and Tilly Boraks—encouraged me at every turn, even when it meant life for them was about to get weird.

I would not have been able to write this book without the financial support of Davidson College and the Smith Richardson Foundation. I was able to finish it thanks to the generosity and extraordinary flexibility of the Fulbright US Scholar Program, especially its executive director in Taiwan, Randall Nadeau. The views expressed are my own, not those of Davidson College; the

Smith Richardson Foundation; the Fulbright Program; the US Department of State or any of its partner organizations; or any other institution, agency, or individual.

Finally, I would like to thank Susan McEachern, my editor at Rowman & Littlefield, for her patience and her faith.

1

How Mao's China Became the "Factory to the World"

For the first three decades after its founding, the PRC's economy was isolated, unstable, stagnant, and unproductive. Its citizens were underemployed, immobilized, impoverished, and deprived. Basic goods—rice, wheat, soap, cloth—were rationed, and even the simplest "luxuries" were unavailable. But even if material comforts had been available to ordinary Chinese, the stigma attached to any "selfish" act surely would have made it hard to enjoy them. The nation's economy was wildly out of balance. It squeezed the agricultural sector (leaving farmers chronically underfed and occasionally starving) in order to finance state-owned heavy industry while denying citizens access to all but the most essential consumer goods. Mao-era policy makers rejected trade, markets, private ownership. In short, they rejected business.

And yet, in the three decades after the Mao era ended, the PRC gained the title "factory to the world." Thirty years of skyrocketing growth, including eighteen years when gross domestic product (GDP) growth averaged over 9 percent per year, made China the world's second-largest economy and one of its top trading nations. In 2018, China accounted for 28 percent of the world's manufacturing exports (it was slightly less in 2020). It is the world's biggest exporter by value and the world's second-highest recipient of foreign direct investment. It is a key supplier to leading multinational corporations, from textiles to technology. And while most of its manufactured goods are exported under foreign brands, some Chinese companies, such as Huawei and Lenovo, are household names in the West.

China's transformation from an autarkic, anti-business bastion to a leading player in global markets is one of the great mysteries of our time. How did this closed economy with minimal experience in consumer manufacturing or international trade become a central player in global production?

Plenty of countries have tried to develop strong industrial economies capable of competing on a global scale. Some have succeeded, but more have failed. And none (with the possible exception of post–World War II Japan) has come close to matching the velocity or extent of China's rise as a manufacturer and exporter. The states most similar to China—those making the transition from communist to capitalist institutions—have struggled to hang on to the industry they had under communism, much less expand into global markets on a large scale. Without doubt, Chinese people deserve much of the credit for their nation's success. They have worked hard, and tirelessly, to construct a brighter future. But hardworking people are everywhere, and all too often, their efforts are thwarted, and the brighter future never appears.

WHAT MAKES CHINA DIFFERENT?

One difference between China and other nations is Beijing's policy approach. Since the economic reformer Deng Xiaoping took power in 1978, China has followed an experimental model of development that has allowed new forms of economic activity to grow up alongside its existing institutions. Rather than selling off its state-owned enterprises (SOEs) in a spasm of "shock therapy," Beijing made decisions about the fate of SOEs based on their performance and potential, famously "grasping the large and releasing the small" (*zhuada fang-xiao*) in order to consolidate successful firms and eliminate those that could not succeed. Experimentalism—captured in another four-character aphorism "crossing the river by feeling for stones" (*moshi guohe*)—allowed China to try out new forms of economic activity without committing to them on a massive scale. Special economic zones (SEZs), in particular, were a successful experiment that Chinese leaders expanded and built upon, to great effect.

But export-oriented industrialization requires more than good policy and a hardworking labor force. It requires companies that can produce goods that customers in other countries want to buy, at a price those customers are willing to pay. Without customers, the best production methods in the world will manufacture only disappointment. When its export drive began, China's stock of capital was small, and its technical level—while impressive in some heavy industries, including defense equipment—was abysmal in light manufacturing. For thirty years, it had ignored consumer goods; it had punished and shunned people who had experience as managers of market-oriented businesses and made entrepreneurs into pariahs. Where, then, did the knowledge come from to produce goods in response to demand (as opposed to central planning guidelines)? How did Chinese companies learn to attend to quality and service? How did Chinese producers find their way into foreign markets?

The answer to these questions is foreign investment—and not just any foreign investment. Many foreign companies that put money into China early on found themselves locked in joint venture projects with state-owned enterprises whose business practices could not be changed. The investors who transformed management practices and connected factories in China to international markets were the ones who went into China and opened their own shops. The earliest, most pervasive, most numerous, and most influential of these were investors from Taiwan and Hong Kong, the *Taishang* and *Gangshang*. As Ming-chi Chen and Yi-feng Tao, two of Taiwan's most astute academic observers of cross-Strait economic relationships, have written, "Within China's massive process of transformation, *Taishang* [Taiwan-originated entrepreneurs] were the most important source of foreign investment for export manufacturing and a critical behind-the-scenes provider of stable support for China's maturing developmental model."[1]

Taiwanese investors brought more than money to China. They brought modern business practices that Chinese players would have taken decades to develop on their own, and they introduced Chinese localities, workers, and (eventually) firms to the foreign partners whose manufacturing contracts enabled China's explosive export growth. In the words of You-tien Hsing, "Taiwanese investors managed to improve productivity and to transfer managerial know-how and the capitalist ideology of efficiency to China, and thus paved a fast lane for local China to link up with the world market."[2]

This process started small in the mid-1980s, then accelerated in the 1990s. While trade increased steadily, investment (at least that which was reported to the Taiwanese government) was more variable, but the overall pattern is clear: both trade and investment increased rapidly over these decades. According to Taiwanese government statistics, the rates of increase were fastest in the 1990s, when annual investment growth averaged 146 percent and trade increased an average of 34 percent per year, but they were starting from a base of nearly zero. From 2001 to 2013, trade increased an average of 24 percent per year and investment increased at a rate of 19 percent per year, even with a huge drop in 2008 and 2009 due to the global financial crisis. These compounding year on year increases resulted in a massive increase in absolute terms over the decade 2001 to 2010.

The central claim of this book is that without *Taishang*, the PRC economy as we know it today would not exist. That is a bold assertion, and it deserves powerful evidence. Unfortunately, some of the most basic questions—how many *Taishang* are there? how much did these "key foreign investors" actually invest?—are surprisingly difficult to answer.

No one can say with certainty how many Taiwanese are doing business, living, working, or studying in mainland China. The most popular estimate is one million, but that is more of a convenient round number than an actual figure. Serious scholars admit it is impossible to know, and some who look closely at population data believe one million is a low guess. In 2014, Taiwanese people made about three and half million direct trips to the PRC and another two million to Hong Kong. (For comparison, they made three million trips to Japan and just under half a million trips to the US in that same year.) But knowing the number of trips doesn't tell us how many *different* people traveled. Many Taiwanese travel back and forth regularly, others go for short trips, while some go and stay for long periods. So even if we could know how many individual Taiwanese were in the mainland on a given day, we wouldn't know how many actually live there since many are short-term visitors. Plus, long-term residents include not just investors (*Taishang*) but also their dependents, professional managers and staffers (known as *Taigan*), and students (*Taisheng*). The numbers add up: according to the Chinese government, there were more than twelve thousand Taiwanese students (*Taisheng*) seeking degrees on the mainland in 2019.

Pinning down the amount of money Taiwanese have invested in the PRC is at least as daunting a challenge as determining how many are living there. Both Taipei and Beijing keep records of capital inflows and outflows, of course, but their numbers differ significantly, and both governments admit their figures are inaccurate. The biggest reason is that an unknown but substantial portion of the money Taiwanese invest in the mainland is funneled through back channels, third parties, and shell companies. At first, *Taishang* invested indirectly because they wanted to evade restrictions imposed by Taiwan's government, but firms continued to invest indirectly even after Taipei relaxed its restrictions. (Setting up an offshore channel is expensive, so once it's there, it makes sense to use it, but indirect investment has tax and privacy benefits, too.) Scholars have published estimates of the total based on informed guesses about how much Taiwanese money enters China surreptitiously, but the real total is impossible to know. But even if we assume the amounts shown in the figure below are low, the trends the chart reveals are accurate, including the skyrocketing increases in both trade and investment during the first fifteen years of this century.

As if these measurement challenges were not enough, there's another, even tougher puzzle to solve: in order to know how much Taiwanese investment there is in China, we also need to figure out what we mean by "Taiwanese."

The most straightforward way to define "Taiwanese investment" is "money invested by companies that are registered in Taiwan." Unfortunately, much of the money Taiwan-registered companies transfer to the mainland is not reported to either side, so even by that definition, it's impossible to

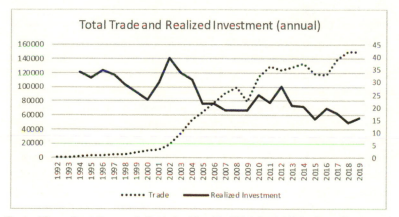

Trade: "Cross-Strait Economic Statistics Monthly," Mainland Affairs Council, accessed August 26, 2020, https://www.mac.gov.tw/News_Content.aspx?n=2C28D363038C300F&sms=231F60B3498BBB19&s=042EB117967ABAE7. Investment: "Approved Mainland China Investment," Statistical Yearbook of the Republic of China, accessed August 26, 2020, https://www.dgbas.gov.tw/public/data/dgbas03/bs2/yearbook_eng/y048.pdf.

measure accurately. One way Taiwan-registered companies evade investment restrictions is by setting up offshore shell companies. Early on, Hong Kong was a favored location for indirect investment, but Taiwanese soon added more distant havens—the British Virgins Islands (BVI), Cayman Islands, Panama—to their itineraries. Their activity had a big impact: in 2010 the British Virgin Islands were the second-largest source of external investment in the PRC economy (after Hong Kong). According to experts on both sides of the Taiwan Strait, in the mid-2000s, 70 to 80 percent of the PRC's inbound investment from the BVI, Cayman Islands, and Panama originated in Taiwan. (A portion of the remaining third came from PRC investors sending money on a "round trip": out to the Caribbean, then back into the PRC as foreign investment eligible for preferential treatment.) The portion of Hong Kong's investment in the mainland that originated in Taiwan is even harder to estimate, but it is substantial.

Even if we could trace all the investment dollars back to Taiwan-registered companies, we still wouldn't really know the full extent of Taiwanese investment in China. Many Taiwanese firms are multinational; they have business units registered in several countries. For example, Taiwan's leading electronic device manufacturer, Hon Hai/Foxconn, has units in Singapore, Malaysia, India, the US, and more. Likewise, one of Taiwan's top food processing companies, WantWant, is now a subsidiary of a holding company registered in Singapore—a holding company WantWant itself created. Another of Taiwan's leading food processors is Weichuan. It is owned by Kangshi Foods, a company founded in the mainland by Taiwanese investors and listed on the Hong Kong stock market. Given these complicated ownership structures, how do we know whether a company is Taiwanese or not? Perhaps the trickiest case is SMIC (Semiconductor Manufacturing International Group), a company founded in China by a Taiwanese American engineer who had worked at Texas Instruments and Taiwan's semiconductor pioneer, TSMC. Although the company was registered in China, because its founder, top executives, and technology all had roots in Taiwan, Taiwanese think of it as at least partially a *Taishang* firm.

Whether a particular company "counts" as Taiwanese depends upon who is doing the counting. The governments in Taipei and Beijing are interested in investment flows, whether out of Taiwan or into the PRC. Meanwhile, PRC local officials care less about where a company is registered or listed than they do about who owns it. If the boss is from Taiwan, the company is Taiwanese, regardless of its formal registration. As a Chinese local official explained it to me, they "investigate" companies to find out where they're "really" from. *Taishang* firms are prized because they bring big benefits to Chinese localities, and they integrate into the localities more easily than most other international firms. And by lifting the local economy, they also help boost the local officials' careers. For all these reasons, this book defines Taiwanese firms the same way PRC local officials do: Taiwanese companies are those that were founded in Taiwan and those that are controlled by people who were born on the island.

According to Taiwanese government figures, in early 2016, more than seventy thousand Taiwanese firms had operations in mainland China, and registered investment exceeded $150 billion. That's a big number—and the real number was almost certainly even bigger. Those seventy thousand Taiwanese firms employed millions of PRC workers. Foxconn alone employed as many as 1.3 million, making it the PRC's largest private employer. But these numbers are only part of the story. Many of the most consequential *Taishang* contributions cannot be quantified. How can we put a price on gaining access to global supply chains? What would it cost to learn to manage a business well enough to satisfy the quality standards of a company like Nike or Apple? What is the value of Teresa Teng's voice awakening Chinese from the nightmare of the Culture Revolution to call them into her musical world of romance and beauty? What would a society pay to revive ancient religious traditions that have been all but wiped out? These are just a few of the priceless contributions Taiwanese have made to China's post-Mao reawakening that are explored in this book.

NOTES

1. Chen Ming-chi and Tao Yi-feng, "Quanqiu ziben zhuyi, Taishang yu Zhongguo jingji fazhan" [Global capitalism, Taishang and China's economic development], in *Taishang yu Zhongguo Jingji Fazhan* [Taishang and China's economic development], edited by Tien Hung-mao and Gao Wei-feng, 51–65 (Taipei: Institute for National Policy Research, 2010), 52.

2. Hsing You-tien, *Making Capitalism in China: The Taiwan Connection* (Oxford: Oxford University Press, 1998), 10.

2

Taiwan's "Economic Miracle"

Buzz Lightyear's eyes widen in horror when he finds the words "Made in Taiwan" stamped on his arm in the animated film *Toy Story*. The mark is proof that his nemesis, cowboy Woody, was telling the truth: Buzz Lightyear is not a real spaceman but a mass-produced toy. For adults watching the film, the "Made in Taiwan" insignia is a laugh line, a comic reference to their childhood, when "Made in Taiwan" was synonymous with cheap consumer goods—especially plastic toys.

Not many children watching *Toy Story* in theaters would have gotten the joke. They would have had few, if any, Taiwan-made toys in their collections, for by the time the film came out in 1995, plastic toy manufacturing had shifted almost entirely to mainland China. For today's kids, "Made in China" plays the role "Made in Taiwan" played for their parents—a role "Made in Japan" played for the previous generation.

Taiwan's journey from an agricultural backwater to a manufacturing powerhouse so successful that it became a punchline is one of the most fascinating economic stories of the twentieth century. The primary focus of this book is an even more intriguing story: how Taiwan's journey landed the island in just the right place at just the right time to drive the People's Republic of China's rise to its status as "the world's factory." To understand how Taiwan helped China take off, we first need to understand Taiwan's economic path.

Taiwan's history as an exporter is long, with many intriguing twists and turns. The fourteen-thousand-square-mile volcanic island sits astride the Tropic of Cancer, and its semitropical location gives it long growing seasons and abundant rainfall. Meanwhile, its topography—including mountain peaks up to thirteen thousand feet—blesses the island with an extraordinary variety of climatic and geological conditions. That geography, which is dominated by broad plains in the west, a towering mountain spine at the center, and a narrow strip of level land to the east, provides the substrate for accumulating layers of human settlement, each of which contributes its own cultural and economic coloration.

Taiwan's verdant landscapes first attracted human inhabitants as much as fifteen thousand years ago, when the ancestors of today's Indigenous peoples took up residence on the island. These Austronesian-speaking populations were Taiwan's first exporters, supplying deer skins, antlers, and meat to traders from China, Japan, and Holland.

During the Ming dynasty (1368–1644), smugglers, fishermen, and pirates plying coastlines from Japan to the South China Sea used Taiwan as a refuge. Their presence added a new human stratum distinct from the first, although they blended at the edges. In 1624, Dutch naval forces established a military presence in southern Taiwan, near present-day Tainan. In addition to trading with their Indigenous neighbors, the Dutch built forts to protect a growing population of farmers who had moved to the island from the Chinese coast. The farmers, whom the Dutch encouraged to migrate from the mainland, produced rice and sugar for export. Two years later, the Spanish established a presence in northern Taiwan with forts of their own, and for about twenty years, the Dutch and Spanish operated parallel outposts on the island.

The Europeans' efforts to attract Chinese settlers got a boost from tough times in mainland China, a hundred miles away across the Taiwan Strait. In the 1620s, famine wracked Fujian, the Chinese province directly opposite Taiwan. To relieve the pressure, seafaring warlord Zheng Zhilong encouraged Fujian's governor to provide financial incentives to farmers willing to move to Taiwan. The Chinese stratum in Taiwan's population thickened.

Zheng Zhilong ran a huge (albeit illegal) shipping and trading enterprise based in Taiwan. When the Dutch used their military advantage to expel him from the island, Zheng turned his fleet over to the Ming navy. His status as an admiral-for-hire won him the title "admiral of the coastal sea." Zheng

Zhilong's grandson, Zheng Chenggong, followed in the family business and received an honorary title of his own. His nickname, "Guoxingye" or "the old man with the national name," was rendered "Koxinga" by Europeans, giving Zheng Chenggong the name by which he is known in Western histories.

When Manchu invaders overthrew the Ming dynasty in 1644, the Zheng family split: Zheng Zhilong sided with the Manchus while his grandson remained loyal to the Ming. Zheng Chenggong's efforts to reverse the tide of history and overthrow the Manchus' newly formed Qing dynasty were unsuccessful, but he prevented the Qing from capturing Taiwan and even managed to drive the Dutch off the island in 1661. During the twenty years Zheng Chenggong and his descendants ruled Taiwan, they expanded the amount of land under cultivation and introduced Chinese elite culture—including Confucian education. In 1683, Zheng fighters fell to Qing forces under Admiral Shi Long. For the first time, Taiwan was under the jurisdiction of a government headquartered in mainland China.

The era of Qing rule was a fascinating time in Taiwan's political and economic history. On the one hand, its status could hardly have been lower; it was a prefecture within Fujian Province until 1885, and Qing officials regarded it as one of the least desirable posts in the entire empire. Its inhabitants were a mix of Indigenous people, many of whom lived beyond the reach of any state institution, and ethnic Chinese farmers accustomed to minimal government and rugged conditions. Neither population was easy to manage; according to a Qing maxim, the island saw a major rebellion every five years, a minor rebellion every three.

The Qing's administration of Taiwan was, in the words of Taiwanese historian Wu Rwei-ren, "preventive, indirect and incomplete."[1] The Qing court tried to restrict migration, but the pressures of a burgeoning population in Fujian worked against those efforts, and Taiwan's population continued to grow. Efforts to restrict trade to a single port on each side of the Strait were similarly unsuccessful. The best the empire could do was to try and contain the rebellions.

Despite its restive population, the island's economy blossomed under the Qing. Vast new lands were opened to cultivation, spurred on by privately funded waterworks projects that irrigated huge areas of central Taiwan. As the supply of irrigated land and farmers to work it increased, Taiwan became a major supplier of rice, sugar, tea, indigo-dyed cloth, fish, and timber to

mainland China. Because of the island's topography, links between population centers up and down the west coast were weak. Traveling across the
Strait to the mainland was often safer and easier than moving north or south
on the island itself.

Inter-island trade and transportation became more important in the nine-
teenth century. When Western powers defeated the Qing in the Opium Wars,
they forced Beijing to sign treaties opening its ports—including those in
Taiwan—to foreign traders. The treaty port system gave Western merchants,
officials, and missionaries a foothold on the island. Taiwan was spared the
worst miseries of the declining Qing empire, including the catastrophic Taip-
ing Rebellion that devastated China's breadbasket and killed tens of millions
in central China, but fallout from the Qing's decline reshaped Taiwan's destiny when the dynasty lost the disastrous Sino-Japanese War of 1894–1895.

The Sino-Japanese War was fought mainly on the Korean peninsula, but
the spoils Japan demanded from the Qing included Taiwan. The Qing agreed
to hand over the island, and in 1895, Taiwan was folded into the Japanese empire. Then, for fifty years, Taiwan and the mainland followed divergent paths.
Although few Japanese individuals remained on the island after World War
II ended, those five decades of Japanese rule had enduring social, cultural,
and economic consequences for Taiwan. The Japanese era thus represents yet
another distinct stratum in Taiwan's human development.

From 1895 to 1945, while Taiwan's attention was turned toward the Japanese home islands to the north, mainland China was racked by a series of
catastrophes that inspired efforts to build a strong, modern nation. The rebellions, changes of government, civil wars, and foreign invasions China suffered
between 1895 and 1945 forged modern Chinese nationalism, but they echoed
only distantly in Taiwan, colony of Japan. The psychological distance between
Taiwan and the mainland during the Japanese colonial era had long-lasting
consequences. To residents of the mainland, the early twentieth century was
a period of struggle in which a new, modern Chinese nation was born; that
struggle is central to China's contemporary self-image. It is difficult for mainland Chinese to understand how Taiwanese can be unmoved by this history,
but for Taiwanese, those events took place long ago in a land that felt, at the
time, far away.

On Taiwan, a foreign state's colonial ambition again spurred economic
progress. Its new rulers were determined modernizers, and they brought

equal zeal to their colonies as to their home islands. In fact, for Japan's Meiji government, demonstrating its effectiveness as a colonizer was a critical component of a strategy both defensive and ideological. The Meiji leaders believed the best way to win the West's respect was to adopt Western economic, political, and military techniques—including the economic exploitation of colonies. They set Taiwan up as a model colony, one whose success would stand as proof of Japan's superior civilization.

Colonization was demeaning and restrictive; it made Taiwanese second-class citizens on their own island (although they had previously been subjects—not citizens—of the Manchu Qing empire). The Japanese left little room for political participation by Taiwanese. They brushed aside efforts in 1895 to enlist Western support for an independent Republic of Formosa and harshly suppressed political dissidents throughout their fifty-year reign. The colonial government even discouraged Taiwanese from pursuing nontechnical education and professions. As World War II approached, Tokyo forced Taiwanese to forswear many aspects of their Chinese identity and eventually enlisted thousands to take up arms on behalf of the expanding Japanese empire.

While colonization may have hindered Taiwan's political development, it was a boon to the island's economy. The effort to transform Taiwan into a model colony emphasized economic development, beginning with agriculture. Taiwan exported significant quantities of rice, sugar, camphor, and fruit to Japan throughout the first half of the twentieth century, thanks to Japanese-led improvements in infrastructure and agricultural processing industry. Infrastructural investments included detailed city plans for the island's two largest cities and a railroad that provided the first efficient north-to-south connection in the island's history. The Japanese also built roads, telegraph systems, power plants, and an electric power grid, and they expanded the irrigation and water control projects begun during the Qing era. A water purification plant came on line in 1908 that provided potable water to 120,000 Taipei residents—an extraordinary achievement for the time and place.

The colonial government also invested in human capital, including public health, and in less than a decade, it markedly reduced the incidence of deadly infectious diseases such as cholera and smallpox. It built a medical college in Taipei and hospitals and clinics throughout the island. Education was also a priority: by the 1940s, nearly 60 percent of Taiwanese adults were literate (in Japanese) and three-quarters of children attended school. Public education

used Japanese as the language of instruction and emphasized modern subjects, but many Taiwanese families supplemented this learning with a traditional Chinese education at home. Meanwhile, Taiwanese were understood to
be subjects of the Japanese emperor but not fully Japanese. As World War II
approached, the government implemented policies aimed at assimilating the
Taiwanese and promoting greater loyalty to the empire.

The impending war also brought new economic opportunities. By the
early twentieth century, Taiwan had already developed agricultural processing industries, but manufacturers soon broadened their activity to include
higher-value industries. Japanese capital—both state and private—dominated
the sector, but Taiwanese working in Japanese-owned firms acquired skills
and capital to start their own companies. Japan's invasion of China in 1931
increased the demand for industrial goods, and manufacturers in Taiwan
stepped up their production to meet it. By 1940, Taiwan's heavy industry and
consumer manufacturers were supplying markets in Japan as well as Taiwan.
By the mid-1940s, the old economy of subsistence agriculture and basic commodity trade had matured into one where scientific farming techniques were
widely used and industrial production was becoming widespread.

Taiwan's "Japanization" ended abruptly in 1945. Tokyo's unconditional
surrender included relinquishing all conquered territories, including Taiwan. The Allied governments regarded the Republic of China (ROC) as the
successor to the Qing dynasty, which had fallen in 1911. At the Cairo Conference in 1943, Roosevelt and Churchill agreed that certain Japanese-held
territories—including Taiwan—should be handed over to the Republic of
China at the end of the war, and they referenced that commitment in the
agreements ending the war. Thus, when Japanese troops and civilians left
the island, soldiers and administrators from the Chinese mainland took their
places. They represented a government that, while nominally democratic,
operated along authoritarian lines, with a single party, the Nationalist Party
or Kuomintang (KMT) and its leader, Chiang Kai-shek, at the helm.

Taiwan's transition from Japanese to ROC rule was not easy. While many
Taiwanese looked forward to the end of Japanese colonization, the appearance of the ROC forces on the island made them uneasy. The troops who
arrived were a ragtag bunch—many of them conscripts from rural China who
were underfed and tragically ill-equipped for modern warfare. Taiwanese accustomed to the Japanese imperial army's spit and polish were aghast to see

disheveled soldiers disembarking from their troop ships armed with paper umbrellas and cooking pots. Stories quickly circulated of mainland soldiers stealing bicycles they had no idea how to ride and poking faucets into walls, expecting water to flow.

If many Taiwanese found the installation of Chinese government on the island disappointing, from the Nationalist government's standpoint, sending its most capable forces to Taiwan would have been an unforgivable error. For the central government, Taiwan was a sideshow—a peripheral territory that needed to be brought under control but was not expected to offer much in the way of resistance. The nation's best soldiers were needed for a far more important task: defending the ROC from a communist takeover.

When Japan surrendered in 1945, mainland China was ravaged by invasion and wracked by internal dissention. Most nations recognized the Kuomintang-led ROC as the nation's legal government, but the Chinese Communist Party (CCP) had a very different vision for China's future. These competing forces and ideologies reflected the decades-long search for a solution to the crisis of the Chinese nation, a search to which millions of mainland Chinese had dedicated their lives. For Taiwanese, those struggles were distant, barely relevant. Japan's surrender returned them to the Chinese nation-state, but it did not prepare them to belong in the China they were about to join.

The ROC leadership recognized the ambiguous relationship between Taiwan and the mainland. The Nationalists viewed Taiwanese with suspicion; after all, they had fought and died for the same Japanese empire that had so recently occupied and plundered China. They also thought of Taiwan as an unimportant place, one that existed to serve the Chinese heartland. For four years after "Retrocession"—the return of Taiwan to Chinese control—the ROC regarded Taiwan and its people as a low-priority concern.

Taiwanese expected more. The island's economy was damaged during the war, including by US bombers targeting its relatively advanced infrastructure. Shortages of food and other goods and skyrocketing unemployment left Taiwanese in dire need of government help, but the mainland economy was in even worse shape than their own. Instead of protecting Taiwan, the KMT-appointed governor encouraged the two sides of the Strait to integrate economically, and Taiwan soon was infected by the hyperinflation that was devastating the mainland economy. In 1948, inflation exceeded 1,000 percent, and during the first half of 1949, it topped 3,000 percent. To make matters worse, Nationalist leaders treated Taiwan's economic assets as national resources that could be redeployed to the mainland. Entire factories were dismantled and reassembled on the mainland. By the end of 1945, Taiwan's industrial output had dwindled to a third of its prewar peak.

Corruption, too, spread from the mainland to Taiwan. ROC officials took bribes and confiscated property. Within months, Taiwanese were expressing nostalgia for Japanese law enforcement, which they remembered as strict but also fair and predictable. A popular saying went, "The dogs have gone; the pigs have arrived."

Tension between local Taiwanese and newly arrived soldiers, administrators, and their dependents reached its peak in early 1947. On February 27, a police officer in Taipei struck a woman he was arresting for selling cigarettes in violation of the state's tobacco monopoly laws. When a crowd gathered to defend the woman, an officer shot and killed a bystander. Protests continued on February 28; another shooting that day sparked a series of uprisings across the island. Taiwanese attacked police stations, military installations, and government offices. Many officials fled, and within a few days, Taiwanese civilians controlled most of the island.

Taiwanese elites worked with ROC officials to negotiate an end to the crisis, but the government soon lost patience. The fact that the KMT had not planned for an occupation force in Taiwan did not mean they would not send one if it was needed, and in early March, ROC troops landed in the north and south. They immediately began using deadly force to bring the population to heel. On March 10, the governor cut off negotiations with local leaders and began rounding up dissidents and Taiwanese elites, many of whom were murdered outright or executed on flimsy charges. At least ten thousand Taiwanese died during the series of events known as the 2-28 (February 28) Incident.

The ROC was able to crush resistance to its rule in Taiwan, but it was not able to defeat a much larger adversary: the Chinese Communist Party. The Communists' appeal had many facets, but one of the most important advantages they enjoyed was economic. Areas of China under Nationalist control had suffered decades of economic chaos. Attempts at land reform and other forms of relief failed in the face of opposition from elites determined to preserve their privileges, while the Communists, unconcerned with cultivating political support from local bigwigs, were able to implement popular economic initiatives. Over the course of 1948 and 1949, Communist forces rolled back the Nationalist army until only Taiwan and a few outlying islands remained in KMT hands. On October 1, Mao Zedong declared the founding of the People's Republic of China in Beijing. Two months later, the last remnants of the ROC government, including Chiang Kai-shek himself, evacuated to Taiwan. These 1,200,000 new arrivals, known as Mainlanders or '49ers, added yet another layer to Taiwan's migration history.[2]

The fall of the ROC on the mainland radically altered Taiwan's status. Instead of a sideshow, the island became—virtually overnight—the sanctuary of the ROC state. Just as Zheng Chenggong had done three centuries earlier, Chiang Kai-shek vowed to fight on, to battle back to the mainland and restore what he viewed as the legitimate Chinese state, the ROC. And like Zheng, he would wage his fight from a base on Taiwan.

Taiwan's sudden transformation into the sole remaining territory of the ROC, the fortress from which the KMT would reverse its misfortune, had implications for every aspect of Taiwanese life and society, including economics. Once small and peripheral, Taiwan was now large and central. The ROC government quickly recognized the necessity to build Taiwan's economy into one capable of supporting its ambitious agenda—and to correct the errors that had led to its downfall on the mainland. That is not to say the KMT approached Taiwan with humility; on the contrary, it was determined to make the island a bastion of Chinese nationalism from which it would recover the mainland. In pursuit of this mission, the KMT adopted four imperatives: political conformity, nationalist zeal, economic development, and military might.

The Nationalist government's political strategy provided a foundation for its economic planning. It rested on national institutions that, while paying lip service to democracy (and incorporating competitive, regularly scheduled local elections that were genuinely democratic, although limited in scope), were fundamentally authoritarian. Political power was reserved for the KMT; dissidents were routinely purged and persecuted. The national bureaucracy answered to the president and party, not to constituencies in society that might have fought to preserve their own interests.

A key objective of KMT leaders was to avoid the mistakes in economic planning and policy that had so weakened the ROC government on the mainland. In a 1950 speech, Chiang Kai-shek blamed his government's defeat by the Communists on its neglect of the "people's livelihood"—one of three principles ROC founder Sun Yat-sen laid out as the foundation of the young republic. That principle, he said, must be the basis of the party's work going forward. At the same time, KMT officials were no doubt relieved to discover that Taiwan was an unexpectedly promising venue for implementing their new and improved developmental scheme.

Taiwan entered the postwar era with the fundamentals for rapid economic development already in place. It had a basic transportation and communications infrastructure, a well-educated workforce, rudimentary industry, and a well-developed culture of handicraft manufacturing and trade. It also had a long history of exporting agricultural products and natural resources.

The prewar foundation was not enough, however, to fully explain the economic success that followed. When the Japanese withdrew from Taiwan in 1945, they left behind an island that was, in many ways, less economically promising than many other newly decolonized places—including Taiwan's neighbor to the south, the Philippines, where GDP per capita was 40 percent higher than Taiwan's in 1950.

How, then, did Taiwan move up the developmental ladder so quickly? Why was Taiwan able to achieve developed-world living standards while the Philippines, Indonesia, Malaysia, Thailand, China, and other East Asian countries struggled economically? What was the magic behind Taiwan's economic miracle? The secret to this alchemy was a near-perfect balance between two ingredients: an ecosystem of small, highly networked family firms and an environment crafted by a supportive, pro-development state that allowed those firms to thrive. Taiwan's small and medium-sized enterprises, or SMEs, are the topic of chapter 2. In this chapter, we explore the institutional framework that allowed those firms to flourish.

Losing mainland China was a massive blow to the ROC. Its homeland, the nation it had claimed for almost forty years, was lost. Its loyalists were scattered: more than a million to Taiwan; thousands to Hong Kong, Southeast Asia, and the West; millions more left behind in the newly formed PRC. Its new home, Taiwan, seemed a shaky platform on which to rebuild. To top off this litany of woe, the US withdrew its support from what top American officials had decided was a doomed regime.

Then, on June 25, 1950, the game-changer: Kim Il-sung's North Korea invaded South Korea. America's worst fear—communist expansion into the fragile postwar states of Northeast Asia—was coming true. President Harry Truman ordered an abrupt change in US policy toward the ROC. The US abandoned its hands-off approach in favor of direct political, military, and economic support to help the ROC fend off the Chinese Communists. Taiwan, along with Japan and South Korea, was now a frontline state in the US battle to contain communism.

The most immediate support came in the form of the US Seventh Fleet, which moved into the Taiwan Strait two days after the Korean War began, crushing any hope the CCP might have had for invading Taiwan. Washington deepened its commitment in 1951 when it set up the Military Assistance Advisory Group and began supplying the ROC with military aid. In 1954, the US and ROC formalized their alliance with a mutual defense treaty.

The US was instrumental to the ROC's political and economic survival as well as its military defense. By throwing its weight behind the Chinese government headquartered in Taipei, it ensured that the PRC would not replace the ROC in international bodies, including the United Nations, which allowed Taipei to represent China—a permanent member of the Security Council—until 1971. The US also assisted with economic rebuilding, often transferring resources and successful experiences from occupied and postoccupation Japan to Taiwan. The US Agency for International Development provided money and advice, while the Joint Commission on Rural Reconstruction served as an on-the-ground conduit for US expertise and money flowing into Taiwan's agricultural reforms. In 1961, Taiwan's top economic official, K.Y. Yin, described US aid in the early 1950s as "a shot of stimulant to a dying patient."[3]

If the US involvement seemed heavy-handed at times, ROC leaders were, for the most part, happy to have it. They were well aware of the danger they were in; they understood that their troubles on the mainland had been amplified by their failure to sweep aside vested interests and implement needed changes. As Thomas Gold points out in his classic account of Taiwan's development, *State and Society in the Taiwan Miracle*, Washington and Taipei were in a "dialectical relationship that succeeded because enough Chinese—backed by the Generalissimo [Chiang Kai-shek]—realized clearly the urgent need for reform and were committed to it, and the Americans provided the wherewithal, and sometimes the pretext, to set it in motion."[4]

To reform state policy, the KMT first needed to reform itself. Party leaders acknowledged the faults that had led to their defeat on the mainland, everything from failing to enact land reform to allowing uncontrollable inflation. Their analysis of the disaster was unflinching; their goal was to avoid similar mistakes going forward. From 1950 to 1952, the KMT replaced its Central Executive Committee with a Central Reform Committee, signaling its determination to complete thoroughgoing reforms in personnel, discipline, ideology, and policy. The reform agenda was aided by the fact that most KMT members who moved to Taiwan were motivated by patriotism; as Gold points out, few KMT opportunists chose the island as their place of refuge.

The KMT entered the reform era with two interrelated goals: to strengthen Taiwan and to build it into a launching pad from which to recover the mainland. While they believed recovering the mainland to be their sacred mission and destiny, as well as the source of the state's legitimacy, KMT leaders understood that developing Taiwan was an indispensable step toward that end. For Taiwan to perform its designated role, it would require both economic and political work.

The 2-28 crackdown in 1947 may have suppressed active resistance to KMT rule, but it also infused local society with fear and animosity toward the ROC state, the KMT party, and the '49er minority. An alienated population was hardly a good foundation on which to base such an ambitious project as mainland recovery. So while real democracy was a long time in coming— Taiwan's first opposition party formed only in 1986, and the island held its first popular presidential election a full ten years after that—the KMT used economic policy and limited local self-government to move millions of Taiwanese from grudging compliance to active support.

Moving those millions began with an ambitious, far-reaching land reform. Back on the mainland, KMT leaders knew that the misery of landless peasants needed to be addressed, but political resistance stymied their attempts at land reform. The political environment in Taiwan could hardly have been more different. Taiwanese landowners had no connections or leverage in the KMT. During the 2-28 Incident, rural elites faced brutal repression, a trauma that ensured their political submission. Those experiences, combined with the regime's willingness to suppress opposition of all kinds, left little danger that the landlord class would interfere with the land reform plan.

Taiwan's land reform program was not a matter of simple confiscation and redistribution. Landowners were compensated for their land, and farmers were required to pay for the land they acquired, albeit on highly favorable terms. Land reform included agricultural extension services, training, and marketing assistance to help farmers upgrade their skills and access more sophisticated markets and higher-value crops. Farmers associations, in particular, afforded farmers a huge range of opportunities—from coordinated marketing of farm products to loans to political participation—that increased their incomes, skills, and confidence.

The first phase of land reform began in 1949 with a state-mandated rent reduction from the standard 50 percent of the harvest to 37.5 percent. This initial step alone boosted the incomes of about three hundred thousand farm families. At the same time, the state sold publicly owned land to its tenants, for a price of two and a half years' harvest to be paid in kind over ten years.

The next phase of the reform is referred to as the "Land to the Tiller" reform. Convinced that family farming would boost agricultural productivity, the regime required landholders who rented land to others to sell most of their land to the state. They were compensated with bonds and shares in state-owned firms. (Many sold off those assets, but those who held them enjoyed a high rate of return as Taiwan's economy boomed in the '60s and '70s.) Tenants and laborers purchased the land from the state with thirty-year, low-interest loans. Turning renters and laborers into owners doubled the percentage of land that was cultivated by its owners. As predicted, agricultural production and productivity spiked: in one decade, per-acre rice yields increased by almost 40 percent, even as farmers diversified out of rice and into more profitable cash crops.

The land reform had far-reaching benefits. It increased the quantity and quality of food while reducing its cost and freeing labor for the industrial sector. It spurred technological upgrading, raised rural incomes, reduced the income gap between farmers and others, and broke the grip of landowners on rural communities—all without the brutality and dislocation of the PRC's Maoist version of land reform, which relied on violent confiscation. It helped farmers acquire the skills and capital they later would use to enter the manufacturing economy, and it raised their status in society. Finally, it gave farmers an entrée into the state, which both empowered them and gave them a reason to support the KMT-dominated regime. Despite entering Taiwan as an occupying power, the KMT's economic policies, beginning with land reform, won it the backing of millions of ordinary Taiwanese.

Land reform was a critical first step in Taiwan's economic recovery and development, but the leadership's ambitious long-term plans required an even bigger second step: industrialization.

The policy makers the ROC government empowered to make these decisions were not politicians but technocrats—professional planners with strong technical skills who were given wide latitude to set policy. Because the KMT's top leaders recognized that political pressure from vested interests had derailed important reforms on the mainland and contributed to the regime's defeat, they took pains to insulate economic policy makers on Taiwan from most political interference.

Two men, K.Y. Yin and K. T. Li, were so central to Taiwan's development that Ezra Vogel, a top scholar of East Asian development, dubbed them the "super technocrats." Between them, Yin and Li guided ROC economic policy through four successful decades. Both were brilliant planners who enjoyed the confidence of the ROC's most powerful men, Chiang Kai-shek and his son (and successor) Chiang Ching-kuo. Under the Chiangs' protection, Yin and Li cultivated an army of staffers in numerous economic ministries, agencies, and commissions who were entrusted with Taiwan's economic revival.

Yin and Li came from similar backgrounds. Born in mainland China, they moved with the ROC government to Taiwan as adults. Both were scientists— Yin studied engineering, Li physics—not economists (Li reportedly had no formal training in economics at all). Their policy programs were informed by economic research, but both were pragmatists who put results ahead of economic orthodoxy. In their youth, both men lived abroad in English-speaking countries, and they also spent time working in industry, which may help explain their ability to craft policies that met the needs of manufacturers and private firms as well as the state. Yin and Li also were acute observers of their own work; each published numerous essays and reports analyzing Taiwan's development. And the two men each served in a wide variety of government posts, sometimes several at a time.

K. Y. Yin took the first shift, leading Taiwan through the import substitution phase of its development, from the early 1950s until his death in 1963. K. T. Li took over as Taiwan's top technocrat after Yin died; he helped launch the island's export-oriented development phase and carry it into the era of high-tech industry. When he died in 2001 at the age of ninety-two, Li was still in public service, providing economic guidance to President Chen Shui-bian. Few economic managers can match the dedication and skill Yin and Li brought to their work, the fruits of which are evident to this day, in Taiwan's economic successes and now in the PRC's as well.

The technocrats' core task was to transform Taiwan from an agricultural to an industrial economy, a transformation that required capital, labor, and technology. The land reform contributed by sparking an increase in agricultural productivity that enabled the island's farmers to produce more than they needed to survive. That surplus allowed the state to support an urban population swollen with refugees from the mainland and to put many of them to work improving Taiwan's infrastructure. It also freed many rural Taiwanese from agricultural labor, making them available to industrial businesses coming back on line in the wake of World War II. While much of the farm surplus was transferred to the state—most farmers paid their taxes and land reform debts in rice, at a rate that favored the state—rural Taiwanese experienced rising incomes. And those rising rural incomes fueled demand for the manufactured goods infant industries were producing.

In short, the land reform launched a virtuous cycle of burgeoning consumer demand, rising living standards, growing industry, and expanding infrastructure. In the initial stage, K. Y. Yin and other technocrats emphasized import-substitution industrialization. Instead of allowing Taiwanese to buy what they needed from foreign manufacturers, Taiwan's government restricted imports by tightly controlling the supply of foreign exchange. Dollars, marks, pounds, and yen were available mainly for investment goods—industrial equipment, for example—that state economic managers believed would contribute to long-term growth. Meanwhile, the importation of luxury goods was tightly restricted—although Chiang Kai-shek continued to ride in enormous Cadillac limousines.

The import-substitution approach included many policy tools. Even before the civil war ended, the ROC government had set up the Taiwan Production Board (TPB) to oversee industry on the island. The TPB and its successor, the Economic Stabilization Board (ESB), played a critical role in guiding the ROC economy through its perilous early years on Taiwan. In 1958, Taipei assessed the worst was over, and the ESB was dissolved.

Terminating the ESB did not mean the ROC state was withdrawing into a laissez-faire approach. State intervention in the economy continued under a plethora of offices and commissions charged with executing the import-substitution strategy. Firms seeking to enter markets with strong consumer demand found capital and credit on generous terms, as well as a favorable tax code and a tariff regime and import restrictions that allowed infant industries to avoid price competition from well-established foreign companies.

In order to ensure those consumer-oriented firms had what they needed to keep goods flowing, the government acquired or created state-owned companies to supply everything from raw plastic to logistical services. The inputs pouring out of those upstream state firms flowed downstream to the private companies making finished goods. The synergistic relationship between the two sectors nurtured an active and competitive private sector while ensuring that bottlenecks upstream would not cause droughts down below.

Taiwan's consumer manufacturing success stories include thousands of companies that started small during the import-substitution era, but it also includes a few that got their start during the Japanese colonial era, including Taiwan's most famous consumer manufacturing giant, Tatung Corporation. In 2018, Tatung's consolidated revenue was more than two billion US dollars, but the company grew from modest roots. Its precursor was the Xie Zhi Business Enterprise, founded by Lin Shang-Zhi in 1918 as a construction company. The Japanese colonial government contracted with Xie Zhi to construct significant public buildings, including the Executive Yuan complex, which houses many of Taiwan's government offices today. As World War II heated up in 1939, the company founded an iron and steel manufacturer called Tatung Iron Works. When the war ended, it moved into electrical motors and appliances and quickly established itself as the leading brand of locally made household goods.

More common than the Tatung-style large-scale manufacturers were the small and medium-sized enterprises—SMEs—that proliferated in the '50s, '60s, '70s, and '80s. Nearly all of these were started by small-scale entrepreneurs with limited skills and capital—the people Taiwanese call "black-handed bosses" because they got their hands dirty on the factory floor. One such firm is the Fu Tai Umbrella Group, whose rags-to-riches founder grew his company from a ten-person start-up into the world's largest umbrella manufacturer.

Over the course of the 1950s, import substitution reached its limits. GDP growth slowed, and local markets became saturated. K. Y. Yin was particularly troubled by evidence that those he called "profiteers"—people whose earnings came not from productive activity but from the arbitrage opportunities afforded by foreign exchange restrictions and import quotas—were corrupting the ROC economy. To provide the expanded markets and competitive pressure Taiwanese firms needed to keep growing, in 1958 government strategists unleashed a new approach: export-oriented industrialization.

After several years in a protected domestic market, Taiwan's firms had the basic skills and resources they needed to begin selling goods abroad. They also enjoyed a substantial cost advantage compared to manufacturers in their major export markets, the US, Japan, and Western Europe. Nonetheless, moving from the shelter of import substitution to the big, bad world of global trade was a daunting prospect. Taiwanese firms were fortunate to have two key allies as they entered that world: US economic policy makers and the ROC government.

From the onset of the Cold War, the US was determined to prevent its frontline Asian partners—Japan, Taiwan, and South Korea—from slipping into the kind of economic misery that had nurtured communist movements around the world. To that end (and to propel American companies' technical and managerial upgrading), the US encouraged its allies' economic development. Between 1950 and 1965, the United States gave Taiwan more than one hundred million dollars in nonmilitary aid; financial and technical assistance from the US were central to Taiwan's agricultural transformation and import-substitution industrialization. The anti-communist imperative also inspired the US to open its market to Taiwan's manufactured goods, which fueled Taiwan's transition to export-driven development. Taiwan also had the good fortune to be following a few years behind Japan in implementing export-oriented policies. As a result, ROC policy makers were able to emulate Japan's successes—while avoiding some of its mistakes.

The first steps toward export liberalization came in 1958, when the KMT Central Standing Committee passed K. Y. Yin's proposal to reform the foreign currency system, lower import barriers, and encourage exports. While many government officials and businesspeople worried that Taiwan's economy was not ready for international competition, the reforms showed immediate benefits. Over the next few years, the state put in place a wide range of policy measures designed to encourage exports, including changes to banking laws and tax policy. As in Japan's developmental state, domestic consumers sometimes paid the cost—in higher tariffs on imported goods, for example—of the state's aggressive export promotion.

In addition to these reforms, the ROC government selectively supported industries and firms it believed had particularly strong export potential. In 1958, the government hired Stanford Research Institute consultants to identify areas of competitive advantage for Taiwan. They singled out plastics, synthetic fibers, and electronic components as industries in which Taiwan could expect to thrive, and their predictions—backed up with supportive policies—proved accurate.

At first, Taiwan's ample supply of workers gave the island a significant cost advantage over more established manufacturing locales. As industrial employment became more widespread, wages and incomes increased, but labor productivity increased even faster. The gap between wages and productivity was artificially high, thanks to state-imposed restrictions on labor activism (including the near absence of independent unions) and the self-exploitation that characterized the island's innumerable small family firms.

The surplus created by the productivity/wage gap enabled Taiwanese to save and invest at extraordinarily high rates, which drove a virtuous growth cycle. That cycle was reinforced by the state's determination to ensure a reliable supply of key industrial inputs such as power, metals, petrochemicals, and plastics. While most of the firms producing finished goods for export were SMEs, large companies, most of them state-owned, dominated upstream industries. The combination of low wages, stable inputs, and favorable government policies attracted international investors as well as Taiwanese. Taiwan was an appealing alternative to the US, Europe, and Japan, all of which saw rising labor costs and tightening regulation in the 1960s and 1970s. As the environmental movement took hold in Japan and the West, Taiwan became something of a haven for "dirty" manufacturing.

Some foreign companies chose to access production opportunities in Taiwan through direct investment, but most chose a different model. They contracted with locally owned firms to purchase items produced in accordance with the buyer's specifications. This "contract manufacturing" allowed foreign companies to obtain the goods they needed without tying up investment capital, and it enabled Taiwanese SMEs to raise their technical level and build capacity without bearing the risk and expense of brand building, marketing, and design. How Taiwan's small and medium-sized firms became world leaders in contract manufacturing—a strategy they transferred to mainland China—is the topic of the next two chapters.

NOTES

1. Wu Rwei-ren, "Fragment Of/f Empires: The Peripheral Formation of Taiwanese Nationalism," *Social Science Japan*, no. 30 (December 2004): 16–18.

2. The Chinese word for '49ers is *waishengren*, which means "people from outside provinces." Families that arrived in Taiwan before the Japanese takeover are called *benshengren*, or "people from this province."

3. Quoted in Stephan Haggard and Chien-Kuo Pang, "The Transition to Export-Led Growth in Taiwan," in *The Role of the State in Taiwan's Development*, edited by Joel D. Aberbach, David Dollar, and Kenneth L. Sokoloff (Armonk, NY: M. E. Sharpe, 1994), 60.

4. Thomas Gold, *State and Society in the Taiwan Miracle* (Armonk, NY: M. E. Sharpe, 1986), 58.

3

"Second Spring"

Taiwan's Traditional Manufacturers Discover Mainland China

When Taiwan's export-oriented manufacturing was hitting its stride in the mid-1970s, mainland China had not yet put on its running shoes. But twenty years later, athletic shoe manufacturing (along with many other industries) had all but disappeared from Taiwan as one firm after another moved its production across the Taiwan Strait. The speed of the change is hard to exaggerate. As late as 1986, Taiwan's government still was clinging stubbornly to its "three nos" policy toward the PRC: no contact, no negotiation, and no compromise with the Communist leadership in Beijing. Taiwanese were forbidden to travel to the mainland. Trade was out of the question, investment inconceivable. Given the economic and political chasm between the two sides in the 1970s, no one imagined that within a decade most of Taiwan's traditional manufacturing would pick up and move to the mainland.

Even if Taiwanese had been allowed to set up operations there, mainland China was not an attractive destination for foreign capital in the mid-1970s. The PRC was in a radical phase; both its rhetoric and its policies were deeply hostile to business. The PRC economy was just emerging from the disastrous Great Leap Forward and Cultural Revolution, both of which battered whatever traces of China's private economy had survived Communist rule up to that point. Meanwhile, China's leadership was locked in a life-and-death battle between a moderate faction surrounding Zhou Enlai and the leftist radicals who had led the Cultural Revolution. As long as Mao was alive, political deadlock made economic reform impossible.

Mao's death in September 1976 provided the moderates with their long-awaited opportunity. Without the mighty Chairman's protection, the radicals' political bankruptcy was soon revealed. Zhou's death in 1975 left Deng Xiaoping as the moderates' leader, and when the radicals (personified in the notorious "Gang of Four") fell, Deng's path to power was clear. By 1979, Deng had settled into place as Mao's successor. Although he transferred his formal positions to others, Deng remained China's paramount leader and managed the affairs of state from behind the scenes until his death in 1997.

Deng Xiaoping was a Communist, but he believed economic development was a necessary precondition for China's successful implementation of communist social and economic institutions. To achieve economic development, Deng was prepared to relax Mao's prohibitions on business and engagement with the outside world—an approach captured in his famous slogan, "Reform and Opening." He recognized that developing China's economy required allowing foreign trade and investment. One of his first—and most potent—initiatives was to create special economic zones (SEZs) to promote export processing trade.

China's first SEZ advocate was Zhou Enlai. In the early 1970s, Zhou began sponsoring trips abroad for Chinese economic policy makers to see how other nations managed their economic affairs. After years of isolation and Maoist propaganda, many of these officials were stunned to learn how prosperous and technologically advanced the non-communist world had become. They were keen to bring the benefits of modernity to China but reluctant to expose Chinese society to the individualism and greed they believed pervaded capitalist societies. As self-contained geographical and economic units, SEZs offered a safe structure within which China could develop trade-based industries with the potential to bring the benefits of the late-twentieth-century global economy to the Chinese people—while protecting their socialist values.

Zhou was particularly interested in an SEZ in southern Taiwan. The Kaohsiung Special Economic Zone opened as an export-processing zone—an industrial park whose tenants were exempt from certain taxes and regulations—in 1966. The special zone attracted foreign investors looking to take advantage of Taiwan's labor force at the lowest possible cost. Within two years of opening, the zone met its investment, export value, and employment targets, prompting the government to expand the model to several other locations. Special economic zones were an important item in a package of export-promoting policies that pushed Taiwan's average annual GDP growth rate above 10 percent throughout the 1960s and 1970s.

Zhou Enlai recognized the value of the SEZ model to economies that were rich in labor but poor in investment and technology. He praised the Kaohsiung model to foreign leaders, and he instructed PRC officials to look into establishing an export-processing zone based on the Kaohsiung example. At a State Council meeting, Zhou chided his ministers for falling behind Taiwan: "Hey Mr. Foreign Trade Minister, you're not as good as Yen Chia-kan [Taiwan's premier]. He established an export processing zone in Kaohsiung, and has really developed their foreign trade. . . . In the past, China did not possess the right conditions. Now, the situation has changed. We must think a little bit more about how to do this."[1]

Deng Xiaoping shared Zhou's enthusiasm for the special zone model, so bringing Zhou's plan for SEZs to fruition was one of his top priorities. In 1980, he brushed aside the misgivings of CCP leftists and pushed through plans for four SEZs. Three of the four—Shenzhen, Zhuhai, and Shantou—are in Guangdong province, near Hong Kong. The fourth, Xiamen, lies directly opposite Taiwan. The original SEZ investors were Hong Kong residents and ethnic Chinese businesspeople from overseas; many were entrepreneurs with roots in Guangdong and Fujian whose families had migrated to Southeast Asia. Like the Taiwanese a few years later, they benefited from their familiarity with southern Chinese languages and cultures. Indeed, even though Taiwan was still following the "three nos" policy in the early 1980s, SEZ authorities already had their eye on Taiwanese investment. In 1984, six years before Taiwanese authorities formally approved investment into the mainland, Xiamen adopted investment incentives aimed at attracting Taiwanese investors, known in Chinese as *Taishang*.[2]

Beijing signaled its eagerness to engage Taiwan economically by creating scores of policies and regulations aimed at luring Taiwanese investors. In 1981, a top PRC official, Ye Jianying, put forward a proposal for unification of Taiwan and the mainland in which he called for strong economic engagement between the two sides, including direct transportation, trade, and postal/telecommunications links—what came to be called the "three links." In 1984, Shanghai and other cities became "open cities" in which foreign trade was to be aggressively pursued, and two years later the "coastal development strategy" extended that status to most of coastal China. The coastal development strategy folded 284 municipalities with a population of more than 160 million into a giant SEZ within which foreign-invested companies were freed from all manner of regulations, restrictions, and taxes. The State Council adopted preferential regulations for Taiwanese investing in the SEZs in the early 1980s; in 1988, Beijing adopted a law entitled "Regulations for the Encouragement of Investment by Taiwan Compatriots."

In short, foreign investors looking to do export-promotion trade enjoyed an open, trade-friendly environment, and among those foreign investors, *Taishang* enjoyed the best conditions of all. Chinese firms faced a very different legal and regulatory environment. PRC-based companies—most of which were state-owned enterprises (SOEs)—existed in a partially reformed milieu shaped by rules that retarded their growth and competitiveness. Those rules, in combination with the foreign firms' huge head start over their Chinese counterparts, made it all but impossible for China's domestic firms to compete for export manufacturing opportunities. The preferential treatment enjoyed by *Taishang* thus put the Taiwanese firms at an advantage relative not only to other foreign companies but to China's domestic companies as well. That made *Taishang* attractive targets for grassroots officials seeking to develop their local economies.

The decision to encourage Taiwanese investment was driven in part by politics—Communist Party head Zhao Ziyang observed that unification would be easier if coastal China's standard of living matched Taiwan's—but it had economic motivations as well. As Murray Scot Tanner put it, "Twenty-five years of torrid economic growth in China have almost obscured the fact that in 1979 Beijing almost certainly needed Taiwan more than Taiwan needed China . . . [which] desperately lacked the capital, technology, and managerial expertise that Taiwan possessed in abundance."[3] China needed the kind of development only capitalist firms could provide, but it was not yet ready to let its own firms embrace capitalist models. Encouraging foreign investment allowed Beijing to spur development while protecting its domestic actors from capitalist contamination (or so it seemed).

At first, Taiwanese were cautious about accepting Beijing's invitation. While a few Taiwanese channeled investments into China through third parties, most Taiwanese businesses did not dare take advantage of the opportunities offered in China's burgeoning SEZs and special Taiwanese investment zones as long as Taipei followed its no-contact policy. That policy changed in 1987, when President Chiang Ching-kuo opened the door for Taiwanese to visit the mainland for humanitarian purposes. Between 1945 and 1949, more than a million '49ers had moved with the Nationalist government to Taiwan. Many of them left families on the mainland, never imagining they would be unable to return for four decades. Chiang's intent in relaxing the ban on Taiwanese traveling to the mainland was to give aging '49ers a chance to pay respects to their ancestors and reunite with their families before they died.

The China those early visitors encountered was an intriguing combination of backwardness and potential. In terms of technology and living standards, the mainland was far behind Taiwan, but its very backwardness made it an appealing target for investors. In the late 1980s, traditional manufacturing in Taiwan was being squeezed between global markets' demands for low-priced goods and Taiwan's rising currency value, increasing wage and land costs, and growing regulation. For manufacturers of low-tech products such as shoes, clothing, furniture, and toys, China's SEZs—with ample land ready for industrial development and an army of underemployed rural Chinese ready to work for a tenth of the prevailing wage in Taiwan—promised a way out of the cost trap.[4] Taiwan's government provided further impetus when it eased restrictions on capital exports—a necessary next step in Taiwan's shift from low-end manufacturing to a higher value-added role in the global economy.

As far as Taiwan's small and medium-sized export manufacturing companies were concerned, China's economic opening came at exactly the right moment. Rising costs and an appreciating currency were undermining traditional manufacturers' competitiveness, but the firms thrived in the mainland's lower-cost environment, allowing them to enjoy what they called a "second spring."

Beijing's decision to start the process in a handful of SEZs also worked to the *Taishang*'s advantage, and it contributed to a peculiar geographical distribution of Taiwanese investment. Certain cities—including Dongguan in the south and Kunshan in the Yangtze River delta just west of Shanghai—are known as "Little Taipeis." And even outside those cities, it's hard to find a town that has just one Taiwanese company: they tend to move in packs. Both of these patterns date back to the SEZ era, although for different reasons. Taiwanese firms first entered China through SEZs in the Pearl River delta and

Fujian. As the crow flies, Fujian is the closest Chinese province to Taiwan, but direct air and sea links opened only in 2008. Without direct shipping, the Pearl River region's proximity to Hong Kong—the main transshipment point for money and goods going in and out of China—gave it an edge over other regions.

Until 1992, Taiwan forbade investment in the mainland, and specific restrictions persisted long after the blanket ban was lifted. It was only in 2008 that the two sides finalized comprehensive, direct cargo links and allowed Taiwanese passengers to fly directly from the island to destinations in the mainland. Until that year, in the absence of direct financial and transit links, Hong Kong was a critical stopover for people, money, and goods. The shortest distance between Taiwan and mainland China, it turned out, was through Hong Kong.

The lack of direct transit links was one of many hardships *Taishang* suffered because of the tense political relations between Taipei and Beijing. Cross-Strait passengers wore a path through the Hong Kong airport, from the mainland China arrivals area to the Taiwan-bound departures lounge and back. At each end, hundreds of weary businesswomen and -men sat hunched over their mobile phones, swapping out SIM cards. The trip wasted time—it stretched the eighty-minute flight distance between Taipei and Shanghai into a full day's journey—and money, not to mention jet fuel, and made it difficult for mainland-based workers to return to Taiwan for short visits. The distance was hard on company budgets and *Taishang* families, so it's not surprising that direct flights were a central *Taishang* demand through the 1990s and into the 2000s. Meanwhile, cargo transshipment costs cut into *Taishang* firms' profits. But the lack of direct transport links was good for the burgeoning industrial zone around Hong Kong.

Buoyed along by the large volume of goods and travelers entering through Hong Kong as well as the political and economic infrastructure of the nearby provincial capital of Guangzhou, the southern SEZs blossomed, and a huge number of *Taishang* manufacturers set up shop in the Pearl River region. Dongguan, in particular, became a virtual Taiwanese city. By 1992—just five years after Taiwanese were first allowed to visit the mainland—one small town near Guangzhou was home to more than four hundred Taiwanese-owned shoe factories.[5]

The SEZ at Xiamen in Fujian was not quite so conveniently located, but it had other advantages that helped it attract Taiwanese investment. Most Taiwanese SME owners have ancestral roots in Fujian, and the island's most common native tongue is Minnan, a Fujianese language. The century-long separation of the two sides produced some differences in the spoken dialect, but Taiwanese entrepreneurs and Fujianese officials found an easy companionship in speaking Minnan. After decades under the thumb of Mandarin-speaking officials from their respective capitals, Minnan speakers from both sides could hardly be blamed for enjoying the opportunity to cut their linguistic overlords out of the conversation.

Beyond language, Taiwanese and Fujianese share other ties that eased *Taishang* entry into the mainland through Fujian. Many Taiwanese families—even clans that came to the island in the seventeenth and eighteenth centuries—know where in Fujian their ancestors' migration began. *Taishang* were able to activate their ancient connections to facilitate business ties. They donated to local institutions, hosted banquets, and sponsored festivals. In every case, local officials—especially those responsible for promoting economic growth—were honored guests. These relationships opened the door to further investment, which in turn generated wealth for another round of "business development."

The cultural affinity between *Taishang* and their mainland counterparts was strongest in Fujian, but it gave Taiwanese throughout China an advantage over foreign investors without Chinese ancestry. As anyone who has ever tried to make even the simplest deal can attest, wining and dining is a big part of doing business in China. Chinese value social connections to their partners and clients; would-be investors need to know how to cultivate the right kind of relationships, or *guanxi*. Everything from how you hand over your business card to where you seat your guests at a dinner party matters. Taiwanese etiquette for these interactions is, if not identical to the mainland version, at least close enough to allow *Taishang* to enter Chinese social networks relatively smoothly—and even serve as go-betweens for third-country investors.

Many accounts of Taiwan's successes in the PRC mention the cultural ties between Taiwan and the mainland as an advantage *Taishang* enjoyed over other investors. That effect was real but not unlimited. China's economic and political institutions were and are very different from Taiwan's, and they play a far bigger role in business. *Taishang* are excluded from certain kinds of relationships, and even when they can participate, the cultural parallels are not always as great as one might imagine. In Taiwan, for example, exchanges of gifts and hospitality are a way of cementing an existing relationship. In the mainland, the *Taishang* quickly learned, gifts—even bribes—very often *are* the relationship. As one *Taishang* explained it to me, "In Taiwan, we exchange benefits because we're friends. In China, they're friends because they exchange benefits." It's a fine distinction, but one *Taishang* had to learn to navigate if they hoped to succeed in the mainland.

Understanding how to cultivate politically connected partners was especially important because when *Taishang* began arriving en masse in the late 1980s, China was still in the early stages of its reform process. The vast majority of its economy was state-owned. Many small enterprises were collectives owned by local governments or "red hat" firms, companies run by individuals but registered as collectives for political protection. The private economy was very limited, and even joint ventures between foreign and Chinese companies typically involved state firms as the Chinese partner. Openly private enterprise, whether Chinese or foreign-owned, was very much the exception, and working outside the mainstream economy of interlocking public entities was not easy.

One of the complications facing *Taishang* was China's dual-pricing system. Under partially reformed socialism, many commodities had two prices: a lower one for entities whose political status and connections qualified them for privileged access and a higher one for those who lacked such connections. To leap over barriers and minimize cost premiums, foreign entities such as *Taishang* firms needed locally grown partner-protectors who could access goods at or near the state price. Acquiring use rights to land, locating contractors and materials for building construction, assembling a work force, connecting to water and power, securing affordable transport, and countless other activities—almost any task was easier with a local partner.

Building relationships with local partners required sensitivity to PRC law and etiquette as well as a boundless capacity for hospitality, including endless rounds of eating and drinking. Managing these relationships contributed to the *Taishang*'s tendency to locate close to one another. Staying in the same regions enabled them to introduce newcomers into existing social networks and provide support when things went wrong. While many *Taishang* encountered problems in the mainland—some of them very serious—there was some safety in numbers.

China's SEZ-led development was a roaring success, and China's leaders could see where the exports were being generated. They quickly expanded the size of the areas in which export-oriented manufacturing and foreign investment were allowed. In 1995, less than a decade after Taipei lifted the ban on investment in the PRC, China went from a net importer of manufactured goods to a net exporter.[6]

Looking back at the early years of Taiwanese investment in the mainland, it is jarring to realize how much China's economy has changed in just a few decades. In 2020, foreign firms' primary concern is that they will be pushed out of China by its ever-more-capable home-grown companies. But thirty years ago, foreign companies were not only the leaders of China's export economy—they *were* its export economy, and intentionally so. Beijing wanted the foreign exchange and revenue that came with export manufacturing, but it was unwilling to expose domestic firms to the influence and risk of the global market. Instead, it adopted policies that all but handed over its export-manufacturing sector to foreign-invested enterprises (FIEs). Concessionary policies enhanced FIEs' competitiveness relative to manufacturers outside of China, and they also reinforced those firms' competitive advantage over China-based companies that might want to enter the same industries. In short, Beijing made it nearly impossible for local firms to join the burgeoning export sector. Instead, it directed the opportunities to firms from Hong Kong, Taiwan, and other foreign countries.

These favorable conditions are obvious in retrospect, but they were much harder to recognize in the late 1980s. In fact, *Taishang* entered China on high alert. Investors in the first wave were driven by desperation; as *Taishang* experts Tain-Jy Chen and Ying-Hua Ku put it, "survival was their sole consideration."[7] Low wages and common language notwithstanding, mainland China was still an alien place for Taiwanese in the 1980s. The two sides had been separated for nearly all but a few years since 1895, and they were technically at war after 1949. Taiwan's entrepreneurs may not have paid much attention to the anti-Communist propaganda they had been hearing all their lives, but nothing in their past experience gave them any reason to be optimistic about what they would find in a land ruled by the dreaded "Communist bandits."

Adding to the risk of the unknown facing *Taishang* in the 1980s was a complete absence of legal protection by their own government. If something went wrong (and despite the bright overall picture, much did go wrong for many individual investors), *Taishang* were on their own. Although the Taiwan Strait had become a demilitarized zone—alternate-day shelling was a thing of the past, and missile tests were still in the future—there still was no official communication between the two sides—no investment treaty, tax agreement, or consular protection.

With direct investment still technically illegal, first-wave investors funneled the money to rent factories and equipment through Hong Kong and other offshore investment platforms. The practice of bringing money into China indirectly continued even after Taipei lifted its restrictions on direct investment. The decision to rent facilities, meanwhile, was part of a strategy to minimize expenditures on nonliquid assets. That same caution prompted the *Taishang* to hire workers and buy materials on a strict as-needed basis. In short, the early *Taishang* kept fixed assets and sunk costs to a minimum.

Another way these early manufacturers managed risk was by replicating the business practices that had served them well for the previous two decades on Taiwan. They focused on contract manufacturing for international brands, using the same clustering approach as in Taiwan. Instead of dribbling across the Strait one firm at a time, entire supply chains picked up and moved to the mainland en masse. Just as groups of *Taishang* firms huddled together in the Pearl and Yangtze River deltas and Fujian, within those regions, groups of related firms set up shop next door to one another.

The first-wave investors were just getting settled in the mainland when a political earthquake shifted the ground under their feet. The 1989 Beijing Spring protests and the crackdown that followed were a disaster for China, but they were a boon to Taiwanese investors because they enlarged the *Taishang*'s share of China's manufacturing economy.

The 1980s were a period of unprecedented political opening in the PRC. Where Mao's China had been a nation of surveillance, propaganda, and control, under Deng Xiaoping, Chinese were permitted to speak and think for themselves to an extent not seen since before the PRC's founding in 1949. Energized by the new atmosphere, students and others took to the streets to agitate for political reform in '83, '85, and '87, with each round of demonstrations growing bigger and bolder than the one before it.

Hu Yaobang was a reform-minded leader whom Deng had designated as his successor. Within the CCP, the anti-reform faction singled him out for criticism, so when he lost his position, many pro-reform Chinese saw his demotion as a setback for economic liberalization. Hu passed away in January of 1989; his death prompted students at Beijing's universities, including many veterans of previous protests, to launch a series of demonstrations in April calling for Hu—and the liberal reforms associated with him—to be rehabilitated. Within a few days, the students had occupied Tiananmen Square, Beijing's massive—and highly symbolic—central plaza.

The protests attracted global attention; the Western press dubbed the movement "Beijing Spring." With the eyes of the world upon them, China's leaders were loath to break up the protests. But as the student takeover of Tiananmen Square dragged on with no sign of abating, the government decided to act. On May 20, the leadership declared martial law in Beijing and ordered the military into the city to clear the square. Incredibly, the people of Beijing rose up to protect the protesters, flooding streets and blocking key intersections to prevent the military from reaching Tiananmen Square. Military commanders notified the government that the city could not be taken without violence and pulled back their forces.

For several days, the residents of Beijing controlled the city while the troops held their ground on the outskirts of town. The leaders' patience was finite, however, and on the night of June 3, they brought in fresh troops and ordered them to restore normalcy to the city. The army entered in tanks and armored personnel carriers, rolling over barricades and gunning down protestors and passers-by alike. Within a few hours, Tiananmen Square was empty, and an unknown number of Beijingers—students and nonstudents—were dead.

As the crackdown unfolded, horror and dread gripped the international community. Especially in the West, the student protests had evoked an enthusiastic response. Many Western commentators had predicted years earlier that China's economic reforms would inspire a political transformation, and the Tiananmen protests looked like the beginning of that change. Instead, they were brutally crushed, and Chinese were jerked back into the Maoist nightmare of political prosecutions, forced self-criticism, and nonstop propaganda.

To show their outrage and pacify domestic publics demanding action against the Chinese leadership, numerous foreign governments imposed economic sanctions. The World Bank estimated that foreign investment applications dropped by 75 percent in the wake of the crisis; the rate of increase of direct foreign investment in China fell from 38 percent in 1988 to 3 percent in 1990. According to the Chinese government, the crisis sparked a 50 percent drop in foreign loan agreements and sharply increased China's borrowing costs. The *Wall Street Journal* estimated China could lose a billion dollars in tourism revenue as a result of the crisis. China's trade deficit doubled from 1988 to 1989, although by 1990, it was running a trade surplus—no doubt in part due to export restrictions in several countries. Some of those restrictions—including US and European Union bans on military sales to China—were still in place decades later.

The Tiananmen crisis dealt a sharp blow to the PRC economy. In the summer of 1989, the government pulled back from its reform-and-opening policies—and multinational companies pulled out. Foreign investors wondered whether China was ready to be incorporated into the global economy—if politics could override economics at any moment, how could their money be safe?

The vacuum that formed when other foreign investors fled might have broken China's export drive but for the Taiwanese. Instead of fleeing the vacuum, *Taishang* rushed in to fill it, not for political reasons but because they saw a business opportunity. Meanwhile, their own government had done little to facilitate cross-Strait investment, and so could do little to impede it; instead, it lifted restrictions on imports from the mainland in the summer of 1989. A year later, Taipei began registering indirect investment in the mainland, effectively legalizing the practice.

In the end, the Tiananmen crisis interrupted China's economic rise only briefly. In the spring of 1992, Deng Xiaoping used a tour through the manufacturing hubs of southern China to signal his support for a return to rapid growth, including foreign investment. Deng singled out Shenzhen, the fastest-growing of the SEZ-centered export areas, as a model. Within a few years, foreign companies had flooded back, and China's economic growth trajectory picked up where it had left off. By 1992, its GDP growth rate had rebounded to 14 percent from its 1990 low of 4 percent.

When the dust settled on the Tiananmen crisis—and it settled quickly, as the promise of cheap Chinese goods soon drowned out cries for human rights—little had changed. China was still an authoritarian state whose people enjoyed few political rights, and the West was still importing an ever-increasing volume of manufactured products from the PRC. But for *Taishang*, the incident was significant, for it gave them an opening to expand their share of mainland manufacturing and further entrenched them as a critical—and reliable—source of investment in coastal China.

Most of the firms that moved to the mainland in the first wave were contract manufacturers in traditional industries. The move made them more competitive, which was critical to their survival. But many did more than just survive: they upgraded and improved both their business practices and their products. Especially for high-end manufacturers, the relationships with branded companies that had been forged in Taiwan flourished and deepened in the 1990s. In the process, the very nature of contract manufacturing was transformed.

Contract manufacturers are required to balance three competing values: quality, timeliness, and cost. Different clients rank these values differently. For some, ensuring consistent quality is more important than finding the lowest price. For others, such as companies that chase fast-changing fashion trends, getting goods delivered on time may be the top priority. And for some buyers, price is decisive. *Taishang* firms' particular strengths are quality and timeliness. The move to China helped *Taishang* manufacturers keep their prices competitive while maintaining high quality standards.

"Quality" means more than just delivering goods that meet the standards set in a contract. For international brands, "quality" also includes the quality of the contracting experience itself—the confidence international buyers have that their manufacturing partners will do a good job with minimal drama. It may be possible to get a similar product at a lower price, but if the delivery is late, the quality is uneven, or the interaction is stressful, it might make sense to pay a little more. Another danger is losing proprietary technology and designs to competitors. In China, where intellectual property protection is notoriously lax, design theft was a serious risk.

Finding the right balance of quality, timeliness, discretion, and price was a lesson Nike Inc. learned the hard way. Nike was born a design and marketing company with no manufacturing capacity. From the beginning, it relied on contract manufacturers for all of its production. Nike's original suppliers were in Japan, but in the early 1980s, the company began working with contract manufacturers in South Korea and Taiwan, including Pou Chen and Feng Tay. As the PRC's reform and opening deepened over the course of the decade, its low labor costs caught Nike executives' eyes, and they began shifting the most labor-intensive step in its production process—final assembly—to Chinese companies. To ensure high quality, Nike continued to use contractors in Taiwan to manufacture the components that the Chinese firms assembled.

What the company soon discovered, however, was that the strength of Taiwan's shoe industry was the unique combination of small, specialized firms working in densely networked geographic clusters. That combination gave Taiwan's shoe industry the flexibility to keep pace with Nike's constant design changes without sacrificing quality in production. Managing these complex supply chains was beyond the capacity of the mainland-based footwear assembly firms; the process required a level of coordination among suppliers, assemblers, and Nike's home office that Chinese firms simply could not achieve. It also required contractors who would never leak information about new designs and technologies. In order to sustain the high level of quality, reliability, and timeliness on which the brand depended, Nike needed Taiwanese (and South Korean) contractors to be in charge of the entire production process.

Once Nike recognized that Korean and Taiwan-based production networks had become an indispensable link in its global production chain, it developed a more strategic approach to managing its contracting relationships. Developed partners, such as Feng Tay, were given long-term contracts to produce top-end Nike products. Volume producers, including Pou Chen, were charged with keeping the supply of high-demand Nike products flowing to consumers, while developing sources partners, including Pou Chen subsidiary Yue Yuen, had the job of extending high-performance production practices into new (read: cheaper) locations. These arrangements allowed Nike's long-term suppliers to help the company manage its expansion into new markets. It also gave the long-term contractors a very high degree of autonomy in managing the supply chain—including the workforce in China and other low-wage countries.

As Nike discovered, however, there is even more to manufacturing in today's globalized world than getting the best product quality for the lowest price. "Quality," it turns out, extends even to the quality of the labor and environmental conditions in the manufacturing process. In the 1990s, American consumers began paying attention to the "high cost of low prices," especially when it came to the conditions under which some very high-profile brands were being manufactured. Taiwanese and Korean subcontractors delivered a reliable supply of high-quality goods at competitive prices, but their operations left Nike and other brands vulnerable to a new challenge: the anti-sweatshop movement. Anti-sweatshop activists sought to make Nike and similar firms responsible for working conditions in facilities where their products were made—whether or not it directly controlled them.

In the early 1990s, human rights and labor rights groups called attention to the poor working conditions in many overseas apparel factories linked to US brands. Labor rights activists attacked US companies for purchasing goods produced under sweatshop conditions in Indonesia, Pakistan, Vietnam, and China. The movement picked up steam mid-decade after a couple of high-profile incidents, including a tearful televised confession by celebrity Kathie Lee Gifford that clothing sold under her name at Walmart had been manufactured in Honduran sweatshops that used child labor. Anti-sweatshop and anti-globalization activists decided that Nike, given its high profile and international reputation, would make a prime target for their movements; the company became a leading target for a wide range of labor, economic, and environmental activists.

A 1996 photo of a Pakistani child laborer sewing a Nike soccer ball received extensive media coverage, and in 1997, an Ernst and Young audit of a Korean-owned Nike supplier in Vietnam turned up serious violations of Nike's health and safety standards. In 1996, President Bill Clinton's labor secretary, Robert Reich, brought together anti-sweatshop activists, branded companies, and American unions to craft labor standards for the apparel industry. A 1998 report from Reich's Apparel Industry Partnership included a proposal for an industry code of conduct as well as monitoring guidelines. If the industry thought participating in the White House project would quiet its critics, however, it was disappointed. The anti-sweatshop movement was about to become even more powerful.

In the fall of 1997, a group of activists on the Duke University campus formed Students Against Sweatshops to pressure the university administration to require suppliers of Duke-branded merchandise to meet labor standards and eliminate sweatshop labor. In early 1998, Duke's president announced that the university would require companies manufacturing licensed products for Duke to commit to improving labor conditions, raising wages, allowing monitoring of factories, and recognizing workers' right to unionize. Duke's successful model was copied on other campuses, and soon there were Students Against Sweatshops groups on campuses from Berkeley to Yale. The White House–sponsored Apparel Industry Partnership invited universities to join its newly formed monitoring organization, the Fair Labor Association.

The anti-sweatshop student movement posed a powerful challenge to Nike, which held licenses to athletic gear for many universities and colleges in the US. The company responded quickly to the pressure, promising to improve wages and working conditions in factories that made Nike-branded products and to allow inspectors to visit its plants. By 1997, it had labor affairs departments at its Oregon headquarters and in Asia. The company sponsored training sessions for contractors, including many of its own suppliers. In 2001, Nike held such a workshop in Taipei.

A central challenge for Nike and other brands was that they did not actually operate the factories making their products. In order to deliver on their promises to the activists, they needed the cooperation of the contractors who operated the overseas factories and managed their subcontractors. For the contractors, it was not enough to comply with Nike's code of conduct in their own facilities; they also had to oversee subcontractors, many of whom were working in countries whose legal standards were less stringent than Nike required. Just as Nike relied on its contractors to supply high-quality sweatpants, it now also relied on those contractors to supply proof that those sweatpants were not being made in sweatshops.

In 2002, Nike restructured its contracting practices under the "Future Vision" plan, a program aimed at rehabilitating the brand's image by improving Nike's ability to monitor the manufacturing process and meet its corporate social responsibility goals. Nike eliminated some of its contractors and tightened its ties with those that remained. Five companies, including Taiwan's Pou Chen and Feng Tay, achieved the status of Manufacturing Leadership Partners, completing their transformation from Nike's contractors to its partners.

Between 1990 and 2010, the athletic apparel industry was transformed, and Taiwanese companies were at the center of that transformation. Today, very few shoes bear the mark "Made in Taiwan," but Taiwan-based companies still dominate global branded-shoe production. Their corporate strategies emphasize diversification, both of their product mix and their geographic expansion. The Pou Chen Group is the world's largest supplier of branded athletic shoes—not only Nike, but Reebok, Asics, Under Armour, Adidas, New Balance, Puma, and others, as well as casual shoes such as Converse and Timberland. Feng Tay makes shoes for Clarks, Rockport, and Doc Martens as well as Nike and other athletic brands. It also makes in-line skates, ski boots, ice hockey equipment, and top-of-the-line golf balls and soccer balls. Both companies invest in research and development activities in Taiwan and are looking to add manufacturing capacity in Vietnam, Indonesia, India, and other countries. They have become, in other words, multinational corporations in their own right, with the patents and investments to prove it.

In 1978, the People's Republic of China did about twenty billion dollars in international trade; its exports totaled less than ten billion dollars. Economists characterized it as a developing country likely to experience slow growth for the foreseeable future. Meanwhile, the up-and-coming export-manufacturing economies were in Latin America. Textile manufacturing was flowing out of the southern United States and into Mexico and Central America. Just twenty years later, though, the PRC's export economy was skyrocketing. In 2000, China had two hundred fifty billion in export earnings, most of it from manufactured goods. It was the world's biggest exporter of shoes, toys, and athletic apparel, and it had become a key link in global commodity chains. The companies that made those goods were overwhelmingly foreign, including thousands from Taiwan.

In retrospect, China's transformation into a consumer manufacturing powerhouse seems overdetermined, almost inevitable, but no one predicted its rise, and even as it was picking up steam in the 1990s, few imagined it would achieve the heights it did. So how did poor, rural China become the factory of the world? This is a complex question; the answer has many parts, but we cannot explain China's shift to export-oriented manufacturing without taking into account the myriad industrial firms with roots in Taiwan. These firms arrived in China fully equipped with capital, technology, equipment, management, and customers. Just add labor—a resource in ample supply in China—and export manufacturing was under way. Without those firms—and their resources, expertise, and connections—it is hard to imagine when (if ever) China's export-oriented manufacturing sector would have reached takeoff velocity.

NOTES

1. Quoted in Lawrence Reardon, *The Reluctant Dragon: Crisis Cycles in Chinese Foreign Economic Policy* (Seattle: University of Washington Press, 2002), 165.

2. Michael West Osborne, *China's Special Economic Zones* (Paris: Development Centre of the Organisation for Economic Co-operation and Development, 1986), 111.

3. Murray Scot Tanner, *Chinese Economic Coercion against Taiwan: A Tricky Weapon to Use* (Santa Monica, CA: RAND National Defense Research Institute, 2007), 37.

4. Hsing You-tien, *Making Capitalism in China: The Taiwan Connection* (Oxford: Oxford University Press, 1998), 18.

5. Hsing, *Making Capitalism in China*, 4.

6. World Integrated Trade Solutions, "China 1994 Import Partner Share," World Bank, https://wits.worldbank.org/CountryProfile/en/Country/CHN/Year/1994 /TradeFlow/Import/Partner/ALL/Product/manuf.

7. Chen Tain-Jy and Ku Ying-Hua, "Quanqiuhua xia Taiwan dui dalu touzi celue" [Taiwan's mainland investment strategy under globalization], in *Jingji quanqiuhua yu Taishang dalu touzi* [Economic globalization and Taishang investment on the mainland], edited by Chen Te-shung (Taipei: Ink Publishing, 2008), 16–17.

4

From SME to ODM

Taiwan's Integration into Global Manufacturing Networks

In *Toy Story 3*, spaceman Buzz Lightyear is held prisoner at Sunnyside Day-care until his friend Barbie takes advantage of her erstwhile sweetheart Ken's vanity to pull off a rescue. The platonic relationship between fashion doll and spaceman action figure (not to mention the movie's G rating) prevents us from finding out for sure, but depending on her age, there's a good chance that under her turquoise unitard Barbie carries the same mark as Buzz: Made in Taiwan.

In 1967, the Mattel Corporation entered into a joint venture with the China General Plastics Corporation to manufacture toys at a plastics factory in Taishan, a small town just outside Taipei. Two years later, the factory began producing Barbie dolls. The production model used at Taishan's Meining doll factory is called original equipment manufacturing, or OEM. Under the OEM model, Meining and its subcontractors produced goods exclusively for Mattel using designs Mattel provided. OEM manufacturing is a type of contract manufacturing, one Taiwan excelled at in its export-manufacturing heyday.

The Barbie factory was so successful that the joint-venture company soon added three more factories nearby; by 1983, they employed eight thousand people and produced half of the world's supply of Barbie dolls: twenty thousand per day. The four factories directly owned and controlled by the joint venture specialized in assembling and packaging dolls, as well as making Barbie heads, torsos, limbs, hair, and clothing.

CHAPTER 4

To supplement the work carried out in the factories, hundreds of smaller companies joined the production process as subcontractors, an arrangement known as a "center-satellite" factory network, which was used by many multinational companies in Taiwan. These small factories and workshops—some of them little more than a sewing machine in a living room corner—painted dolls' faces, attached and styled their hair, and sewed many of their outfits. They also helped with dressing and packaging Barbies. Some workshops also did plastic injection, producing tiny Barbie clutch purses and miniscule Barbie stiletto heels in molds provided by Mattel. Altogether, Mattel and its contractors employed a third of Taishan's workforce, even as the once-sleepy village grew into a city whose population rivaled Boston's.

The end of "Barbie Town" is another familiar story: by the mid-1980s, Taiwan was no longer a competitive location for manufacturing inexpensive plastic toys. Rising wages were part of the picture, but higher prices for land and logistics, new regulations, and an appreciating New Taiwan Dollar added to the cost of manufacturing in Taiwan. The young women who had flooded into the factories and the housewives who labored in their spare moments assembling Barbie's infinite wardrobe lost their jobs when Mattel moved the Taishan factories to China and Malaysia in 1987. Nonetheless, the town never lost its self-image as Barbie's second home, and in 2005, it opened the Taishan Doll Museum, a testament to the role industrial doll making played in the town's history. The museum documents the life of Meining factory workers, including photos, pay stubs, and other memorabilia. Some nostalgic former employees work as docents at the museum; some even teach visitors how to design and sew outfits for Barbie's distinctive figure.

Reading the tale of Taishan Barbie, it's hard not to wonder: Why Taiwan? In a world full of countries hungry for development, why choose a village in Taiwan as the birthplace for half the world's Barbies? What made Taiwan so much more successful than others in managing the transition from import substitution to export-oriented industrialization? The answer to that question is interesting and important. It tells us a lot about the strengths Taiwanese businesses possessed when they moved to the mainland and also about the challenges they encountered as they tried to transplant their unique—and uniquely successful—business model to a new location.

Taiwan's export success rested on three legs: open markets, supportive government policy, and a vibrant entrepreneurial sector. The previous chapters covered the first and second legs. They explained the reasoning behind Washington's decision to allow imports from Taiwan and its neighbors to enter freely, and reviewed the government policies that allowed Taiwan to develop its manufacturing prowess. But what about the entrepreneurs? Where did they come from, and how were they able to take advantage of opportunities so efficiently?

There's no question that Taiwan began manufacturing goods for export at the ideal time. It was the height of the Cold War, and the US was eager to support friendly countries on the borders of the communist world; Washington was happy to overlook its allies' undemocratic politics and mercantilistic economic policies, so long as those allies were equally happy to fight the spread of Soviet and Chinese influence. It was also the apex of American manufacturing. US companies held the top spot in countless high-value industrial food chains, so they were content to share opportunities for low-value manufacturing with friendly countries.

While US government policies ensured Taiwanese manufacturers' access to a rich consumer market, Taiwanese government policies ensured those firms had what they needed to keep the merchandise flowing. But markets and inputs alone do not make a thriving export economy. They are necessary, but not sufficient, conditions. Without firms willing and able to make the products consumers want at prices they're willing to pay, nothing happens. The final link in Taiwan's success was the proliferation of small firms that supplied goods to the US and other export markets at prices that were hard to beat. Over time, those small and medium-sized enterprises—SMEs—adopted new technologies and business strategies. As their skills improved, they grew from order-based manufacturing through long-term contract manufacturing to original design manufacturing (ODM). Today, for example, Apple relies on its Taiwanese suppliers not only to make the iPhone but to engineer new components and achieve steady improvements in quality and functionality.

Taiwan was able to grab a disproportionate share of export production in large part because its SMEs were more able than their competitors in other countries to respond to global demand. Taiwan was and is what sociologist Gary Hamilton calls a "demand-responsive economy."[1] Only a few Taiwanese companies are known for their ability to create demand by developing new products and marketing them to consumers. Most Taiwan firms' strength lies in their ability to supply goods to companies that have built demand through design, marketing, and branding but don't have the capacity to produce their products at a price the market will bear.

Demand-responsive industry needs to be fast, flexible, reliable, and independent. Ordinarily, these traits are hard to combine. Speed is usually the enemy of quality. Being flexible often means putting innovation and change ahead of steadiness and reliability. Being reliable implies you're in a long-term relationship, but being independent means you're keeping things casual. So how did Taiwan's small and medium-sized enterprises manage to combine all these traits in one package?

Small size is a big part of the answer. Most SMEs were founded by individual entrepreneurs investing their personal or family resources (or a combination of family money and money borrowed from friends). Partnerships were uncommon, joint stock companies extremely rare. Most companies started the way Fu Tai Umbrella, the company profiled in the preface, did: somebody took his life savings and invested it in a business. The classic SME began with an entrepreneur who learned his skills, not as an engineer or an MBA student, but as a factory worker or apprentice. Once he (and the founder is almost always a man, although his wife will likely be a key player in his business) acquired the know-how he needed to enter the trade, he found an empty building in a dusty rural crossroad or grimy urban intersection and went to work. And going to work meant doing everything the company needed, from loading trucks to signing contracts. These "black-handed bosses" were at least as comfortable operating a lathe or sewing machine as writing up an invoice.

Founding a small business is notoriously risky, and that was no less true in Taiwan in the 1950s, '60s, and '70s than in other places and times. Most of the people who founded SMEs had few other opportunities; they were looking for an escape from agriculture or industrial labor. Few came from white-collar sectors such as government, education, and state-owned enterprise management because those forms of employment were more stable, remunerative, and prestigious than becoming a black-handed boss. White-collar professions strongly favored '49ers—those who had come to Taiwan after World War II. Many native Taiwanese (those whose families had come to the island decades or centuries earlier) might have preferred jobs in the state sector, but the lack of opportunity left them with little choice but to form small businesses. Ironically, once business replaced government as the driver of growth and prosperity on Taiwan, this division of labor left many native Taiwanese better off than most '49ers, at least financially.

SME founders retained ownership of their businesses as they grew, creating in Taiwan an economy based on a vast number of small family firms. In 1954, over 99 percent of Taiwanese firms had fewer than one hundred employees; forty years later, the percentage was 98 percent.[2] The preference for entrepreneurial family businesses is partly cultural: Taiwan has a strong norm that being a boss is preferable to working for someone else. Taiwanese have a saying: "It's better to be a chicken's head than an ox's ass," and they mean it. Chen Tian-fu, the Umbrella King, left a comfortable office job in the banana business to get his hands dirty making umbrellas. Andy Huang, founder and head of Pretty Fashion, which at one point supplied one in four wedding dresses sold in Europe, quit his steady job as a sales manager at Northwest Airlines to found a string of unsuccessful businesses before starting Pretty Fashion. Theirs is a trajectory countless Taiwanese have followed. The popularity of leaving a big company to form a small one, the fissiparous tendencies of Taiwanese business, the relentlessly entrepreneurial mentality throughout the society—these are the traits that created an economy in which small and medium-sized enterprises could employ 80 percent of the nation's workforce and produce most of its exported goods. As late as 1996, a decade after firms first began moving to the mainland, SMEs still produced a majority of Taiwan's exports. According to one estimate, in the mid-1980s, there was one registered business for every eight Taiwanese adults; in 1985, companies with fewer than three hundred employees represented 62 percent of the workforce and 65 percent of exports.[3]

A second cultural factor reinforces the preference for being a boss. While European inheritance norms traditionally privileged the concentration and preservation of wealth—the first son inherited, the rest found something else to do—in Chinese tradition, family property is divided after the death of the patriarch—not always right away but eventually. The expectation that one's sons would someday split up their father's creations motivated fathers to prepare for that moment.

Instead of giving each son a job within the same corporate entity, Taiwanese entrepreneurs tended to create multiple entities, sometimes in industries quite distant from the original business. So, for example, Chen Tian-fu diversified from umbrellas into aluminum caps, bicycle spokes, and umbrella frames. Diversification—which was not absolutely limited to direct relatives—had other benefits as well. For one thing, it spread risk. If one business failed, the others might thrive; all the family's eggs were not in a single basket. Nonetheless, there was no question that the businesses were related; they did not spin off into fully independent entities but remained linked through interlocking management and (as long as the patriarch was alive) through the father's iron-fisted leadership.

In short, Taiwan's SMEs grew through proliferation, not expansion. Instead of making the original company larger and larger, SMEs often hived off a new company when they reached a certain size. But even as they were decentralizing management and diversifying lines of business, Taiwan's SME founders kept a tight hold on another key production factor: capital. Here again, culture matters. In traditional Taiwanese families, wealth is shared, so revenue generated by one company within a family group was assumed to be available to the others. Each firm's profits could be used as investment capital by others in the group. Allocating that capital was one of the patriarch's most important responsibilities. Sharing assets and revenues enabled many entrepreneurs to self-fund their start-ups, and it also allowed unprofitable firms to close because core personnel (i.e., family members) could easily find another position within the group—or start a new business in a more promising industry.

Being able to close unsuccessful businesses is an important virtue of Taiwan's SME economy because demand responsiveness requires extreme flexibility. Because Taiwanese firms were so flexible, they tended to rush into new product lines en masse, flooding the market and driving down profits, a phenomenon they called "swarming bees." This combination—decentralized production with centralized financing—allowed Taiwanese entrepreneurs to take advantage of new opportunities without getting stuck in unprofitable sectors.

The most successful firms took advantage of what Gary Hamilton calls the "gold rush" nature of Taiwan's export economy.[4] During the California gold rush, companies that sold prospectors their supplies earned far more than the prospectors themselves. Similarly, Taiwanese companies that moved up the value chain to provide inputs to production were more profitable than those laboring at the bottom of the chain assembling finished goods. Fu Tai

Umbrella founder Chen Tian-fu became the umbrella king not by assembling umbrellas but by manufacturing umbrella parts.

Few firms have the first-mover advantage (and forward-looking management) that allowed Fu Tai to flourish once umbrella manufacturing became a low-margin industry. Most Taiwanese SMEs never became queen bees but remained part of the swarm of drones. They needed to move in and out of business quickly in order to find niches where profits still could be made. The structure of Taiwanese family firms maximized their chances of navigating to success through the thicket of risk and opportunity that is demand-responsive manufacturing.

Another advantage Taiwanese SMEs enjoyed in export manufacturing was their high productivity, which rested significantly on firm owners' self-exploitation. Taiwanese SMEs were operated by entrepreneurs—not investors. Business owners expected to do production-related tasks alongside managerial and administrative tasks, and they expected family members to pitch in, too. Instead of paying wages, entrepreneurs in family businesses used firm revenues to provide for their employed family members; self-exploitation extended to the entire family. Wage bills were low also because contract manufacturers needed few marketing, sales, or managerial employees. Rather than maintaining a permanent sales staff, firms pooled their resources to send representatives to trade shows to solicit business.

Sharing a booth at a trade show is just one example of cross-firm cooperation among Taiwanese SMEs, and it points to another critical asset they enjoyed: networking. At the heart of Taiwan's manufacturing success—early and late, on Taiwan and on the mainland—are relationships: relationships with coworkers and employees, relationships with suppliers and customers, relationships with partners and competitors. The ability to form and sustain the kind of relationships that have enabled Taiwan's businesses to thrive is rooted in the island's tight-knit, heavily networked society.

In 1996, Gary Hamilton wrote:

> It is somehow understandable that huge business groups in Japan or South Korea, linking sometimes thousands of firms of different sizes together and exploiting their internal synergies, can concentrate their research and development efforts and their production expertise to manufacture some of the world's finest products. It is much more difficult to understand—as one walks down

dusty streets in central Taiwan and sees family after family working around
tables in their storefront homes that are open to everyone's view, or as one
drives in the countryside and sees small concrete boxes located in the midst of
rice fields that are factories employing only handfuls of people—how someone
here, in these locations, could be producing a piece of a part that will go into a
component that is in 50% of all the computers worldwide. Taiwan's business
organizations achieve both economies of scale and economies of scope, and
they do so because they utilize the resources contained in Taiwan's densely
networked society.[5]

Hamilton goes on to describe two types of networks in which SMEs participated. The first, the family enterprise group, was a free-standing financial
and production network centered on a patrilineal family. We have already
seen how collaboration among companies within the same family group
helped SMEs compete and thrive. The second type of network—the *guanxi*,
or relationship, network—extended beyond the family. *Guanxi* networks rest
on shared identities that allow Taiwanese to invoke norms of trust and reci-
procity that enable an extraordinary degree of economic cooperation.

The overlap between family networks and *guanxi* networks is extremely
dense, and it gave rise to significant economic efficiencies. The high degree of
trust among friends allows firms to take risks, to seize "stretch" opportunities.
Contract manufacturers could sign contracts without knowing exactly how
they would meet them because they had large networks of potential partners
that could be mobilized to meet the contract terms. Likewise, they dared to
extend generous financial and payment arrangements to their partners because they trusted that they would be paid. For example, postdated checks are
a common form of loan in Taiwan—so common that Taiwan's central bank
tracks their interest rates. Looser payment terms helped to maximize the efficiency of capital by making it possible for firms to commit to transactions
that otherwise would have been impossible to finance.

Network-based production maximized both speed and quality because
breaking down the production process into steps and assigning them to different firms kept each workshop's production process simple and specialized.
Disaggregating the process in this way was possible thanks to another of Taiwan's SME innovations: clustered manufacturing. All the firms participating
in a particular production chain set up their workshops close together, clus-

tered around the final assembly plant. Given Taiwan's small size and lax land-use regulations, groups of producers could set up shop pretty much wherever they wanted, including in rural villages and small towns. Land and labor were cheap in the countryside, and workers had alternate income sources—mainly agriculture—to fall back on when their labor wasn't needed.

The subcontractors that sprang up in Taishan to sew Barbie costumes, mold Barbie shoes, and "plant" Barbie hair were a variation on this theme. The assembly plant around which they had clustered was itself not an SME but a joint venture involving a foreign company, but their function—performing discrete, limited tasks in a much larger production process—was typical. The assembly plant directed materials to household workshops, each of which completed its step in the production process before passing the goods on for the next stage of processing. This kind of production still happens in Taiwan: I saw an industrial sewing machine being used for piecework in a private home in central Taiwan in early 2020.

Production networks helped Taiwan pull off the tricky combination of speed, quality, reliability, and independence. Once a network was established, individual firms had less need for marketing than ever since they could count on the network to provide orders. They reduced risk while maximizing innovation and ensuring access to capital. Another benefit: the density of networks ensured wide access to information about new products, market demand, and production techniques. Taiwan's SMEs were famously nimble—leaping from product to product, constantly retooling to accommodate the next season's orders. We can attribute much of that nimbleness to the networked nature of the SME economy.

One particularly important type of network is the rotating credit cooperative, or *hui*. For individuals and firms that cannot meet their capital needs out of personal assets, *hui* provide a convenient alternative to formal credit. Throughout most of the export-oriented industrialization period, the state's credit policies were biased toward large companies, forcing SMEs to rely on informal sources of financing, including *hui*. According to Shui-yan Tang, informal credit markets contributed more than a third of money lent to private enterprises in Taiwan prior to the 1990s.[6]

Hui are invitation-only credit societies created by individuals entirely outside the banking and legal system. As such, they rely entirely on trust among the members. They generally last a few months to a few years, about one month per member. During that time, each member contributes a fixed sum of money each month. Payouts can take a variety of forms. In some *hui*, the recipient of the month's contributions is chosen by lottery, making the *hui* a savings vehicle. In others, the contribution scheme is set up so that those who choose to cash in early end up paying more than those who wait until the end to collect the kitty. Some *hui* allow members to bid for the kitty along the way, which provides a small interest payment to the others. However it is organized, the point of a *hui* is to pool resources so that each member has access to a lump sum greater than he or she (many *hui* are operated by women) could accumulate alone. Even today, when most Taiwanese have ready access to bank credit, many still participate in *hui*. The loan societies don't require proving credit worthiness or other paperwork, and if managed carefully, they can provide a nest egg just when it's needed.

Of course, *hui* have a huge downside: if someone defaults or absconds, there's no collateral to seize—really no way to avoid losing one's investment, which, if you were planning to wait until the end to cash out, can be considerable. The whole edifice rests on trust, which means relationships. Like clustered manufacturing, *hui* are possible because of the densely networked nature of Taiwan's society. People who live in the same town, who see each other every day, who know one another's parents and children, who do business together, cannot easily walk away from a *hui* obligation. Taiwan's population of just under twenty-four million may sound like a lot, but socially, it's a small world. Busted *hui* are surprisingly rare.

Taiwan's SME economy was a perfect environment for *hui* to thrive. Dense social networks and tightly woven business networks made *hui* a safe way to concentrate resources at a time when small infusions of capital could make a decisive impact on firms' ability to participate in export manufacturing. And because those firms were able to join the global economy, Taiwan's standard of living rose swiftly in those decades, earning it a high position in the global per capita income rankings. The small size of the firms also helped preserve a relatively egalitarian distribution of wealth and income.

It is important to acknowledge the downside of the SME economy, too. Self-exploitation (and the exploitation of family members) is still exploitation. Millions of Taiwanese labored under grueling conditions, deferring the enjoyment of their newfound economic security into the future. As Ping-Chun Hsiung has written, Taiwan's particular form of capitalist production assumed—indeed required—that women would do all the household work and child care while also laboring in what she calls "living rooms as factories" for little or no wages.[7]

Taiwan's loose zoning regulations meant that factories—some of them processing dangerous or toxic materials—were located in residential areas. Pollution from small workshops fouled farmland and degraded living conditions for local people. Residents of high-rise apartment buildings were forced to live with the noise and dirt from industrial operations in neighboring units. And not all SMEs were successful; Pretty Fashion's Andy Huang was hardly the only entrepreneur to experience failure. Indeed, his ultimate success is less typical than his repeated bankruptcies. Still, the SMEs were the beating heart of Taiwan's export-led development. Their energy built the world's seventeenth-largest trading economy.

SMES MEET MNCS

In a nutshell, here's what worked in Taiwan: family-owned companies staffed by members of tight social networks making the most of the state's policy of giving the private sector free rein in downstream manufacturing while maintaining a strong state presence upstream to ensure a steady supply of industrial inputs. These elements, combined with open markets in the West, made it possible for Taiwan's SMEs to become the most vibrant and competitive in the world. But they were not enough to keep Taiwan's manufacturing firms in business over the long haul.

Taiwan's SMEs began as straightforward contract manufacturers filling orders for simple goods designed by clients overseas. They compensated for their low technological level by controlling costs. Family-based networks kept wages low while diverse lines of business minimized idle time for workers and facilities. Inevitably, however, as Taiwan grew wealthier, labor costs began to rise. At the same time, Taiwanese began to demand better working and environmental conditions. "Black-handed bosses" wanted their children in school—not the factory. At the same time, production technology was improving and clients were upping their expectations for product quality and logistical efficiency. Taiwanese firms were forced to upgrade their operations constantly to keep pace with an ever-more-complicated manufacturing environment. This process had important consequences for both the Taiwanese companies and their foreign clients.

Upgrading changed the relationship between Taiwanese firms and their clients in many ways. First, it raised the firms' technical level so that they could contribute more intellectual content to the products they made. Fu Tai Umbrella provides a good example of this shift. As more and more companies began making umbrellas and umbrella parts, Fu Tai kept its lead by upgrading its operations from OEM (original equipment manufacturing) to ODM—original design manufacturing. ODM contractors don't just produce to the specifications provided by their clients, as OEM firms do. Instead, ODM firms incorporate research and development in their business model. They offer design services to their clients, they tweak old products, and they create new ones. For Fu Tai Umbrella, that meant inventing new umbrella designs—multi-fold, automatic, self-closing—while at the same time supplying higher value-added components to other companies to assemble. In the process, Fu Tai became a major source of patented technology for its overseas partners, including Totes.

Upgrading also tightened the ties between Taiwanese contract manufacturers and their foreign clients. Improving the quality, reliability, and technical sophistication of their products made Taiwanese contractors, in the words of Chang-ling Huang and Suk-jun Lim, "indispensable partners" to multinational companies (MNCs).[8] As partners, the Taiwanese firms no longer competed on price alone but also on the quality and consistency of the products and services they provided. That gave them breathing space in an increasingly global, hypercompetitive manufacturing environment. A good example of this type of partnership can be found in the tight linkages between Nike, the American athletic shoe giant, and its Taiwanese contractors, Pou Chen and Feng Tay.

Shoes were one of Taiwan's first manufactured exports. The Taiwanese Plastic Shoes Exporters Association was founded in 1968, not long after Taiwan's shift to export-oriented industrialization began. In 1970, there were about seventy-five registered footwear firms on the island, a number that grew nearly tenfold in next ten years and peaked in 1988 at 1,245.[9] By the mid-1970s, Taiwan's share of the US footwear market was over 40 percent. American manufacturers mobilized to protect their market, and in 1977, the US imposed quotas on shoe imports from Taiwan and South Korea. Fighting Washington's protectionist measures was a key reason Taiwanese companies founded a broader trade group—the Taiwanese Footwear Manufacturers Association—in 1978.

In 1962, Phil Knight conceived the idea of importing high-quality running shoes from Japan. With help from his former track coach and Japanese suppliers, Knight's creative designs became popular among serious runners. Knight's biggest innovation was his decision not to open manufacturing facilities but to outsource all of his company's production, keeping only the design and marketing in-house. In 1971, Knight hired contract manufacturers to make shoes under a new brand: Nike. Production costs in Japan were rising steadily, and by the end of the decade, Nike had transferred its business to contract manufacturers in Taiwan and South Korea. By 1982, 86 percent of Nike's athletic shoes were made in Taiwan and Korea. In 1983, the firm began contracting with Taiwan's Pou Chen Corporation, a family-owned company founded in 1969 that had been doing contract manufacturing for the German athletic shoe brand Adidas since 1979.

Chasing lower costs is typical behavior for companies that outsource production, but cost is not the only variable they consider. Nike's business model pays attention to cost, but other priorities are at least as important. For Nike, athletic shoes are a fashion product, and that puts it in what experts call the "design-sensitive market." In the design-sensitive market, contract manufacturers must produce many different patterns at a high level of quality on a tight schedule—without leaking design information to competitors (including "knockoff" firms that copy their designs at a lower quality and price). Meeting the demands of the design-sensitive market requires reliable workers, clever management, and close ties between the branded firm and its contract manufacturers.

Nike discovered just how important those qualities were when mainland China opened itself to trade and investment in the early 1980s. China was just emerging from decades of low growth and slow development, so costs were low. State-owned companies were eager to partner with foreign brands to bring jobs, money, and technology to China. Nonetheless, Nike abandoned its efforts to contract directly with Chinese firms after four years of trying. The mainland companies could not meet Nike's requirements for quality, speed, reliability, and secrecy. In a design-sensitive market, lower costs can carry a high price.

After its disappointing foray into mainland China, Nike strengthened its ties with its suppliers in Taiwan and Korea. It seemed their production model had emerged victorious, but their victory was short-lived; the escape from price pressure was only temporary. As the cost of production continued to rise in Taiwan, even the best manufacturing firms found themselves squeezed between clients' demand for lower prices and workers' expectation of higher wages, which rose as much as 10 percent annually in the late 1980s. During that time, Taiwan was a leading supplier of shoes to the world; footwear was its third-largest export. But in less than five years the shoe factories were gone—relocated to mainland China.

NOTES

1. Gary G. Hamilton and Cheng-shu Kao, "The Asian Miracle and the Rise of Demand-Responsive Economies," in *The Market Makers: How Retailers Are Reshaping the Global Economy*, edited by Gary G. Hamilton, Benjamin Senauer, and Misha Petrovic (Oxford: Oxford University Press, 2011).

2. Wan-wen Chu, "Industrial Growth and Small and Medium-sized Enterprises: The Case of Taiwan," Academia Sinica, accessed November 24, 2020, http://idv .sinica.edu.tw/wwchu/SME%20TW.pdf, p. 25.

3. Tyler S. Biggs, "Heterogeneous Firms and Efficient Financial Intermediation in Taiwan," in *Markets in Developing Countries: Parallel, Fragmented, and Black*, edited by Michael Roemer and Christine Jones (San Francisco, CA: ICS Press, 1991), 169.

4. Gary Hamilton, *Patterns of Asian Capitalism: The Cases of Taiwan and South Korea*, Working Paper Series no. 28, Program in East Asian Culture and Development Research (Davis: University of California, Institute of Governmental Affairs, 1990), 18.

5. Gary G. Hamilton, "Organization and Market Processes in Taiwan's Capitalist Economy," in *The Economic Organization of East Asian Capitalism*, edited by M. Orru, N. Biggart, and G. Hamilton (Thousand Oaks, CA: SAGE, 1996), 257–258.

6. Shui-yan Tang, "Informal Credit Markets and Economic Development in Taiwan," *World Development* 23, no. 5 (1995): 845.

7. Ping-Chun Hsiung, *Living Rooms as Factories: Class, Gender, and the Satellite Factory System in Taiwan* (Philadelphia, PA: Temple University Press, 1996).

8. Huang Chang-ling and Suk-jun Lim, *Globalization and the Corporate Strategies: South Korea and Taiwan's Footwear Industries in Transition*, paper presented to the Annual Meeting of the American Political Science Association, Philadelphia, Pennsylvania, 2006.

9. Lu-lin Cheng, *Embedded Competitiveness: Taiwan's Shifting Role in International Footwear Sourcing Networks*, Unpublished PhD thesis, Department of Sociology, Duke University, 1996.

5

The 1990s

From Umbrellas to iPhones

In the 1980s, China's opening was a novelty; it had a tentative, experimental feel. For many in the West, the 1989 Tiananmen Crisis seemed to bring that experiment to an end, but they were wrong. Three years later, Deng Xiaoping's "Southern Tour" signaled Beijing's determination to revive reform and opening. Western investors read that signal and rushed back to China, ushering in a new phase in China's economic opening. After 1992, there could be no doubt: economic reform—including a fierce commitment to export manufacturing and foreign investment—was in China to stay. That confirmation prompted a second wave of Taiwanese investors to turn their sights to the mainland. It also put China—and its key foreign investors, especially *Taishang*—at the forefront of globalization.

China's economic transformation offered a new lease on life to the SMEs that had driven Taiwan's economic miracle, but the island's leaders worried that those firms' eagerness to move their operations to the mainland was putting Taiwan's economic and political independence at risk. Even more concerning was a new wave of cross-Strait investment dominated by companies farther up the production chain, including the high-tech firms that had replaced the island's rapidly disappearing traditional manufacturing companies. The second part of this chapter explores Taiwan's high-tech development, but before moving to that topic, we need to pause to consider how Taiwan's policy makers responded to the rush of Taiwanese firms to the mainland.

CHAPTER 5

In 1990, Taipei rescinded its official ban on indirect investment in the mainland; a year later, it repealed the so-called Temporary Provisions Effective during the Period of National Mobilization for the Suppression of the Communist Rebellion, an anachronistically labeled set of rules put in place in the 1940s to keep the two sides apart. Taiwan's business community was extremely bullish about opportunities for growth in China: by 1996, mainland-bound investment totaled nearly 5 percent of Taiwan's gross domestic product.[1] Legalizing their activity opened the door for investors to begin advocating for a more liberal investment climate. Their enthusiasm was so intense, in fact, that Premier Lien Chan accused Beijing of mobilizing *Taishang* to pressure Taiwan's government—an accusation that would be repeated many times in the coming decades by politicians of all stripes.

Taiwan's economic bureaucrats were reluctant to give in to the business community's gung ho impulses. They saw both political and economic risks for Taiwan in becoming overly dependent on the mainland economy. The economic risks are obvious: for a country that manufactured its way into the top tier of world economies, offshoring manufacturing is a risky move. But what were the political risks?

Both sides in the Chinese civil war, the Nationalists and the Communists, believed in a unified Chinese nation that included Taiwan. The KMT's plan was to use Taiwan as a platform from which to fight its way back to control over the mainland; the Chinese Communist Party's plan was to develop a military capable of "liberating" Taiwan by force. By the 1970s, it was clear that neither side was in a position to defeat the other, but both governments were still imagining a united future. But beginning in the late 1980s, Taiwan's political system democratized rapidly, and citizens began raising questions about unification. Some even advocated declaring Taiwan an independent nation and getting rid of the "Republic of China" label altogether.

The PRC government was determined to prevent Taiwan from gaining recognition as an independent state; it made it clear with words and actions that it was willing to use military force to block such an outcome. As for unification, Beijing was equally committed but less urgent. It was willing to wait for conditions to be right for unification, but that didn't mean leaders in the mainland were not happy to encourage those conditions when they had a chance to do so. Economic integration between the two sides, and the people-to-people exchanges that inevitably followed, were exactly the kinds of trends the PRC government believed would help the conditions for unification to ripen.

The PRC's efforts to recruit Taiwanese investors had both economic and political motivations, and so did Taiwanese leaders' discomfort with the velocity of cross-Strait investment. President Lee Teng-hui worried about the economic consequences of the rapid migration of resources to China, but Lee and his advisors also worried that overdependence on the PRC economy would leave Taiwan vulnerable to Beijing's political pressure, including pressure to enter negotiations aimed at ending the two sides' political separation. And even though Lee was, at that time, an advocate of eventual unification, he was dead set against unification on Beijing's terms.

In 1991, Taipei adopted regulations mandating government approval of investments over a million dollars and restricting investment outside the labor-intensive manufacturing sector. Still, the business exodus continued, with companies farther up the value and production chains following downstream assembly firms across the Strait. In 1992, the PRC lifted regulations that had prevented foreign (including Taiwanese) companies from manufacturing personal computer products in the mainland. That decision sparked a spike in Taiwanese computer companies' mainland investment.

As more (and more valuable) manufacturing activities shifted across the Strait, Taiwanese economists began to worry that cross-Strait investment could hollow out the island's manufacturing sector. President Lee Teng-hui responded to this anxiety with a series of policy moves aimed at reducing the flow of Taiwanese capital, technology, and talent to the mainland. In 1994, he inaugurated a "Go South" strategy to encourage Taiwanese firms to invest in Southeast Asia. Investing in Malaysia, the Philippines, Indonesia, and Thailand, the president argued, would allow Taiwan to access the low-wage manufacturing platforms they needed to remain competitive without the political risk investing in the mainland entailed.

While the Go South program did increase Taiwanese investment in Southeast Asia and advance Taiwan's diplomatic goals, it diverted very little investment from the mainland. *Taishang* continued to direct most of their investment to the mainland—where they had no formal status or protection at all, much less government financial support. A 1994 Ministry of Economic Affairs survey found that fewer than 20 percent of firms planned to invest in Southeast Asian countries in the coming years, compared to almost 50 percent that planned to invest in China.[2] And when the Southeast Asian currency crisis erupted in 1997, Lee's Go South policy was effectively dead. To slow the pace of cross-Strait investment growth, Lee turned to more forceful means.

In March 1996, Lee Teng-hui won Taiwan's first democratic presidential election. He was so popular that he managed to capture a majority of the vote in a four-way race. Most Taiwanese shared Lee's concerns about the risks of cross-Strait investment, but they also understood that the economic opportunities in the mainland could not be ignored. That ambivalence has been baked into Taiwan's politics ever since, and it is evident in the policies of a series of presidents: Lee Teng-hui, Chen Shui-bian, Ma Ying-jeou, and Tsai Ing-wen.

Six months after the 1996 election, Lee rolled out yet another new policy aimed at slowing the pace of cross-Strait investment: "avoid haste, remain patient" (*jieji yongren*). The policy rolled back initiatives that would have eased investment restrictions and subjected high-tech and infrastructure investments to review and approval by government agencies. It limited the amount Taiwan-listed corporations could invest in the mainland, and it set a fifty-million-dollar maximum on individual investments. In 1997, Lee's government promulgated new, even more restrictive investment guidelines—which many companies evaded by funneling their investments through third parties. Lee's government pressured Formosa Plastics, Taiwan's largest manufacturer and biggest employer, into abandoning its bid for a power plant construction contract in southern China that was worth nearly four billion dollars. Despite all these efforts, approved investment totals did not decline significantly.

The fact that Formosa Plastics was investing in power generation reveals another important reason for Lee's discomfort with the trajectory of the cross-Strait economic relationship: by the mid-1990s, the vogue for cross-Strait investment had spread from traditional SME manufacturers to Taiwan's large, upstream firms. SMEs were entrepreneurial ventures, funded largely outside formal credit markets; they carried minimal risk for the larger economy. They were born and died, neither heralded nor mourned by Taiwan's central government. For a small firm to move to the mainland was not a significant loss, and if it did well, its growth could generate gains for the island: jobs for Taiwanese managers, investment in R&D, contracts for services, and repatriated profits and taxes.

Big firms like Formosa Plastics were a different story. They were tied into the export-manufacturing sector as suppliers of basic inputs and logistical services, but they also were part of Taiwan's "top tier" economy. Their contributions were critical to the island's prosperity. The biggest firms had been involved in overseas investment for some time—Formosa Plastics has had operations in the United States since the early 1980s—but for Taipei, they were the bedrock on which the island's export-oriented manufacturing boom was built. The possibility that they, too, might transfer operations to the mainland raised alarms, but designing policy measures to combat the trend was no easy matter.

In sum, the political and economic implications of Taiwan firms' move to the mainland were complex. Electronics assembly is not that different from traditional manufacturing: the products such companies make are high tech, but the operations they perform are labor-intensive and require little technical know-how. Being in the mainland made those firms competitive and expanded the market for high value-added components made in Taiwan, so the overall effect on Taiwan's economy was positive. In fact, the benefits Taiwan received from this triangular trade were so great that in the late 1990s, Taipei became an energetic advocate for the PRC's incorporation into the World Trade Organization (WTO), a position that continued even under Democratic Progressive Party (DPP) president Chen Shui-bian. Nonetheless, a May 2000 editorial in the Sino-skeptical *Taipei Times* captured islanders' ambivalence: "PNTR [Permanent Normal Trade Relations status] and WTO entry will certainly bring economic benefits to China and its trading partners, including Taiwan, and they are to be welcomed. But we should not believe that they are a panacea for the many political and security issues that remain to be addressed."[3]

Chen Shui-bian was elected in March 2000. He was a member of the Democratic Progressive Party, making him the first Taiwanese president from outside the Kuomintang, the party that had ruled the island since 1945. The DPP was founded in 1986 with a twofold mission: to fight for democracy and to put Taiwan's own development ahead of the KMT's goal of unifying China under the ROC flag. Although the DPP was known for its skepticism about the mainland and its strong preference for continued separation—even independence—from China, in 1999, Chen ran on a platform that was friendlier to cross-Strait economic development than those of his opponents, both of whom came from within the KMT political machine.

Chen hoped to use economic cooperation and trade to build a more normal relationship between Taipei and Beijing. He advocated opening direct air and shipping links (following up on the "three links" [postal, shipping, and trade] first suggested by China's Ye Jianying), signing an investment protection agreement, and exchanging representative offices with the mainland. He also criticized Lee Teng-hui's "avoid haste, be patient" approach; after less than a year in office, he introduced the slogan "proactive opening, effective management," suggesting Taiwan should accelerate the growth of cross-Strait economic relations while continuing to maintain some state supervision over the process. Early in his presidency, Chen acceded to an important PRC demand: authorizing private organizations to carry out negotiations on behalf of government agencies. He also relaxed investment restrictions. In short, Chen Shui-bian was far from the enemy of cross-Strait economic development he was later accused of being.

Under Chen, the pace of cross-Strait economic relations accelerated sharply: according to Taiwanese government statistics, cross-Strait trade increased an average of 50 percent per year during his first term. "Effective management," it turned out, was far more difficult than "proactive opening." Within four years, China became Taiwan's largest export market, due in part to clever work-arounds that reduced shipping costs despite the absence of direct transport links. When Chen left office in 2008, cross-Strait trade was nine times what it had been in 2001. Investment trends were more interesting. After a short boom in investment following the PRC's entry into the WTO, investment actually declined. The problem was not Taipei—the Taiwanese authorities approved plenty of new investments—but the business environment on the mainland.

The dot-com crash in 2000 and the two sides' nearly simultaneous entry into the World Trade Organization in 2001 intensified the pressure on Taiwanese firms to lower their costs by entering the Chinese marketplace. Neither the PRC government nor the KMT-led legislature was willing to work with Chen to install effective management tools, so this rapid growth took place largely beyond the reach of state authority. Shortly after his second term began in 2004, after years of struggling to lift Taiwan's sagging economy, a sadder, wiser Chen reversed the adjectives in his slogan to read "proactive management, effective opening."

THE RISE OF TAIWAN'S ELECTRONICS INDUSTRY

Neither Lee nor Chen worried much about sunset industries moving to the mainland: it was clear by 2000 that Taiwan's traditional manufacturers could thrive in the mainland in ways that were simply impossible if they remained on Taiwan. Another reason they were content to see traditional manufacturing disappear was that Taiwan's economic mix had shifted drastically during the 1990s. No longer dominated by low-tech contract manufacturing, Taiwan had become a technology powerhouse. The firms Taiwan was worried about losing to the mainland in 2000 were not making toys and umbrellas; they were making integrated circuits and computer hardware—industries into which Taiwan's government had poured enormous resources. The change in the island's industrial structure was an important motivator for Lee and Chen's efforts to slow the trend toward mainland-based manufacturing.

Taiwan's high-tech revolution was decades in the making. In the 1960s, foreign investors began contracting with Taiwanese firms to make radios, televisions, and small electronic devices. In the 1970s, Taipei launched institutions tasked with incubating high-tech industry on the island. In the 1980s, the leadership focused its attention on enhancing the island's technological prowess and innovative capacity. Building on its tradition of vibrant SMEs and public-private partnerships, Taiwan's government helped private firms become suppliers of a huge range of high-tech products, from semiconductors to motherboards to notebook computers. Even as Taiwan's traditional manufacturers were flooding across the Strait, the information technology revolution was creating new opportunities for Taiwan-based manufacturers. During the 1990s, electronics and IT products' share of Taiwan's exports nearly doubled, from 11 percent to 21 percent.

Taiwan's electronics industry encompasses two broad sectors. They developed in rough parallel, but their trajectories, both in Taiwan and on the mainland, differ in important ways. Electronics manufacturing services (EMS) companies build and assemble electronic components and devices for branded companies. Taiwan's EMS sector includes world-famous companies such as Foxconn and Acer, but it is in many ways an extension of Taiwan's traditional manufacturing into the information technology age. Taiwan's other high-tech sector makes the brain cells of electronic devices: semiconductors and integrated circuits (ICs). These firms—including Taiwan Semiconductor Manufacturing Corporation (TSMC), which makes more than half the world's semiconductors—are a wholly new economic phenomenon, both for Taiwan and for the global economy.

The EMS firm Foxconn has received more news coverage—both good and bad—than just about any other Taiwanese firm. The positive coverage focuses mainly on the company's spectacular growth and its strategic position as a key supplier of devices for Apple (in 2012, Morgan Stanley estimated that Foxconn represented 65 percent of Apple's production) and other famous electronics brands—about 40 percent of the world's consumer electronics output in 2020. The negative coverage stems from a rash of suicides in 2010 when at least fourteen workers in "Foxconn City"—a huge factory complex in Shenzhen—took their own lives.

At the time, Foxconn was China's largest private employer (and it remains the largest as of 2020), with well over a million workers, and the world's largest supplier of electronic devices. It accounted for almost 4 percent of China's total exports.[4] Foxconn's explosive growth rested on assembly lines staffed by workers who put in long days of often tedious labor and spent their nights in dormitories on the factory grounds. The spate of suicides alerted labor activists to the factories' harsh conditions, even prompting a *Wired* reporter to ask himself, "Did my iPhone kill 17 people?"[5]

While conditions at Foxconn's Shenzhen factory appeared harsh to many Americans, the company's defenders pointed out that working conditions in its plants were better than in many Chinese factories. The canteens and dormitories that feel restrictive to outsiders were built to ensure that Foxconn's workers—many of whom come from far away to work for the company—can find safe, affordable food and lodging close to their workplace. The hours are long, but many workers are eager to earn the extra wages that come with overtime. And while fourteen suicides in one year seems like a lot, the plant where the deaths took place employed about three hundred thousand workers, yielding a suicide rate below China's national average.

Apple and Foxconn responded to the pressure from nongovernmental organizations (NGOs) and consumers with a program of reforms aimed at improving working conditions, but both companies remained under scrutiny by labor rights organizations. In 2019, China Labor Watch, a watchdog based in New York, released a report alleging violations of Chinese labor laws at Foxconn's iPhone factory in Zhengzhou. Apple denied many of the report's claims, but both Apple and Foxconn acknowledged some violations. The nature of the accusations suggests the external pressure to reform Foxconn's labor practices has been effective: instead of accusing the company of driving workers to suicide, the 2019 report's main accusation was that Foxconn had too many temporary workers and was paying too much overtime. The swift responses from both corporate giants promising to address these issues underscored just how sensitive they are to this kind of criticism.[6]

Foxconn's founder, Terry Gou, could not have been happy to have his company become a household name because of a suicide outbreak. But as the introspective *Wired* writer quoted above explained, by 2010, Foxconn had become "a billion-dollar avatar of globalization, and they were feeling the rubbernecked gape of international scrutiny." To most international observers, Foxconn was the rubber-hits-the-road embodiment of the high-tech economy, where meeting the demand for the latest electronic gadget means asking thousands of anonymous Chinese workers to put in extra hours of grueling labor. To Taiwanese, however, Foxconn's international exposure had a different meaning: it was both a triumphant success story and a cautionary tale, a reminder of the risks and dangers facing even the most successful Taiwanese companies on the mainland.

Taiwanese companies first gained experience in manufacturing electronic devices in the 1960s, thanks to foreign direct investment (FDI). By working in foreign-owned and joint-venture factories, Taiwanese learned to build radios, television sets, calculators, and other devices. Their mastery of miniaturization, audio equipment, and video displays was perfectly suited for the next generation of electronic devices: electronic games, monitors, and personal computers. While foreign investment was crucial in the early phase, the cost of entering the market was relatively low, and by the early 1980s, Taiwanese private capital was driving electronics to become Taiwan's top export sector.

EMS production bears many similarities to Taiwan's traditional manufacturing practices. EMS companies work as contract manufacturers for foreign brands; their approach to production is not so different from that of contract manufacturers in traditional industries. They emphasize efficiency and cost reduction, and they use co-located supply networks that allow individual firms to master specialized tasks and ensure reliable delivery of components for final assembly—a practice that is well-suited to the modular nature of modern electronics. Just like contract manufacturers making running shoes, Taiwanese device makers use disaggregated production networks to stay nimble and keep pace with rapidly changing markets. And just like Nike, Totes, and Mattel, IT brands need suppliers they can trust to produce high-quality goods on a short product cycle without leaking proprietary information. Once again, Taiwanese firms fit the bill.

Taiwan's high-tech manufacturers moved to the mainland for the same reason traditional manufacturers did: they needed to lower their costs. The first to go were low value-added products such as mice, keyboards, and computer cases. Those items were followed by power supplies and scanners in the mid-1990s and motherboards and desktop monitors a few years later. When Taipei eased investment restrictions on high-tech firms after the dot-com bubble burst, notebook makers began shifting their assembly operations to China. In 1992, 90 percent of Taiwanese PC hardware firms' output was made on the island itself; three years later, that percentage had fallen to 70 percent, and China's share was rising.[7]

As with traditional manufacturing, once labor-intensive assembly operations moved offshore, firms farther up the supply chain followed the assembly plants to the mainland. The need for proximity to their customers was irresistible. In a paper published in 1997, only about five years after device makers began moving to the mainland, the economist Chin Chung wrote, "Judging from this persistent trend of FDI toward the PRC, close production cooperation combining Taiwanese capital, managerial skills, and OEM reputation with Chinese land and labor seems an irreversible trend well into the future."[8] That trend, Chung said, left Taiwan's PC industry at a crossroads.

Foxconn founder Terry Gou exemplifies the classic Taiwanese SME success story—with a high-tech twist. Born in 1949, Gou founded Foxconn at age twenty-five with a handful of employees and 7,500 dollars in start-up funds. He began, like so many other Taiwanese SME bosses, by molding plastic parts. Gou was ambitious, smart, and a great salesman. In the early 1980s he developed a specialty in plastic connectors for electronic devices. He supplied parts to the electronic game maker Atari, and during a legendary eleven-month sales tour in the United States, he expanded his client base to include many US electronics firms. Gou led the company through an astonishing period of growth: from 1995 to 2010, Foxconn's annual sales grew by more than 30 percent in all but four years.

In 1991, Gou listed Hon Hai, the division of Foxconn devoted to EMS, on the Taiwan Stock Exchange with the goal of raising capital to expand its operations into China. He chose a village near the boomtown of Shenzhen in Guangdong province as his mainland base. In his Chinese factories, Gou developed production techniques aimed at maximizing efficiency and cutting costs to the bone. Foxconn is known for its huge factories housing vertically integrated production processes that merge made-from-scratch elements (he's still molding plastic) with modular components—some of which are also made by Foxconn, while others are sourced from other firms.

The word "Foxconn" may conjure up images of young women standing at interminable assembly lines soldering iPhones (and such scenes certainly do exist), but Foxconn is more than a twenty-first-century sweatshop. The company is engaged in substantial R&D activities, and its plants employ highly skilled toolmakers and engineers who constantly tweak and refine the manufacturing process. In 2014, the company finished eighteenth in the world (and first in Taiwan) in the race for US patents (TSMC overtook Foxconn in 2017 as the island's top patent applicant). Gou's approach to high-tech manufacturing is so successful and so original that *Bloomberg Businessweek* called him "Henry Ford reincarnated."

Foxconn is at the pinnacle of the electronic device manufacturing world. In early 2016, it bought Sharp, a huge but troubled Japanese electronics maker, for more than six billion dollars. It was the largest foreign takeover of a Japanese technology company in history, and it showed Gou's self-confidence and ambition. The deal also helped seal Foxconn's position as the number-one supplier to Apple. One of Gou's objectives with the purchase was to advance Foxconn's efforts to diversify its product mix and make more components in-house—steps that are necessary if it is to build its value-added and increase profits. Sharp's strength in electronic display technology was aimed at helping Foxconn build its intellectual property. After the purchase, Sharp returned to profitability after years of weak performance, inspiring other Taiwanese firms to consider acquiring Japanese companies.

Like his predecessors in traditional industries, Gou has fine-tuned the art of contract manufacturing for maximum profitability. In the process, he has won a modicum of leverage with his clients by providing excellent service and adding significant value. Apple relies on Foxconn to gear up for massive new-product roll-outs while never wavering on quality and keeping costs competitive. But despite being the best in its class, Foxconn's profit margins are low; its strong performance has brought enormous wealth to Apple but far less to Foxconn itself. In 2008, Apple had a profit margin of 20 percent, which rose to over 30 percent by 2012. In that same span of time, Foxconn's profit margin fell from 2.7 percent to 1.5 percent; sales doubled, but net income increased less than 50 percent. In 2012, Foxconn was paid an estimated eight dollars per unit to build a phone that sold for more than six hundred dollars. Foxconn is spectacularly successful in its market niche, yet the company does not yet sell anything under its own name.

Although most Taiwanese device makers build for international brands, a handful of firms bucked the contract manufacturing trend. Acer is Taiwan's most famous PC brand; it has been in the top five PC makers by market share since 2000. Acer got its start as an OEM contractor for ITT, but as the personal computer industry began to take off, it began selling under its own brand, spinning off its manufacturing to a separate company. Its experience as a contractor certainly made this easier, but so did the industry norm of building to the IBM standard, using Intel processors and the Microsoft operating system. Thanks to these open standards, Acer was able to bring an IBM-compatible PC to market only a year after Compaq released the very first such computer. Asus, which was founded by former Acer engineers, is another important Taiwanese high-tech brand.

The EMS revolution brought a new wave of opportunity to Taiwan's manufacturing sector, but electronics are vulnerable to the same limitations that afflict contract manufacturing in other industries. EMS firms are positioned in the middle of the supply chain, with relatively little value-added. The low barriers to entry that allowed the Taiwanese firms to join the industry are just as low for others hoping to do the same work—recently, Apple has diversified its production to other EMS firms—mostly *Taishang* companies but also some PRC-born firms. Fierce competition leaves device makers with little bargaining power relative to their customers. Even for highly successful EMS firms, profit margins are slender, and buyers are in command. Much of the growth in the sector is in low-price devices, which further squeezes the manufacturers. Foxconn-linked FIH Mobile makes mobile phones for the leading PRC brands, Xiaomi and Huawei, both of which are focused on price and squeeze their suppliers hard.

Even in this tough industry, however, Taiwanese companies have found a way to maximize their leverage and remain profitable by taking advantage of the mainland's low costs and refining the strategies traditional manufacturers have used to stay afloat—especially the *Taishang*-driven manufacturing cluster. The two most important clusters for Taiwanese electronics firms are in the Pearl River Delta, where Foxconn is based, and the Yangtze River Delta region, especially the city of Kunshan. In recent years, however, Foxconn and EMS firms have begun moving operations deeper into China where local governments are still willing to provide preferential conditions to attract new investment and wages are lower (Foxconn's labor costs reportedly doubled between 2010 and 2015). At the same time, Taiwanese EMS firms are turning to automation to cut their wage bills.

Another feature of the Taiwanese EMS industry that resonates with traditional *Taishang* manufacturing is the EMS firms' emphasis on quality, flexibility, and collaboration. As different as their products seem on the surface, Nike and Apple have a lot in common. They both charge a premium for their brand, so their customers expect reliable quality and excellent service. Their products change quickly, and product roll-outs are expensive, highly choreographed affairs. When Michael Jordan stepped on stage in the latest Air Jordans or Steve Jobs previewed a new iPhone for the media, Taiwanese contract manufacturers were hard at work making sure the products the superstar spokesmen were touting would end up in stores on schedule. Whether the product is running shoes or a tablet computer, constant product updates and design changes require a high level of interaction and collaboration between designers and manufacturers. *Taishang* companies' strength in this domain has secured them a strong market share in some very tough industries.

Taiwanese EMS firms make massive contributions to the PRC economy. It is thanks to them that China has become the leading supplier of electronic goods to the world. Directly and indirectly, they provide jobs to several million Chinese and pay taxes to countless Chinese local governments. And by bringing electronics assembly operations to China, they created the opportunity for Chinese companies to enter the supply chain—a trend we will explore in a later chapter. And while the industry is changing fast, as of 2019, Taiwanese firms still dominated the world's EMS market, holding positions one (Foxconn), two (Pegatron), five (Wistron), and seven (New Kinpo Group). The top-ranked PRC-based company, Byd Electronics, was number eight.[9]

Foxconn has a dominant position in EMS, but its counterpart in the semiconductor industry is an even bigger player. In 1985, Morris Chang, the head of Texas Instruments' global semiconductor business, agreed to return to Taiwan to lead the Industrial Technology Research Institute (ITRI), a government-sponsored research and development institute whose mission was to drive innovation and spin off new tech companies. Two years later, Chang founded TSMC (Taiwan Semiconductor Manufacturing Company) with two things: start-up capital from the Taiwan government, local investors, and the Dutch electronics firm Philips; and a revolutionary idea.

In the first few decades of the computer age, most high-tech equipment manufacturers designed and manufactured the computer chips (semiconductors and integrated circuits [ICs]) they needed in-house. By the early 1980s, many electronics companies were looking to outsource this expensive, capital-intensive, and increasingly complex process. Morris Chang's revolutionary idea was to build a company whose sole function was to manufacture chips designed by others—a "pure-play foundry." By 2013, he had built TSMC into the world's leading semiconductor producer, with almost twenty billion dollars in revenue—five times that of its closest competitor. And, like Foxconn's Terry Gou, Chang extended his company's operations into mainland China.

TSMC's origins lie in a strategic debate among Taiwan's officials and entrepreneurs: should Taiwan stretch toward high-tech innovation or build on its existing strengths? Taiwan's traditional expertise lay in contract manufacturing and process engineering—improving products and finding manufacturing efficiencies for items destined to be sold under foreign brands. Many of the island's IT firms found their niche, like Foxconn, in ODM and EMS—manufacturing for others. At the same time, though, some business leaders argued that contract manufacturing was a self-limiting strategy. They urged the government to encourage investment in new technologies and brand development.

Technocrat Y. S. Sun shared the ambition of the latter camp. He spearheaded a government effort to push Taiwan's electronics manufacturing capacity beyond contract manufacturing. Under Sun's guidance, Taiwan's Ministry of Economic Affairs created the Electronics Research Service Organization (ERSO) and ITRI in the early 1970s. Both were envisioned as public-private partnerships that would gradually shift from state subsidies to a licensing-based funding model as the technologies developed under their sponsorship matured. (The subsidies proved to a be a smart investment: in less than ten years, ITRI reduced its government funding to just over half its budget, while ERSO was getting three-quarters of its funding from private sources.)

Among the earliest ITRI and ERSO projects was a pilot facility for fabricating semiconductors using technology licensed from RCA. It was the starting point for integrated circuit manufacturing in Taiwan, an industry that has become extremely important to the island and the world. In 1979, Taiwan unveiled a joint state-private venture, United Microelectronics (UMC), the island's first commercial semiconductor foundry. The company thrived: in 2019, UMC was the fourth-largest semiconductor foundry in the world.

In 1980, Taiwan opened the Hsinchu Science-Based Industrial Park. The plan was to use the park to attract high-tech investment, build Taiwan's capacity for high-tech research and development, and entice Taiwan-born engineers to return from overseas (especially Silicon Valley). Returnees were attracted not only by the powerful opportunity for professional advancement the program offered but also by perks like excellent housing and access to a bilingual Chinese-English school associated with the park. In the decades that followed, the Hsinchu Park incubated a vast array of firms. TSMC, which broke new ground as a contract foundry making chips for clients (as opposed to designing and marketing chips on its own), developed a strong symbiosis with design firms in the Hsinchu industrial park, a relationship that positioned TSMC to thrive as the world's first pure-play IC foundry.

While ITRI and ERSO were—and to some extent continue to be—active players in Taiwan's high-tech sector, they did not seek to squeeze out or overshadow private firms. Their job, as political scientist Leng Tse-Kang has written, was to create an ecosystem in which firms could thrive.[10] To that end, they actively encouraged private investment, which tended to be more aggressive and risk-tolerant than state actors. For example, Acer founder Stan Shih was determined from the start to buck Taiwan's long-standing preference for small and medium-sized companies and grow. In 1988, he told the *New York Times*, "I was tired of the small-company mentality here. Small companies never do R&D." In that same interview, Shih also expressed confidence in Taiwan's high-tech talent pool: "Now we have the engineering talent. We are doing a lot of development on our own."[11] Shih's ambition paid off: his company went from making DRAM chips to developing its own computer brand—the world's fifth largest in 2019.

The "small-company mentality" was never a problem for TSMC founder Morris Chang. His company grew extremely fast (around 25 percent per year), and its massive size soon allowed it to dominate research and development in its industry. Supplying nearly half the global pure-foundry market brought annual revenues in the tens of billions, so its R&D commitment of 5 percent of revenues allowed it to rocket past its competitors to become the technical leader as well as the market leader in its industry.

Like many Taiwanese companies, TSMC puts customer relationships at the center of its business model. The company was founded on a promise never to compete with its customers, and it sees servicing clients as its core mission. While other foundries might be able to match or beat TSMC's prices, few can supply customers' needs so precisely and reliably. TSMC's core customers are design and production firms with no chip-fabricating capacity of their own; TSMC allows them to closely monitor the production process and work with TSMC's engineers to tweak their designs in production. Again, quality, reliability, and collaboration distinguish the Taiwanese firm.

Semiconductor manufacturing is a very different business from device making. Where Foxconn needs a large, semiskilled labor force (although that, too, could change: in 2016 the company replaced sixty thousand PRC workers with robots and announced plans to cut its human work force by 30 percent by 2020, a target it did not meet), TSMC and others in its industry need fewer, more highly skilled workers. The semiconductor industry is capital-intensive, and its firms thrive under ultra-efficient management systems that keep foundries running at full capacity by servicing a wide range of clients with different production schedules and demands. These features have shaped both TSMC's development as a company and its relationship with mainland China.

Given their sensitivity to labor costs and regulation, the move to China was a no-brainer for device manufacturers. But for TSMC, the mainland has few obvious advantages over Taiwan—and some very evident disadvantages. For TSMC, therefore, decisions to invest in the mainland have been driven by the interplay between economic and political considerations.

Economically, moving to the mainland makes less sense for TSMC than for many other Taiwanese manufacturers for several reasons. First, for a long time, China was not a big part of TSMC's market. In 2015, TSMC's global market share in semiconductors was 55 percent; only 8 percent of its sales revenue came from mainland China, compared to two-thirds from North America. That has begun to change: TSMC's sales to Chinese tech leader Huawei nearly doubled in 2019, from 8 percent of the firm's revenues to 14 percent. But TSMC's US business was even bigger; one company—Apple—

accounted for 23 percent of TSMC's 2019 sales. In May 2020, TSMC showed its determination to shore up its US presence when it announced a twelve-billion-dollar investment in new manufacturing capacity in Arizona.

Moving to the mainland also is less urgent for TSMC because the advantages mainland China enjoys in other types of manufacturing—low labor costs, loose regulation—are of relatively little importance to TSMC. The business is capital-intensive, not labor-intensive, and it is a favorite of the Taiwan government. Taiwan's secure legal environment and active protection of intellectual property rights is another important asset—as TSMC's tough (and ultimately successful) legal battles with its main China-based competitor, SMIC, attest.

While the economic case for TSMC to take its business to the mainland is weak, the politics are ambiguous. Both Taipei and Beijing have viewed semiconductors as a strategic industry. For Taipei, that means doing what it can to keep production on the island; for the PRC, it means doing what it can to build its domestic capacity in semiconductor production, whether by enticing foreign companies to invest or by growing domestic companies capable of competing with those foreign firms. Under Lee Teng-hui and Chen Shuibian, Taiwanese policy makers implemented a number of regulations aimed at blocking TSMC from moving its cutting-edge technologies to the mainland. For example, Taiwan's semiconductor manufacturers were prohibited from making eight-inch semiconductor wafers (from which individual chips are cut) on the mainland until foundries capable of producing more advanced twelve-inch wafers were up and running.

Nonetheless, in 2004, TSMC opened a foundry to make eight-inch wafers in Shanghai. According to Morris Chang, the decision was driven by a desire to be close to customers (many of which were international companies with supply chains in China) and China's substantial engineering talent. Taiwan restricted PRC nationals from traveling to the island, which made it hard for TSMC to service its mainland-based clients. The move was also in some sense a hedge against the future—as China's market for semiconductors grows, TSMC wants to be in the best possible situation to enter that market.

All of these factors were important to TSMC's decision, but Harvard business professor William Kirby sees political motivations underlying the decision.[12] First, "being close to customers" is a weak rationale. If TSMC needs to be near its customers, shouldn't it be opening fabs in North America? In fact, Kirby suggests, the desire to have a TSMC plant in the PRC was related to customers' anxiety about the political relationship between the two sides of the Strait. In the event of a Taiwan Strait crisis, chip supplies are less likely to be disrupted if TSMC has manufacturing on the mainland, so putting manufacturing capacity there might have been a way of pacifying nervous clients.

Kirby also believes politics may have influenced TSMC's decision to open the Shanghai plant even more directly. He suggests TSMC's leaders were worried that the Chen administration would continue to add restrictions on its ability to invest across the Strait. The result was a "now-or-never" mentality at TSMC. Kirby finds support for his argument in TSMC's behavior after Chen left office: when Ma Ying-jeou, a more China-friendly president, took office in 2008, TSMC announced that it would build two new twelve-inch wafer foundries in Hsinchu, in addition to expansion plans already under way in Taichung and Tainan. The Ma government also lifted some restrictions on TSMC's cross-Strait investments, including the ban on twelve-inch-wafer production.

Taiwan's domestic politics may have shaped TSMC's investment decisions in the past, but PRC politics has become another important driver. In 2014, Beijing released its National Semiconductor Industry Development Guidelines, followed in 2015 by the "Made in China 2025" initiative. "Made in China 2025" is a comprehensive plan to localize Chinese industry; the semiconductor industry guidelines lay out specific policies for developing China's domestic capacity in semiconductor manufacturing and technology. The guidelines set a target of 20 percent annual growth in China's semiconductor industry and promise up to 150 billion dollars in support for the industry between 2015 and 2025. The Chinese government set a goal of producing 70 percent of the chips used in China by 2025, a huge increase.

The semiconductor guidelines are unapologetically interventionist; they promise to support industry consolidation to support a handful of "national champion" firms capable of competing on the world stage. The plans acknowledged that Chinese companies lacked the technological expertise to meet the stated goals, so they encouraged mergers, acquisitions, and joint ventures to secure technology from foreign firms. An early example was the move by Tsinghua Unigroup, one of the potential national champions in the semiconductor industry, to purchase three Taiwanese firms specializing in chip assembly.

Beijing released its plans for an independent semiconductor industry in 2014; that same year, TSMC announced its plan to open the first 300mm-wafer fabrication plant in China. The specific type of plant is important: a 300mm-wafer fab is needed to produce the type of chips used in mobile phones and tablets, the two devices in greatest demand in China. In 2015, TSMC submitted an application to Taipei for permission to build a three-billion-dollar twelve-inch-wafer factory in Nanjing, China. The factory, which opened in 2018, is the most sophisticated plant of its kind in China.

Taipei extracted concessions from TSMC in exchange for allowing highly advanced technology to cross the Strait. The company agreed to keep its most advanced technology, R&D, and production lines in Taiwan. While the Nanjing plant is a step up for China in technical sophistication, TSMC does have even more advanced technologies—which are staying in Taiwan. Nonetheless, the changes reflect Beijing's aggressive moves in the semiconductor market. The claim that TSMC was breaking new ground in the mainland was undercut by the fact that other manufacturers—Intel and Samsung—already were manufacturing twelve-inch wafers in China. Taiwan's vice minister of economic affairs acknowledged the pressure on TSMC, saying, "It is necessary for Taiwan to amend the regulations to help local semiconductor firms secure a share of the Chinese market as soon as possible."[13]

Securing a share of the Chinese market remains an important goal for Taiwan's high-tech firms, but the Made in China 2025 initiative was an ominous development. The initiative signaled Beijing's desire to squeeze TSMC and other global firms out of the China market. TSMC's Nanjing investment was aimed at avoiding that fate. Taiwanese and other foreign-invested firms will hold market share in the mainland only as long as their technological advantage allows them to sell products no mainland producer can provide. Keeping a technical edge over competitors is the only way to survive now that Beijing has decided to go all-in for the so-called Red Supply Chain.

NOTES

This chapter includes material from a paper I coauthored with Toy Reid entitled "Taiwanese Investors in Mainland China: Creating a Context for Peace?" The paper was published in *Cross-Strait at the Turing Point: Institution, Identity and Democracy*, edited by I. Yuan (Taipei: Institute of International Relations, 2008), chapter 5.

1. Kerry Brown, Justin Hempson-Jones, and Jessica Pennisi, "Investment across the Taiwan Strait: How Taiwan's Relationship with China Affects Its Position in the Global Economy," Chatham House, November 2010, https://www.chathamhouse .org/sites/default/files/public/Research/Asia/1110pp_taiwan.pdf.

2. Cited in Ping Deng, "Taiwan's Restriction of Investment in China in the 1990s: A Relative Gains Approach," *Asian Survey* 40, no. 6 (2000), 967.

3. "Editorial: PNTR Won't Cure All China's Woes," *Taipei Times*, May 26, 2000, p. 12, https://www.taipeitimes.com/News/editorials/archives/2000/05/26/00000 37548.

4. Chun-Yi Lee, "Taiwan and China in a Global Value Chain: The Case of the Electronics Industry," in *Taiwan's Impact on China: Why Soft Power Matters More than Economic or Political Inputs*, edited by Steve Tsang (Cham, Switzerland: Palgrave Macmillan, 2017).

5. Joel Johnson, "1 Million Workers. 90 Million iPhones. 17 Suicides. Who's to Blame?" *Wired*, February 28, 2011, https://www.wired.com/2011/02/ff-joelinchina/.

6. Saheli Roy Choudhury, "Apple Denies Claims It Broke Chinese Labor Laws in iPhone Factory," CNBC, September 8, 2019, https://www.cnbc.com/2019/09/09 /apple-appl-claims-it-broke-china-labor-laws-at-iphone-factory-mostly-false.html.

7. Chin Chung, "Division of Labor across the Taiwan Strait: Macro Overview and Analysis of the Electronics Industry," in *The China Circle: Economics and Electronics in the PRC, Taiwan, and Hong Kong*, edited by Barry Naughton (Washington, DC: Brookings Institution Press, 1997), 185.

8. Chin, "Division of Labor," 189.

9. Peter Clarke, "Global Top 50 Ranking of EMS Providers for 2019," eeNews Analog, April 19, 2020, https://www.eenewsanalog.com/news/global-top-50 -ranking-ems-providers-2019.

10. Tse-Kang Leng, "Cross-Strait Economic Relations and China's Rise: The Case of the IT Sector," in *Taiwan and China: Fitful Embrace*, edited by Lowell Dittmer (Berkeley: University of California Press, 2017).

11. David Sanger, "PC Powerhouse (Made in Taiwan)," *New York Times*, September 28, 1988, p. D1.

12. William C. Kirby, Billy Chan, and Dawn H. Lau, "Taiwan Semiconductor Manufacturing Company Limited: A Global Company's China Strategy (B),"

Harvard Business School Supplement 320-045, November 2019, revised January 2020.

13. Lauly Li, "MOEA Eases China Investment Rule," *Taipei Times*, August 14, 2015, https://www.taipeitimes.com/News/front/archives/2015/08/14/2003625310.

6

The Rise of the Red Supply Chain

Cooperation and collaboration between *Taishang* and their mainland hosts grew at a breakneck pace in the two decades after Taiwan opened to the mainland in 1987. *Taishang* businesses seized opportunities to earn profits, upgrade their technical capacity, and make themselves indispensable to their overseas partners. But Taiwanese firms were not the only ones making progress during these decades. Domestic Chinese firms were also profiting, upgrading, and working their way into global production chains.

In the 1980s and '90s, PRC local officials were mesmerized by the fast, easy money that foreign investors brought in—they paid less attention to the homegrown firms struggling for a foothold. But those local companies did not disappear. Many of them studied their *Taishang* neighbors assiduously, and by the 2000s, they were starting to attract attention from their own government. Economic and political forces were gathering that were about to accelerate that trend and bring fundamental changes to the *Taishang* world.

The *Nikkei Asian Review* described the trend in 2016: "A fast-growing cluster of mainland companies [is] snatching market share from Taiwanese counterparts, often thanks to massive financial support from the Chinese government."[1] Taiwanese dubbed this new competitor the "Red Supply Chain." As one Taiwanese businessman told political economist Chun-Yi Lee, "We actually helped domestic enterprises to emerge. Many excellent local cadres in my enterprises, after acquiring knowledge and skill, left my enterprise and started their own businesses outside. Once they accumulated more capital, we could not compete with them because they are local people, they could have the lowest expenditure and they have great *guanxi* with the locality."[2]

The changes Taiwanese companies were facing were not just economic; they had political roots as well. On both sides of the Strait, government officials sought to channel economic development in ways that would strengthen their own firms and minimize their vulnerability to the other side. That task was especially urgent for Taipei, where the threat was not just economic but went to the heart of the country's security. Chen Shui-bian tried to slow or at least redirect the flow of economic activity in order to diversify Taiwan's economic ties, but he had limited success. At the same time, Beijing stonewalled Chen's requests to talk about cross-Strait issues. PRC leaders were convinced that Chen was trying to move Taiwan toward independence by driving wedges between Taiwan and the mainland, so they rejected requests for dialogue. In the absence of cross-Strait conversation, economic ties developed according to their own internal logic, largely beyond the reach of legal institutions or state direction.

When *Taishang* first began moving operations to the mainland, most Taiwanese were cautiously optimistic about how things would play out economically. That optimism proved prescient: companies (and their profits) grew, Taiwanese workers gained new employment opportunities, and the political consequences of integrating the two economies turned out to be manageable. But as the two sides grew closer economically, new challenges emerged. In the face of that trend, optimism gave way to ambivalence and then to skepticism. A turning point came in the early 2010s when Taiwan opened its doors to PRC investment and tourists. There was money to be made, but the presence of so many mainlanders on the island was disconcerting; it intensified the sense that Taiwan was losing its freedom of action, becoming dependent on the mainland for its economic survival. Meanwhile, the economics on the mainland were also changing. *Taishang* saw their privileged position slipping away.

In the eight years of Chen's presidency, 2000 to 2008, approved investment in mainland China by Taiwanese firms quadrupled (although PRC figures show that much of that investment was never completed). That left his successor, Ma Ying-jeou, with two massive challenges. First, *Taishang* urgently needed relief from the risks posed by an unregulated economic relationship of unprecedented magnitude. Second, the global financial crisis had thrown Taiwan's export markets into chaos, threatening the island with recession. Ma addressed those challenges in two ways. One was to open a dialogue with the PRC aimed at easing restrictions on cross-Strait economic activity and creating a legal framework for *Taishang* activities. The other was to use Taiwan's cachet to entice mainlanders—and their money—to come to Taiwan.

The dialogue was possible under President Ma because Beijing was willing to engage. That was true in part because leaders in Beijing preferred Ma and his party, the KMT, to Chen and his Democratic Progressive Party; they believed the KMT was committed to unification, at least in theory, while the DPP clearly was not. Beijing's stated rationale for reversing its ban on communication was that Ma agreed to a framework known as the '92 Consensus. During his presidency, Chen Shui-bian rejected the '92 Consensus as a KMT contrivance (the label first appeared in 2000, eight years after the consensus was supposedly forged), but Ma recognized it as a useful device for enabling cooperation with Beijing.

The '92 Consensus originated in quasi-official talks Taipei and Beijing set up in 1992. Their goal was to establish basic infrastructure—things like mail and telephone service and document verification—for the burgeoning economic relationship of the early 1990s. Taiwan set up the nominally independent Straits Exchange Foundation (SEF) and authorized it to conclude agreements with its PRC counterpart, the Association for Relations Across the Taiwan Straits (ARATS). SEF and ARATS became the "white gloves" that allowed the two governments to interact without officially recognizing one another.

During talks in Hong Kong in 1992, the chief negotiators for SEF and ARATS devised an ingenious solution to a fundamental problem. The governments that sponsored them did not acknowledge one another's existence; each believed that it, alone, was the legitimate government of the Chinese nation. For SEF negotiator Koo Chen-fu's side, "China" meant the Republic of China; the vision of unification he represented was unification under the ROC flag and constitution. For his ARATS counterpart, Wang Daohan, "China" meant the People's Republic of China, and unification meant unification under the PRC system. In order to move beyond this impasse, the two men made a tacit agreement: their shared commitment to the idea that Taiwan and the mainland were part of a single Chinese nation was sufficient

to proceed with talks. There was no need to continue arguing over their competing definitions of the Chinese nation. The KMT, Taiwan's ruling party at
the time, defined the '92 Consensus as "One China, with each side having its
own respective interpretation." For the PRC, the heart of the consensus was
"One China," but it didn't challenge the KMT's wording.

Beijing closed the SEF-ARATS channel in 1999 when President Lee Teng-
hui described cross-Strait relations as a "special state-to-state relationship,"
a characterization they said was tantamount to independence. It remained
closed throughout the Chen administration, but the KMT and the Chinese
Communist Party continued to talk—and *Taishang* continued to operate
businesses in the mainland. The party-to-party mechanism allowed for some
progress in cross-Strait relations, as the PRC used the meetings as a venue for
announcing policy changes such as its willingness to permit direct charter
flights between the two sides. It allowed the KMT to take credit for bettering
investors' situation, and it set the stage for a revival of the SEF-ARATS talks
and rapid improvements in the relationship after Ma Ying-jeou took office
in May 2008.

Ma aspired to deepen and codify the cross-Strait economic relationship in
the hope that healthy economic ties would reduce the level of tension in the
Strait and allow the two sides to develop a better political relationship, one in
which they could recognize common goals and manage sources of conflict.
The centerpieces of his approach were a promise that there would be no unification, no independence, and no armed conflict during his presidency and his
commitment to the '92 Consensus as the foundation for cross-Strait dialogue.

Under Ma Ying-jeou and his PRC counterpart, Hu Jintao, referencing the
'92 Consensus was enough to allow talks to go forward. Taiwanese officials
used it to gesture toward the idea of unification as a goal without spelling it
out in ways that would have provoked a backlash at home. And so, within a
month of Ma's inauguration, SEF and ARATS negotiators were meeting in
Beijing, where they made quick progress on multiple issues, include *Taishang*'s most urgent demand, direct flights. In November 2008, the ARATS
chairman visited Ma in Taipei (PRC news coverage of the events described
Ma as the "leader of Taiwan," not the president of Taiwan or the ROC), and
within two years, the two sides had signed eleven agreements on topics ranging from financial cooperation to crime fighting. In June 2010, they signed
a comprehensive Economic Cooperation Framework Agreement (ECFA).

In all, Beijing and Taipei concluded twenty-three agreements during Ma's presidency.

Those twenty-three agreements had an enormous impact on cross-Strait business. They institutionalized protections for *Taishang* on issues such as intellectual property rights; they addressed technical issues like the exchange of meteorological, seismological, and public health information; and they made it much easier to travel. Instead of schlepping through Hong Kong or Tokyo, airlines on both sides finally were able to fly nonstop from airports in the PRC to Taiwan. The ease of travel went both ways: while the number of trips Taiwanese made to the mainland continued the steady rise under way since the late 1980s, reaching more than five million in 2014, under the new agreements, PRC visits to Taiwan catapulted from zero to four million in just six years. Most of those PRC visitors were tourists, and their skyrocketing numbers catalyzed a whole industry devoted to serving *luke*, or mainland guests. The vast majority came on package tours—the preference of both governments since (for very different reasons) neither one relished the prospect of PRC citizens roaming around Taiwan unsupervised. Taiwan also began allowing PRC students to enroll in local universities, which helped postpone a crisis in higher education posed by Taiwan's declining birth rate.

Ma's economic policy was rooted in his conviction that the best way to strengthen Taiwan's economy was to maximize opportunities for cooperation with the mainland and minimize cross-Strait tension. His policies went a long way toward stabilizing Taiwan's economy at a dangerous moment. The global financial crisis sent Taiwan's GDP growth negative in 2009, but it bounced back in the following year to an astonishing 10 percent. Nonetheless, Ma's approach soon revealed its limitations. The fundamental problem was one Taiwan's leaders had recognized for decades but could not avoid: the economic and political conflict of interests between Taiwan and the PRC.

Beijing was happy to use Taiwanese people's money, know-how, and business relationships to generate wealth for China. It was even willing to give Taiwanese individuals and firms special privileges in the hope of winning their political support. But at the end of the day, the goal was always to advance the PRC's interests, not Taiwan's. And while the PRC's interests included political goals that required giving Taiwanese incentives to advocate for Beijing's preferences, PRC leaders were not willing to keep PRC domestic firms on a leash forever. More and more, Beijing used the language of "carrots and sticks" to characterize its policies. As Taiwan soon discovered, all sorts of cross-Strait business relationships could be sticks as well as carrots.

The velocity with which the two sides churned out agreements made Ma's first term a high point in cross-Strait relations, yet even then, trouble was brewing. Cross-Strait relations were only one of many considerations driving PRC leaders' policy decisions, and not everything they did benefited *Taishang*. One ominous development—for *Taishang*, anyway—was the 2008 labor law. The labor law was enacted before Ma was elected, but *Taishang* began to feel its effects only after he took office. The law's main provisions protected employees from arbitrary job loss and increased the penalties on employers who deny employment contracts, withhold wages, or fail to contribute to social insurance benefits. The law was controversial, as many companies—Chinese and foreign-invested alike—worried it would increase the cost of labor and hamper firms' agility. Many—especially domestic PRC firms—turned to labor service contractors and "internships" to skirt the new law.

Obviously, the labor contract law didn't squelch China's economic growth, which has continued through thick and thin in the years since. It did, however, tighten the margins for many *Taishang*, leading some export-oriented firms to look for new locations with lower costs. The pressure to reduce prices was especially acute in the wake of the great financial crisis, which happened just as the cost of doing business in China was rising. In response, some *Taishang* moved deeper into China: between 1998 and 2011, for example, the percentage of Taiwan-approved investment in coastal Guangdong fell from 40 percent to 15 percent of the total, while inland provinces such as Sichuan in which *Taishang* investment was negligible in 1998 registered above 5 percent in 2011.[3] At the same time, many other *Taishang* left mainland China altogether after 2008, a trend sociologist Chih-peng Cheng dubbed the "third large-scale migration of *Taishang*."[4] Many headed to nearby low-wage markets such as Vietnam, but some went farther afield. Others even moved production to Taiwan.

The labor contract law was only one of several factors driving up the cost of production at the end of the decade. Because of those rising costs, the proliferation of agreements during Ma's first term did not speed the growth of cross-Strait economic activity. In fact, the average rates of increase for trade (8 percent per year) and investment (15 percent per year) were lower during

Ma's presidency than under Chen Shui-bian. Still, that annual growth was on an enormous base, so the total volume of trade and investment was still huge.

Even if they didn't accelerate the growth of economic activity, the Ma-era agreements did stabilize and ease the business environment. At the same time, though, they made a lot of Taiwanese very nervous. Just after Ma's inauguration, the percentage of Taiwanese telling National Chengchi University researchers that the pace of cross-Strait economic exchanges was too fast jumped from 20 percent to 30 percent, while the percentage calling the pace too slow fell from 35 percent to below 20 percent. In other words, even before he had a chance to do much of anything, some Taiwanese were already worried that Ma was doing too much. That said, though, it's important to note that throughout Ma's presidency a plurality of Taiwanese said the pace of cross-Strait economic exchanges was "just right."

If concern about the pace and extent of cross-Strait ties was growing during Ma's first term, it wasn't growing fast enough to prevent his reelection in 2012. The economy took a hit from the global financial crisis, but Taiwan avoided the kind of severe downturn that afflicted many other countries, thanks in part to a PRC stimulus program that shielded mainland-based firms from the worst of the recession. Ma also managed to increase Taiwan's international space, another high priority for many voters. Between 2008 and 2012, Taipei opened economic talks with Singapore, New Zealand, and Japan, and Beijing dropped its objections to Taiwan's participation in some international organizations, including the World Health Assembly. Beijing also refrained from poaching Taiwan's existing diplomatic partners.

A central issue in the 2012 election was the '92 Consensus. Ma's campaign contrasted the rapid progress in cross-Strait relations during his first term with the eight years of stagnant political ties—accompanied by uncontrolled, unregulated economic growth—under Chen. He attributed his success to the '92 Consensus, without which, he argued, the relationship would return to Chen-era deadlock. Meanwhile, his opponent, the DPP's Tsai Ing-wen, stuck with her party's rejection of the '92 Consensus. Tsai promised voters that she would maintain the status quo in the Strait, but it was hard to see how she could pull that off without Beijing's acquiescence, which could be gained only by affirming the '92 Consensus.

In the lead-up to the election, both Beijing and Washington openly worried about Tsai's approach. *Taishang*, too, were concerned enough about the possibility of slowing cross-Strait progress to make public statements endorsing, not Ma himself, but the '92 Consensus. Lin Yi-shou, the head of the Kaohsiung-based E United Group called the '92 Consensus "the only and best way to narrow Taiwan's south-north growth gap," while Evergreen Group founder Chang Yung-fa called the '92 Consensus the "foundation for cross-Strait dialogue."[5]

Ma won reelection by a solid six-point margin, but his victory didn't come with a honeymoon. Within a few months, concerns about the pace and extent of cross-Strait economic ties exploded in a series of protests known as the Anti-Media Monopolization Movement. Unlike past critiques that focused on the possibility that overreliance on the mainland market could hollow out Taiwan's economy or give the PRC leverage indirectly, through *Taishang* companies, this movement reflected the growing sense that cross-Strait economic cooperation was infiltrating and *directly* reshaping Taiwan politics. This new trend responded to a subtle shift in Taipei from policies aimed at expanding Taiwanese individuals' and firms' access to China, toward policies that also expanded Chinese individuals' and firms' access to Taiwan.

The catalyst for the Anti-Media Monopolization Movement was a prominent *Taishang*'s attempt to acquire a dominant share of Taiwan's mass media. Want Want Holdings is one of Taiwan's largest prepared food companies, and it is the parent of Want Want China, the PRC's largest rice cracker and flavored milk producer. Its founder, Tsai Eng-meng, has made statements supporting unification. In the mid-2000s, Want Want bought a number of media outlets, including the *China Times*, one of Taiwan's most established newspapers. After the takeover, the media outlets began to take a decidedly pro-China slant. In 2012, a group of investors linked to Want Want decided to buy Next Media, a purchase that would have given Tsai Eng-meng influence, and perhaps even control, over half of all mass media in Taiwan.

The idea that a company with deep investments on the mainland as well as a pro-unification boss might acquire a near-majority share in Taiwan's media enraged many Taiwanese. China-skeptical Taiwanese had long worried that Taiwanese tycoons might put their own desire for business opportunities in the mainland ahead of Taiwan's interests, but the suggestion that one of those tycoons was buying up the island's mass media in order to help Beijing push its pro-unification agenda took their suspicions to a new level.

Protesters went online and into the streets to demand that the government block the sale. They chose "Oppose Media Monopolization" for their slogan to stress the point that overconcentration of media ownership was bad for democracy, but the political affiliation of this particular media "monopolist" was an important driver of their fury. Want Want answered their critiques by attacking the protesters in its news outlets—an act which only reinforced the conviction that Want Want was an enemy of free speech. The controversy raged for months; one protest in early 2013 attracted more than a hundred thousand participants. Ultimately, the government agencies in charge of communications and free trade made it clear that the purchase was unlikely to be approved, and Want Want withdrew its offer in March 2013.

Even in failure, however, the Want Want/Next Media purchase highlighted the Taiwan mass media's vulnerability to mainland manipulation. Taiwanese ownership doesn't prevent so-called Red Media outlets from promoting Beijing's interests. In July 2019, the *Financial Times* reported that *China Times* journalists admitted that their editors took instructions from officials in China's Taiwan Affairs Office. Later that year, a Want Want–linked TV network was fined for its fawning coverage of KMT presidential candidate Han Kuo-yu. In 2020, the network lost its operating license after the National Communications Commission ruled that company officials were injecting their political preferences into its news coverage.

The Anti-Media Monopolization Movement was one of the earliest tangible examples that optimism about cross-Strait relations had given way to ambivalence, even skepticism. This trend, which accelerated quickly during Ma's second term, gained momentum from the increasing visibility of mainland influences within Taiwan. Prior to 2009, the changes in cross-Strait relations had been largely quantitative: year after year, Taiwanese invested more and more money in the PRC, while more and more people went to work on the other side. Taiwanese noticed these trends, but most felt little direct impact—the real action was across the Strait.

Ma's policies were different. Instead of merely adding to the amount of cross-Strait economic activity, they changed the nature and the direction of that activity. Those qualitative changes altered Taiwan's domestic climate and brought cross-Strait economic exchanges into Taiwanese citizens' everyday lives. Two of Ma's policies were especially high-impact: admitting PRC visitors and opening Taiwan to PRC investment.

This book focuses on Taiwanese who live, work, or invest in mainland China, but the truth is most Taiwanese have never been to the PRC. Taiwanese had been aware for decades that their compatriots were going to the mainland, but until 2008, the water to the west of Taiwan was pretty much a one-way strait. In 2007, many Taiwanese had never even met someone from the PRC; Taiwan's tourist authority recorded zero visitors from the mainland that year. But Ma's policy changed the situation—and fast. In 2008, there were 315,000 mainland tourist visits; in two years, the number quintupled to 1.6 million. In 2015, there were more than 4 million PRC tourist visits to Taiwan.[6]

After fifty-five years of near-total separation, PRC people were suddenly everywhere in Taiwan. Or if the tourists themselves were not quite everywhere—the package tours that catered to mainland guests tended to stick to a well-worn circuit of famous sites such as Sun Moon Lake and the National Palace Museum—their tour buses seemed to be clogging traffic everywhere. The sudden arrival of so many PRC citizens created economic opportunities, but it also allowed Taiwanese to observe firsthand the cultural and social differences between mainlanders and Taiwanese that *Taishang* had been describing since the late 1980s. A 2011 study found that cross-Strait encounters had little effect on Taiwanese people's thinking, but they did tend to reinforce negative stereotypes about mainlanders.

The introduction of mainland tourists was a huge qualitative shift in Taiwanese people's everyday life. The effects of the second change—opening Taiwan to mainland investment—were less direct but no less significant. The Ma administration opened Taiwan to investment from the PRC in 2009, and by the end of his term, approved inbound investment from the PRC to Taiwan totaled about $1.3 billion.[7] That was a pittance compared to the money flowing in the other direction, but even on a small scale, investment from an unfriendly power felt like a hostile takeover. The fact that many PRC investments had political objectives only reinforced fears that instead of taking Taiwan by force, the PRC had decided to buy it.[8]

Opening Taiwan to PRC visitors and investors had limited economic consequences (although pockets of the Taiwan economy, especially tourism and higher education, got a big boost), but the political consequences were huge. The Anti-Media Monopolization protests kicked off a series of social movements challenging Ma's opening-up policies. They were followed by two movements, one about gentrification and one about mistreatment of military conscripts, that were not directly related to cross-Strait relations but demonstrated growing dissatisfaction with Ma's government. This series of movements culminated in the 2014 Sunflower Movement, which was a direct consequence of the Ma administration's efforts to promote inbound investment from the PRC.

The catalyst for the Sunflower Movement was the government's request for legislative approval of a twenty-fourth cross-Strait economic agreement, this one aimed at liberalizing the services trade. The Cross-Strait Services Trade Agreement (CSSTA) was more sensitive than previous agreements because it opened the possibility of lower-priced PRC service providers entering Taiwan's domestic market, but the vehemence of the popular response also reflected six years' worth of accumulated anxiety and dissatisfaction with the pace and extent of cross-Strait economic integration.

When the CSSTA was presented for ratification, opponents rushed to the legislative building to protest. The KMT majority wanted to avoid forcing through an unpopular bill on a party line vote, so party leaders agreed to the DPP's demand for a series of public meetings and a line-by-line review of the proposal. When the process failed to move forward swiftly, the KMT legislator charged with shepherding the bill lost patience and decided to put it to a vote on March 18, 2014. In response to his announcement, protesters clambered over the fence surrounding the legislative building and pushed their way into the chamber. The protesters—most of them students—occupied the chamber for twenty-four days. Throughout the occupation, supporters held daily protests as well as ongoing occupations and sit-ins on the streets surrounding the building.

The protesters departed the legislative chamber peacefully on April 10 after the KMT speaker, Wang Jin-pyng, promised that no cross-Strait agreements would be ratified until the legislature passed a law to codify monitoring procedures for all such pacts. It was clear, however, that the CSSTA would be the last such agreement proposed for a long time—the tide of public opinion had turned decisively against the Ma administration's approach. In November 2015, Ma Ying-jeou met face-to-face with Xi Jinping in Singapore, but even this historic gesture—the first meeting between leaders from the two sides since the Civil War—felt beside the point. Taiwanese were no longer interested in accelerating interactions with the mainland. Less than two months after the Ma-Xi meeting, the KMT lost control of the government for the first time since 1945. On January 16, 2016, the DPP's Tsai Ing-wen won a decisive presidential victory and the DPP and its Sunflower-inspired ally the New Power Party (NPP) captured seventy-three of the legislature's one hundred thirteen seats.

In retrospect, it's clear that the quantitative and qualitative changes in cross-Strait relations during the Ma administration were simply too much for Taiwan's society to absorb. Trade and outbound investment are one thing—goods and money moving across the Strait don't change Taiwanese people's everyday lives much. There were voices calling for a slower pace long before Ma's second term, but they focused on abstract concerns and potential problems like the hollowing out of Taiwan's manufacturing. Meanwhile, in the here and now, many Taiwanese were seeing concrete benefits from cross-Strait interactions. But with millions of PRC visitors suddenly turning up at tourist sites across Taiwan, cross-Strait economic interaction was no longer something that happened on the other side. The Ma administration's efforts to codify the process began to seem less like an effort to protect Taiwanese businesses and more like a legal edifice trapping Taiwan in a relationship that many were not sure they wanted. In the process, Taiwan was developing a new dependence on China, in the form of tourists, students, and investors. Their presence produced economic value but in a way that made Taiwan vulnerable, not just indirectly, via the competitiveness of PRC firms or the vicissitudes of PRC policy, but directly, because Beijing controlled the flow of all three. And when Tsai Ing-wen became president, Beijing demonstrated its power—and its disdain for the DPP president—by choking off the flow of tourists. The goal was to stir up opposition to Tsai by making her responsible for the loss of lucrative activity.

Taiwanese manufacturing firms have been quick to chase opportunity and profits across the Taiwan Strait. For the government in Taipei, however, the dramatic and precipitous increase in cross-Strait trade—and especially investment—has worrisome implications. Taipei and Beijing are not friends—far from it—and while neither side seeks a hostile relationship, their goals are very different. In the 1990s, Taiwan's position was that both Taiwan and the PRC were Chinese entities that should be unified someday—as a democratic Republic of China. In the decades since, support for unification has steadily waned as Taiwanese have become more determined to protect their political autonomy and separate identity. Meanwhile, the PRC continues to insist on unification under its flag and political system. For Taipei, facing international isolation and a waning military advantage, allowing the mainland to gain leverage over the island's economy is a frightening prospect.

The fear that overengagement with the mainland might harm Taiwan's interests is not far-fetched. The first wave of cross-Strait investment consisted of traditional manufacturers whose competitiveness rested on finding a low-cost base of operations, but it didn't take long for the higher value-added industries that blossomed in the 1990s to make the move. It was one thing to see industries with little chance of thriving in Taiwan gain a new lease on life on the mainland, but once the bridge was open, companies of all shapes and sizes seemed eager to cross over. Losing manufacturing, including high tech, was bad enough, but losing it to a military rival was deeply worrying to Taiwan's leaders. Nonetheless, by the turn of the twenty-first century, nearly a third of Taiwan's personal computer production was in the mainland. And that was only the beginning.

It was precisely this outcome—the possibility that cross-Strait investment would make Taiwan dangerously dependent on the mainland and strip its manufacturing base—that motivated Taiwan's government to ban direct shipping, flights, and telephone or postal communications until 2008 and restrict the amount and type of investments Taiwanese were allowed to make in the PRC. Compounding the government's concerns was Taiwan's rapidly growing bilateral trade surplus with the mainland. While a trade surplus might seem like a good thing, for Taiwan, asymmetrical trade is risky. It's easier to find new suppliers of goods than to find new customers to buy goods you want to sell, so having a large trade surplus with one trading partner gives that partner dangerous leverage. Making things even more complicated, though, about half of Taiwan's exports to the mainland are electronic components destined to be incorporated into products that are exported from China—devices that are in many cases assembled in the mainland by Taiwan-based firms. That means Taiwan is not really as dependent on the China market as it would seem. In theory, at least, Taiwanese firms could avoid Beijing's pressure by moving final assembly out of the PRC.

One reason Taiwanese businesses were so successful in the mainland early on was, frankly, luck. Taiwanese investors thrived in the mainland because the mainland opened to business at exactly the right moment. But that lucky timing was a onetime event; it gave the Taiwanese investors an astonishing amount of momentum and made some of them fabulously rich, but it did not give Taiwanese companies a permanent advantage in the China market.

In retrospect, the Ma administration's decision to ease restrictions on cross-Strait economic activity may seem unwise, but at the time, it made sense. As of 2006, of China's top ten exporters, eight were Taiwanese electronics contract manufacturers.[9] These companies—and many others—were crucial to Taiwan's economy, and they reminded policy makers of that fact at every opportunity. As they pointed out, profits from their mainland operations made their way back to Taiwan and into the local economy. Taiwanese professionals were able to turbocharge their careers by working for *Taishang* firms in the mainland or for the research and development facilities many high-tech companies maintained in Taiwan—where their intellectual property was protected. *Taishang* also favored Taiwanese financial institutions and business services providers, which further boosted the domestic economy. Even the most sensitive policy changes—such as allowing tourists and inbound investment—created many economic winners in Taiwan.

Over the course of Ma's presidency, the risk/benefit balance gradually shifted away from the logic of ever-increasing trade and investment. The Sunflower Movement was the tipping point, the moment at which we suddenly discovered that apprehension about the dangers Taiwan faced had overtaken the optimistic faith that deeper cross-Strait economic ties were, on balance, good for Taiwan. The concerns that drove the Sunflower protesters were mainly political, but they had economic roots, too: PRC firms were gaining on the *Taishang* in competitiveness, while the PRC government was actively working to dethrone *Taishang* from their leading position.

Meanwhile, Taiwanese were beginning to notice yet another downside of cross-Strait economic integration: inequality. Taiwan's postwar industrialization had produced a remarkably egalitarian distribution of income and wealth. That began to change in the 1990s and 2000s as *Taishang* made big fortunes on the other side of the Strait. To store their new wealth back in Taiwan, they invested in real estate. That drove up the price of housing much faster than wages were rising. Many middle-class Taiwanese—especially young people—found themselves priced out of their hometown housing markets.

Economic, political, and social changes in Taiwan helped slow the pace at which cross-Strait ties expanded, but they were not the only factors. The global environment was also changing in ways that complicated the calculus for *Taishang*, a topic I will explore in chapter 10. At least as important as the changes in Taiwan, however, were changes in the PRC, where the rise of the Red Supply Chain had many *Taishang* wondering: will we be needed, or even welcome, in the mainland much longer? Chun-Yi Lee put it best when she wrote: "The small and medium-sized Taiwanese OEM electronics/IT factories provided a good foundation from which the Chinese electronics/IT industry could take off. The Chinese factories learned from Taiwanese experiences in linking up with the brand companies and cost-effective factory management, and they then out-competed their 'teacher,' Taiwanese manufacturers, as they secured a place in the supply chain."[10]

CHINA'S CHANGING STRATEGY

The PRC governs its economy with Five Year Plans. The eleventh Five Year Plan, which covered the period from 2006 through 2010, revealed Beijing's intention to take China's economy back from foreign investors. The plan was concrete proof of something many Taiwanese had suspected for some time: Beijing was no longer prioritizing Taiwanese and other foreign investment. After decades of special treatment, *Taishang* were starting to find themselves competing on a level playing field—and in some cases, on a playing field tilted in favor of PRC domestic firms. Across a range of industries—from steel and petrochemicals to equipment—China's imports from Taiwan were steadily declining in favor of domestic production.

For decades, the primary concern for Taiwanese authorities was finding ways to help *Taishang* access opportunities in China. Increasingly, though, the challenge for Taiwanese firms was not market access or the overall business environment but competitiveness. The *Taishang* mantra "cost down" was nothing new, but the pressure to lower costs intensified as domestic PRC firms made their way into supply chains. By the time Ma took office in 2008, *Taishang* had a new buzzword: "transformational upgrading" (*zhuanxing shengji*). Transformational upgrading means moving up the value chain in order to remain competitive and profitable even as the cost of production in China rises. Firms that failed to transform and upgrade would not survive the surging growth of PRC firms.

Another option for *Taishang*—especially after the financial crisis of 2008 exposed the fragility of their established markets in North America and Europe—was to focus on China's domestic market, a topic I explore in chapter 8. Moving into the domestic market forced *Taishang* out of the relatively protected export-oriented sector and put them in direct competition with PRC firms. Meanwhile, Ma's market-opening reforms allowed some PRC-based firms to operate in Taiwan, forcing Taiwanese firms to compete in both markets.

During Ma's presidency, management consultants and government officials redoubled their advice to *Taishang* to undertake transformational upgrading in order to remain competitive in an ever-more-challenging PRC market. The advice was extensive but not always consistent. Management scholars Lu Hong-de and Luo Huai-chia advised businesses to think of the years 2011 to 2015 as "Taishang 3.0" and to take their cues from Beijing's twelfth Five Year Plan by switching to services, finance, and green manufacturing and by moving operations farther into the Chinese interior. Chang Pao-cheng of Taiwan's China Productivity Center recommended upgrading *Taishang* management practices to become more efficient, up-to-date, and service-oriented.[11] It was good advice, no doubt, but not easy to put into practice.

One industry that took this advice to heart was bicycle manufacturing. Taiwan's bicycle industry has been part of the scene almost from the beginning of Taiwan's industrial age. Early on, Taiwanese firms did contract manufacturing for global brands such as Raleigh, Schwinn, and Trek. In 1972, King Liu founded one such contract manufacturer, Giant, in a small town in central Taiwan called Tachia. In the early 1980s, Liu transformed Giant from a contract manufacturer to a branded company, opening its first international sales operation in the Netherlands in 1986. In its quest to create its own international brand, Giant left behind its primary client, Schwinn, which ended up filing for bankruptcy.

Giant is one of a handful of Taiwanese companies with a globally recognized brand name. It's famous for both quality and innovation. Giant edged ahead of the competition in the US by shipping its bikes "ready to ride," meaning fully assembled. It picked up speed in the 1990s by developing bikes for new uses; from road bikes to mountain bikes to BMX, Giant was at the cutting edge of an evolving market. The company invests heavily in research and development, which has allowed it to make important breakthroughs for the industry. Giant invented a new compact design that made road bikes lighter and more aerodynamic; it also produced the first carbon-based composite bicycle frames. Both of those innovations were quickly adopted across the industry. In 2002, Giant sponsored a team in the Tour de France. It was a huge step forward for Taiwan, whose companies normally stayed in the background.

Giant's operations follow many of the patterns we've seen in other industries. Giant is the flagship of a manufacturing process that relies on differentiation and clustering. Giant designs and assembles bikes and components, but except for frames, forks, and rims, the components are outsourced to specialized firms manufacturing to Giant's specifications. Giant followed another trend in the early 1990s when it opened a factory in Kunshan, Jiangsu Province's "Little Taiwan." Opening a mainland factory was part of Giant's global strategy, but it also targeted the PRC's fast-growing demand for athletic gear. Meanwhile, Tachia became a key nexus in the global bicycle industry, as the town's Giant manufacturing cluster supported a broad-based ecosystem of cycling-related businesses.

In the early 2000s, Giant was riding high, but its competitors—especially lower-cost PRC manufacturers—were catching up. In the mid-2010s, Taiwan's bicycle industry looked to be in serious trouble, about to be overtaken by the Red Supply Chain. Giant's share price peaked in early 2015 and fell steadily until early 2018, when it suddenly turned around, doubling in the first six months of 2019. Giant's turnaround was a textbook example of transformational upgrading.

Giant had already largely abandoned the low end of the market, where price pressures were intense and profit margins microscopic. It focused instead on building market share in the industry segment devoted to hard-core riders willing to pay four-digit prices for a bicycle. But even there, as Giant's innovations became industry standards, competition on price was relentless. So Giant and other Taiwanese bicycle manufacturers made a transformational upgrade: they started making electric bicycles. Taiwan's electric bike sales to Europe doubled in the first half of 2019. To be fair, European Union anti-dumping duties on Chinese ebikes played a big role in Taiwan's spiking market share. Nonetheless, it was the Taiwanese firms' transformational upgrading that positioned them to benefit from the opportunity.

Transformational upgrading is hard, especially when you're competing with companies that have a strong, determined state behind them. The PRC government's willingness to subsidize industry makes it a formidable competitor. While that can sometimes be counterproductive, as the PRC's electric bike companies discovered when their below-cost exports were shut out of Europe, most of the time it makes life difficult for non-PRC competitors. The industry that has felt the heat from Beijing's industrial policy most acutely is information technology.

In the early 2000s, as economists Barry Naughton and Dieter Ernst observed in a 2005 paper, Beijing's approach to developing information technology was pragmatic and flexible; its goal was to create a sector that would thrive in a globally integrated industry driven by market forces.[12] That meant that China's large state-owned enterprises were not the main targets for IT development; instead, the state facilitated hybrid ownership forms that merged state resources with entrepreneurial management. That is not to say, however, that Beijing left its IT firms to the whims of the market. On the contrary: it continued to subsidize firms' R&D directly and indirectly and to provide tax incentives to encourage domestic firms to buy from one another, even when foreign-invested suppliers offer lower prices. Taiwanese saw those practices as unfair competition.

Compared to the eleventh Five Year Plan, the twelfth Five Year Plan (2011–2015) was an even stronger signal that Beijing was planning to upgrade its status in the global economy from low-cost manufacturer to innovative supplier of services and high-tech goods. As we saw in chapter 5, the 2014 National Semiconductor Industry Development Guidelines took direct aim at Taiwanese and other international IC suppliers by setting a target for Chinese companies to use 70 percent domestically produced semiconductors in their products by 2025 (when the guidelines were released, the PRC was importing about 80 percent of its semiconductor needs). It also promised 150 billion dollars in state money to get the industry to the target. The "Made in China 2025" initiative released in 2015 affirmed the semiconductor guidelines, promising to build a suite of "national champion" firms across the different segments of semiconductor production (design, manufacturing, testing, etc.). According to a Brookings Institution report published in 2020, from 2014 to 2018, government subsidies to the top three PRC chip makers—SMIC, Tsinghua Unigroup, and Hua Hong—represented 40 percent, 30 percent, and just over 20 percent of their total revenue, respectively.[13] Made in China 2025 expanded this state-led model to many other industries, including auto manufacturing, green energy, and aerospace. It also committed vast resources to building China's domestic capacity for research and development in cutting-edge fields such as biotechnology and artificial intelligence. And it ramped up its acquisition of foreign companies whose technology and/or manufacturing capability are deemed strategically valuable. It's interesting to note that although technically the PRC claims Taiwan as part of its territory, it does not see Taiwanese firms as "domestic" for the purposes of these programs.

Concern that *Taishang* were being edged out of China had been building in Taiwan since the early 2000s, but it shot up after the release of "Made in China 2025." The plan declared China's intention to overtake the world leaders in advanced manufacturing by promoting indigenous innovation, reducing China's dependence on foreign technology and components, and advancing PRC companies' global competitiveness in high-value industries. Those policies are a complement to Beijing international strategy of developing new markets through the Belt and Road Initiative and the Asian Infrastructure Investment Bank. Those outward-facing policies have a political goal—expanding China's role in South and Central Asia—but they also are designed to generate demand for Chinese-made infrastructure projects—roads, bridges, ports, airports—and, eventually, consumer goods.

China's big economic competitors, including the US, Germany, and Japan, criticized Made in China 2025 as unvarnished economic nationalism and a violation of free trade norms. They complained that subsidies, compulsory technology transfer, and domestic content targets would give Chinese firms an unfair advantage in global competition and might be inconsistent with China's WTO obligations. Taiwan worries about those same things, but it also has concerns that are specific to the bilateral relationship. Another play in China's game plan is to recruit talent to execute its high-tech development goals, and Taiwan is a ripe target for headhunting.

Here, too, of course, Beijing is borrowing a tactic from Taiwan. Just as Taiwan actively recruited Taiwanese engineers to return from Silicon Valley to work in the Hsinchu Science Park, Beijing has implemented a series of measures aimed at enticing promising tech workers to move to the PRC. The most famous of these is the Thousand Talents plan, an incentive plan for scientists, engineers, and entrepreneurs from many backgrounds to set up projects in the PRC, but China also has programs aimed specifically at Chinese-speaking tech workers. For example, it set up an association in Silicon Valley to promote collaboration between US and PRC firms—something Taiwan had done in 1990. While most of the targets for these programs are PRC nationals studying or working abroad, they also target workers from overseas—including many Taiwanese. Taiwanese firms find it hard to compete; the PRC companies pay salaries far above the going rate for talent in the region, an inducement many Taiwanese believe would not be possible without the PRC government subsidizing Chinese tech firms.

Taiwan is not ceding this battlefield without a fight—not when electronics are a third of Taiwan's exports. Both Taiwanese firms and the Taiwan government are working hard to counter the trend. Taipei's changing policies on technology exports reflect Beijing's aggressive moves in the semiconductor market. Those moves force Taiwan to find a balance between allowing its firms to take advantage of the mainland market and ceding the technological advantage to PRC firms. The 2015 decision to allow TSMC to open a factory in Nanjing exemplifies the former; Taipei's rebuff of an attempt by Tsinghua Unigroup, one of China's would-be semiconductor national champions, to purchase Taiwanese firms specializing in chip assembly is an example of the latter.

The international backlash to Made in China 2025—which includes, indirectly, Donald Trump's trade war—led Beijing to lower the initiative's public profile. In 2019, Chinese Premier Li Keqiang omitted mention of the project from his speech to the National People's Congress—a first since the initiative was unveiled in 2015. Taiwanese policy makers and executives, however, are unlikely to mistake a change in the communications strategy for a rollback of China's ambitions.

Made in China 2025 targeted cutting-edge industries and sectors, which is why it provoked such a strong response from China's trading partners. It's important to remember, though, that even if Taiwan is able to hold onto its advantage in semiconductors, that doesn't mean it has defeated the Red Supply Chain—far from it. PRC firms have been slicing off market share from Taiwanese companies in a whole range of industries. For example, as of 2011, only six domestic PRC firms were licensed to build for the iPhone, but just four years later, there were twenty PRC firms holding that license.[14] Meanwhile, domestic PRC brands were gaining market share: in the first quarter of

2020, four PRC brands—Huawei, Oppo, Vivo, and Xiaomi—made more than 80 percent of the mobile phone handsets sold in mainland China. In short, whether we look at traditional manufacturing, contract manufacturing for global brands, or high tech, Taiwanese firms were feeling the squeeze from their PRC competitors. Chun-Yi Lee captured the zeitgeist just after Taiwan's 2016 election:

> Taiwan has to face the reality that China's supply chain in the coming years may no longer include Taiwanese factories. It is not for political reasons, but for the market-economy principles. The term "Chiwan" has already faded; there are very few companies designing products in Taiwan then manufacturing them in China, because Chinese companies can do it themselves or head-hunt Taiwanese human capital.[15]

Since 1987, Taiwanese firms and individuals have eagerly engaged partners in the mainland; in the process, they contributed massively to China's economic rise. As China's economy grew larger and more capable, PRC entities—central officials, local governments, firms—reevaluated the importance of *Taishang* in the mainland economy. At the same time, Taiwanese entities—officials, companies, and citizens—were increasingly skeptical that more economic exchange with the mainland was the best way to secure Taiwan's economic and political interests. *Taishang*, for their part, had always been driven by business considerations, so as the economic returns diminished, so too did their enthusiasm for new investments. As a result, *on both sides of the Strait*, enthusiasm for cross-Strait economic engagement was waning.

This is not an obvious or one-dimensional trend. Cross-Strait trade and investment remained robust through the second decade of the century. The PRC even introduced new Free Trade Zones aimed at attracting *Taishang* investment. But by the time Ma Ying-jeou stepped down in May 2016, it was hard not to conclude that the era of breakneck integration between the two sides was over.

There is a Chinese saying: indigo dye is bluer than the indigo plant. It means the pupil has overtaken the teacher. As we have seen, *Taishang* taught mainland firms, individuals, and officials how to do business. They brought in money to finance new ventures, they imported technology, and they connected the PRC to the global networks that allowed China to become an export-oriented manufacturing powerhouse. In many industries, PRC firms eventually caught up with their Taiwanese "teachers." They worked their way into supply chains; they developed their own technology; they generated their own surplus for new investment. They were able to do this in part because of the support they received from Beijing but also because they learned their lessons well. And because they had good teachers.

NOTES

1. Kazunari Yamashita, "Taiwan IT sector battles threat of 'Red Supply Chain,'" *Nikkei Asian Review*, March 15, 2016, accessed November 25, 2020, https://asia .nikkei.com/Business/Taiwan-IT-sector-battles-threat-of-red-supply-chain.

2. Chun-Yi Lee, "Social Dimensions of the Changing Cross-Strait Relations in the Case of Taishangs," in *New Dynamics in Cross-Taiwan Strait Relations: How Far Can the Rapprochement Go?*, edited by Weixing Hu (London: Routledge, 2013), 193–194.

3. Jian-Bang Deng, "Marginal Mobilities: Taiwanese Manufacturing Companies' Migration to Inner China," in *Border Crossing in Greater China: Production, Community and Identity*, edited by Jenn-hwan Wang (London: Routledge, 2015), 138.

4. Chih-peng Cheng, "Embedded Trust and Beyond: The Organizational Network Transformation of Taishang's Shoe Industry in China," in *Border Crossing in Greater China: Production, Community and Identity*, edited by Jenn-hwan Wang (London: Routledge, 2015), 40.

5. "1992 Consensus Beneficial to Taiwan," *Xinhua News Agency*, January 14, 2012, accessed November 25, 2020, http://www.china.org.cn/china/2012-01/14 /content_24405190.htm.

6. "Tourism Statistics," Ministry of Transportation and Communications, Tourism Bureau, accessed November 25, 2020, https://admin.taiwan.net.tw/English /FileUploadCategoryListE003130.aspx?CategoryID=b54db814-c958-4618-9392 -03a00f709e7a&appname=FileUploadCategoryListE003130.

7. Chung-min Tsai, "The Nature and Trend of Taiwanese Investment in China (1991–2014): Business Orientation, Profit Seeking, and Depoliticization," in *Taiwan and China: Fitful Embrace*, edited by Lowell Dittmer (Berkeley: University of California Press, 2017), 147.

8. Tsai, "The Nature and Trend," 147.

9. Chun-Yi Lee, "Taiwan and China in a Global Value Chain: The Case of the Electronics Industry," in *Taiwan's Impact on China: Why Soft Power Matters More than Economic or Political Inputs*, edited by Steve Tsang (Cham, Switzerland: Palgrave Macmillan, 2017), 135.

10. Lee, "Taiwan and China," 142.

11. Chang P. C., *Taishang Zhuanxing Shengji yu Yinying Celue Sikao* [Strategic responses to Taishang transformational upgrading], unpublished paper presented to the Conference on Mainland-based Taishang's Transformational Upgrading: Strategy, Cases, and Prospects, Taipei, 2012.

12. Dieter Ernst and B. Naughton, *China's Emerging Industrial Economy—Insights from the IT Industry*, paper prepared for the East-West Center Conference on China's Emerging Capitalist System, Honolulu, Hawaii, August 10–12, 2005.

13. Saif M. Khan and Carrick Flynn, "Maintaining China's Dependence on Democracies for Advanced Computer Chips," *Global China: Assessing China's Growing Role in the World*, Brookings Institution, April 2020, accessed December 15, 2020, https://www.brookings.edu/wp-content/uploads/2020/04/FP_20200427 _computer_chips_khan_flynn.pdf.

14. Gordon Sun, "Evaluating the 'Red Supply Chain,'" Taiwan Institute of Economic Research, 2015, accessed December 15, 2020, http://english.tier.org.tw /V35/eng_analysis/pec3010.aspx?GUID=4f51831c-f5a2-4865-8c74-5a367e31ad79.

15. Lee Chun-Yi, "Green Taiwan vis-à-vis China's the Red Supply Chain," University of Nottingham Asia Research Institute Blog, 2016, accessed December 15, 2020, https://theasiadialogue.com/2016/01/22/green-taiwan-vis-a-vis-chinas -the-red-supply-chain/.

"Borrowing a Boat to Go to Sea"

Taiwanese Business Practices in China

This book started with a mystery: how did the People's Republic of China—a nation that nationalized industry, abolished markets, and appropriated private property in the 1950s, '60s, and '70s—manage to become a world leader in export manufacturing? The first six chapters provided a historical overview of the answer: foreign-invested firms, led by companies from Taiwan and Hong Kong, set up production in the PRC and used Chinese land and labor to manufacture for international markets. In doing so, they created the conditions for Chinese companies to follow, and eventually overtake, the foreign-invested firms.

Without *Taishang* and other international investors, the PRC would have needed many decades to develop its industry and break into global markets. But *Taishang* have done far more than set up businesses inside China's borders that export to the outside world; their influence goes much deeper. Far more important than the money they invested were the new business practices they introduced to the mainland. They showed Chinese managers and firms how to participate in global markets. They integrated Chinese workers into global supply chains. They opened the door for Chinese firms to work with international brands. *Taishang* also introduced new products, industries, and lifestyles to PRC consumers. In the remaining chapters, I will detail some of the ways in which Taiwanese companies reshaped Chinese business, economics, and society.

Chinese has a four-character aphorism for almost everything, and the one that describes how China learned export-oriented manufacturing is "borrowing a boat to go to sea" (*jiechuan chuhai*). In this case, the boat was made in Taiwan.

The rise of the Red Supply Chain means this borrowed boat is not as important today as it was a few decades ago, and its importance will almost certainly diminish further in the future. Mainland-originated firms have learned to do export-oriented manufacturing on their own, and they are forging relationships with customers abroad that don't depend on a Taiwanese connection. But would they be in this position without hitching a ride on the *Taishang* boat? It's hard to see how.

When the first Taiwanese travelers touched down in the mainland in 1987, they found themselves in an economy far different from their own. A decade into its "reform and opening," the PRC economy was still dominated by state-owned enterprises (SOEs). At the grassroots level, local governments were heavily involved in the semiprivate firms known as township and village enterprises (TVEs). Many Chinese who wanted to create businesses registered as TVEs out of fear of the PRC's long-standing stigmatization of private business. Meanwhile, a dual-price system held over from the days of central planning allowed SOEs to acquire inputs at a lower price than other forms of enterprise, and many SOE managers and state officials devoted much of their time to arbitrage and rent collecting in the partially reformed economy.

This was a forbidding environment for small-scale entrepreneurs accustomed to Taiwan's free-wheeling style of capitalism. But for those who dared to enter, the potential rewards were great. China's desire for growth was strong, but its performance was weak. The cost of land was low, and unemployment and underemployment were widespread. Government officials at all levels were aggressively seeking external investment. The slow pace of reform combined with the high ambitions of the Beijing government created big opportunities for smart (and lucky) investors.

By the mid-1980s, Taiwan's traditional manufacturing was losing competitiveness, which meant that the typical *Taishang* pioneer was driven as much by desperation as by opportunity. Even so, those pioneers were not blind to the mainland's potential. They moved cautiously, but they moved. Unlike other foreign investors, *Taishang* eschewed joint ventures. When they invested, they went all-in, relocating to the mainland and managing their operations in person. If they needed managerial help, they hired Taiwanese, not local Chinese. They paid a premium to attract managers they could trust, whose skills had been honed in a true market system. *Taishang* means "Taiwanese businessowner." The white-collar professionals brought in to help the *Taishang* run their mainland businesses came to be called *Taigan*: Taiwanese managers.

Most of the companies that made the move to the mainland were—like so many of Taiwan's small and medium-sized firms—contract manufacturers. The driving force in their decision to uproot their businesses and move them across the Taiwan Strait was their international clients' demand for lower costs. Global brands were happy to continue their relationships with Taiwanese contractors, but price was key; for Taiwanese contract manufacturers, the rising cost of business was squeezing margins to the breaking point. The ability to offer the same product at a lower cost promised *Taishang* both survival and (at least temporarily) a boost in profits.

The first wave of Taiwanese investors created a very specific business model in mainland China. That business model allowed *PRC goods* to enter global production networks, but it did not allow *PRC firms* to enter those networks. Gradually, individual PRC citizens worked their way into managerial positions and learned the business model. Some of them then created their own companies or transferred that knowledge to other domestic PRC firms. Over time, the PRC absorbed, or localized, many features of the business model introduced by *Taishang* in the late 1980s and the 1990s. The Red Supply Chain's emergence was a direct consequence of this learning.

A key feature of the *Taishang* business model is clustering, including Taiwanese firms' tendency to settle in a few mainland provinces and cities. They were attracted to these areas by economic factors, of course, including proximity to ports and SEZs. But they also were looking for safety in numbers. The earliest investors mostly had stand-alone factories; they rented facilities and brought in secondhand equipment from Taiwan. But even the stand-alone factories tended to spring up near one another because *Taishang* were more comfortable that way.

Local governments reinforced the *Taishang*'s ingrained preference for proximity: those that succeeded in attracting *Taishang* tended to double-down on the strategy and recruit even more of them. While Shanghai probably has the largest number of Taiwanese residents of any Chinese city, their economic impact is muted by Shanghai's massive size. But in smaller cities, such as Kunshan (about an hour west of Shanghai, home to several thousand Taiwanese firms), Xiamen (the mainland city closest to Taiwan itself), and Dongguan (just outside Shenzhen, near Hong Kong), *Taishang* have transformed local economies and societies.

The areas of the PRC that have been altered the most by Taiwanese investment are those that opened earliest and most aggressively. During the first wave of investment from Taiwan, two provinces—Guangdong and Fujian—attracted two-thirds of the total capital inflows. Those two provinces were home to some of China's first special economic zones. When Deng Xiaoping wanted to reinvigorate the reform and opening process after the Tiananmen crackdown, he went to Shenzhen, the jewel in Guangdong's economic crown. Guangdong's proximity to Hong Kong made it an obvious choice for investors from the British-held territory and also for *Taishang*, most of whom used Hong Kong as a base for indirect investment and as their own point of entry into the PRC. Early arrivals from Taiwan focused on the Shenzhen suburb of Dongguan, where they built up extensive networks of Taiwanese firms and individuals. This clustering effect was self-reinforcing: as the concentration of Taiwanese companies grew, the area became even more attractive. Taiwanese-style restaurants and leisure facilities soon followed.

Jiangsu province followed a different path to becoming a node for Taiwanese investment. Jiangsu is bisected by the Yangtze River. The economic pattern that developed in the southern portion—the so-called Sunan Model—relied heavily on TVEs and left little room for foreign-invested firms. The town of Kunshan was the exception. Kunshan was too small and rural to develop a vigorous TVE economy, but it had ambitious, forward-looking leaders. They saw the opportunity Taiwanese investors represented, and they jumped at the chance to recruit them. *Taishang* have described the Kunshan city government as service-oriented, always looking for ways to help *Taishang* businesses thrive. The city government has an entire bureau devoted to taking care of *Taishang* and attracting more. The enthusiasm in their office is palpable: they know their work was instrumental in transforming their town into one of China's flagship cities for foreign investment. In 2014, Kunshan celebrated an event that exemplifies that transformation: it welcomed the first degree-seeking students to Duke Kunshan University, an international joint venture that enrolls students from all over China and the world.

Wherever *Taishang* settle in the PRC, they engage in industrial cluster-ing—they locate near other related firms, each of which specializes in a particular production task, working together to produce a finished product. Internally, a cluster is a collaborative environment, not a competitive one. Clustering has been recognized for decades as a way to improve productiv-ity, enable economies of scale, maximize specialization, minimize transaction costs, and promote innovation. Clusters nurture entrepreneurship by sharing capital, technology, and know-how. Even financial resources can be deployed within the cluster to ensure smooth delivery of the final product. The World Economic Forum has designated Taiwan as the world leader in cluster devel-opment; scholars agree that clustering is a key factor in the island's economic success.

Some manufacturing clusters are hierarchical "center-and-satellite" clus-ters. In these clusters, a lead firm coordinates the process, takes care of customer relations, and arranges for the delivery of components that can't be made within the cluster while the affiliated "follower" firms perform indi-vidual production tasks. Other clusters are organized horizontally, with net-works of SMEs collaborating on a particular production process. Both kinds of clusters include firms in the supply chain that, for various reasons, have remained in Taiwan. In the 1990s, it was estimated that at least a third, and perhaps twice that much, of Taiwan's exports to the mainland were bound for *Taishang* companies. For example, despite their "Made in China" labels, assembly operations in the PRC contributed less than 4 percent of the value of the iPhones they produced.[1] Components from Taiwan and elsewhere con-tributed far more. *Taishang* firms also use Taiwan-based partners for business services as well as research and development.

One of the great virtues of clustering is that it allows firms to become ex-tremely specialized, which enhances the quality, reliability, and delivery speed of the finished product. The firms' expertise in their respective tasks allows them to adjust quickly to changes in product design. They use a manufactur-ing model they call "both heads outside": imported materials and components enter China, are assembled into finished products, and are then re-exported to foreign markets. Because firms are specialized to provide components that match components made by others in the cluster (and elsewhere), products become modular, with interchangeable parts that allow for constant innova-tion and easy customization. In the high-tech sector, think of a custom-built

PC that a customer buys over the free Wi-Fi in a Starbucks in Chicago on Saturday night. The US-based brand relays the order to its Taiwan-based supplier on Sunday. The machine is assembled at a facility in southern China from components manufactured in Japan, Korea, Taiwan, and China, and by Friday, it is en route to Chicago. This astonishing feat is called nine-eight-three production: 98 percent of components gathered within three days for assembly and delivery in less than a week. It's possible because of the production processes honed in manufacturing clusters.

Taiwanese were engaging in cluster manufacturing long before they made the move to China, but as it turned out, this form of industrial organization was perfectly suited to the business conditions there. In many industries, industrial clusters moved en masse from Taiwan to the mainland. Once they were there, these clusters became even tighter and more exclusive, inspiring the sociologist Ming-chi Chen to dub them "fortresses in the air" (*kongzhong baolei*).[2] Chen's picturesque image evokes a structure that is self-contained and self-reliant, thickly defended and hard to penetrate, and only loosely tethered to the community in which it is based. It is an apt description.

Supply networks' move to the mainland had surprisingly little effect on their customers. Ownership and management didn't change; the composition of the supply chain was barely affected. *Taishang* continued to frequent trade shows at which buyers from international companies browsed acres of booths offering manufacturing services from injection molding to electronic assembly. The clientele for *Taishang* firms also changed very little, and at first, at least, the products on offer were much the same. Their customers were no doubt delighted when Taiwanese manufacturers passed along a portion of their cost reduction in the form of lower prices. But Taiwanese manufacturers working in the mainland also saw their profits expand. A whole sector of Taiwan's economy went from autumn to a second spring.

The industrial practices that made *Taishang* so successful in mainland China are not unique to Taiwan. In fact, they are a textbook example of what business sociologists call "commodity chain" production. Hopkins and Wallerstein created the term "commodity chain" in 1986 to describe production processes in which a network of separate actors—workers, managers, firms, manufacturers of materials and components—collaborate to manufacture a particular item.[3] Gary Gereffi expanded the focus beyond production to include the producer firms' relationships with the companies that design and market finished goods.[4] Gereffi's studies highlighted a marked shift in manufacturing patterns after the 1980s: he found that more and more production was carried out, not by individual companies acting alone or in small partnerships, but by multinational webs of producers coordinating manufacturing on behalf of branded firms specializing in design and marketing.

Global commodity chains are a critical institution in today's globalized economy. They allow international brands to have their products manufactured at the lowest possible cost with reliable quality by farming out the "easy" tasks to low-wage locations while keeping the more complex manufacturing processes in higher-skill locations. Final assembly can be done wherever the workforce has just the right balance of wages and skills. Meanwhile, the management of the supply chain is also outsourced to contractors who understand both ends of the chain and make the whole intricate mechanism function smoothly.

These buyer-driven global commodity chains are the primary way *Taishang* firms access the world economy. They provide contract manufacturing services to retailers (think Target or Walmart), branded merchandisers (Nike, Apple), and trading firms. *Taishang* are popular outsourcing partners because they provide consistently high-quality products at competitive prices. Importantly, too, they understand the economic and political environment in which branded companies operate. When it comes to export-oriented manufacturing, they *get it.*

Branded companies must balance many competing values: cost, quality, reliability, delivery speed, and security of intellectual property. The ideal mix of these values is different for every company, even for every product, and maximizing these values is a huge management challenge. As manufacturing has become increasingly globalized, Taiwanese contractors have amassed a strong record for delivering what lead firms need at a price they can accept. In the process, they have helped integrate China into global supply chains.

What does it mean to say that these firms "integrated" China into global supply chains? It means that Chinese workers and communities became integral participants in manufacturing for those chains. Taiwan's fortresses in the air employed Chinese workers, paid taxes to Chinese localities, helped finance investments in infrastructure, and boosted China's exports (and with them, its trade surplus and foreign reserves). They worked closely with PRC local officials to secure everything from land to construction services to utilities.

What it does *not* mean is that businesses founded and owned by PRC citizens were integrated into the supply chains. In fact, until the mid-2000s, *Taishang* supply chains rarely included domestic PRC firms. The author Liu Zhentao chose a six-character aphorism to describe the relations between *Taishang* firms and PRC companies: "They got old and died without ever visiting each other" (*laosi buxiang wanglai*).

Getting into Taiwanese supply chains is a challenge for PRC companies for many reasons. To begin with, Taiwanese production clusters and networks tended to arrive in the mainland intact; they did not form organically there, so there were few points of entry for Chinese firms. The fortresses' production processes were already established, with precise coordination timed for just-in-time delivery of components. Even when they were bringing a new item into production, residents of a fortress were unlikely to look outside the walls for suppliers, although in some cases PRC firms are able to enter supply chains by providing a resource that is not available inside the fort.

Another reason PRC-based firms were slow to enter Taiwanese supply chains is that *Taishang* prefer working with one another. They believe Taiwanese partners are trustworthy, while trust between Taiwanese and mainlanders is weak. Within the community of Taiwanese businesses, it's possible to offer favorable terms, even extend lenient financial arrangements, because the costs of cheating are high in a tight-knit, interdependent community. Because mainland Chinese are outside that community, not subject to its social norms or its internal sanctions, they are more likely to violate tacit agreements and take advantage of generosity. And given China's weak legal framework and loose contract enforcement, it's hard to get relief when a Chinese partner cheats. (Chapter 1 in a self-help book for would-be *Taishang* entitled *Ten Required Courses for Going into China* is called "The Law Is the *Taishang*'s Last Line of Defense.") The *Taishang* I have interviewed are convinced that Chinese have a different culture, one that emphasizes self-interest. They think it is safer to keep mainlanders at arm's length. According to an outsourcing manager for an apparel company, "I use connections with other Taiwanese to get things done. Trust is a cost."

Taiwanese investors went into the mainland because they had no choice, although they soon saw the potential for profit. But why did so many Chinese localities welcome them—even to the point of giving them preferential treatment? It is tempting to attribute mainland localities' eagerness to recruit

Taishang to cultural familiarity, but institutional factors provide a more satisfying explanation.

Explaining Chinese localities' hunger for foreign investment is easy. To begin with, China's economy was backward and stagnant at the end of the Mao era; the need for investment far exceeded China's modest stock of capital. The wave of TVE activity in the 1980s boosted living standards in rural China and created much-needed wealth for countless localities. But TVEs were not the answer to China's long-term development. They were undercapitalized and poorly managed; their bosses had no experience in true market economies, and the local governments that "owned" them tended to cannibalize them for short-term needs. Still, the central government's aversion to capitalism protected TVEs from competition from private firms, which were not allowed to grow beyond a handful of employees. Foreign companies were permitted only in the special economic zones. Meanwhile, the PRC's tight restrictions on population movement also made it hard for TVEs to grow because it limited their workforce to the local population.

Beijing's economic policy makers reversed direction in the 1990s, adopting a series of market-oriented reforms focused on urban China. They set aside their fear of capitalism, dropping the limits on how many employees a private firm could hire and encouraging competition and even privatization of some SOEs. The urban economy got another big boost when Beijing revoked restrictions on population movement. Rural Chinese flocked to urban areas for work; in less than a decade, the number of migrant workers doubled, then soon doubled again and again. In 2019, nearly three hundred million Chinese were working away from their registered place of residence.

The TVEs and tiny private firms that had grown up in the 1980s were no match for these well-resourced urban companies, and they soon disappeared. China's economic leaders did not mourn their demise; they were focused on promoting vitality and opportunity in urban areas, and they found foreign-invested enterprises (FIEs) a boon on both fronts.[5] Whether on their own or in joint ventures, FIEs could employ local workers and pay taxes to the local governments, and they brought their own capital, expertise, and marketing channels. Export-oriented FIEs were an even better deal since the income they generated for the Chinese economy came from the pockets of consumers halfway around the world.

Beijing had set the stage for foreign investment in 1980 when it implemented a policy of fiscal decentralization. The new policy permitted local governments to retain much of the tax revenue they collected from local businesses—especially private and foreign-invested firms. Localities also charged land-use fees, which constituted as much as half of some localities' annual revenue, and they were allowed to levy special fees and charges. These policies gave local governments a huge incentive to seek out foreign investment once the doors opened.

Individual local officials also had an incentive to woo foreign investors because attracting investment dollars was a sure-fire way to get promoted. The Chinese Communist Party's promotion system prioritizes officials' performance in economic management; the faster a locality's GDP grows, the faster its officials will move up the ladder. Some localities even established quotas for the amount of investment each official was expected to bring in.

Not only did local governments have a strong incentive to attract investment, they also had extraordinary discretion about how those investments would look, and they used their discretion to compete openly for foreign investment. In 2006, John Q. Tian wrote, "Competition for particularistic foreign economic benefits has produced an 'open-door bandwagon' that has effectively turned local governments into 'commercial republics' where rules can be bent and regulations ignored and laws are used only for reference."[6]

The two biggest costs for foreign manufacturers setting up shop in the mainland are land and labor. Local governments control both, along with countless other arrangements that shape firms' profitability.

China does not have private ownership of land; technically, the Chinese state owns all the land in China, and local governments control the use of land within their boundaries. That gives local governments the ability to manipulate the price of land (or, more accurately, the right to use land) as an incentive to attract investors. Guangdong, one of the most successful of all Chinese cities when it comes to attracting foreign investment, pioneered a policy (which then spread to other regions) of pushing old factories out of desirable areas so they can be replaced by new ones—a policy known as "emptying the cage and swapping out the birds" (*tenglong huanniao*). The businesses that move are compensated, as are the farmers whose land is made available to the relocated factories, so it is in theory a win-win practice. (Chapter 2 of *10 Required Courses* is called "There Is No Such Thing as Win-Win in

China.") According to Taiwanese scholars I've talked to, in Dongguan, whole industries were uprooted when the city decided to upgrade from traditional manufacturing to high-tech.

As for labor, while Chinese localities don't own the labor force in the way they own the land, they can make it easier for companies to recruit and retain workers. One of Kunshan's particular strengths is its proximity to Shanghai—it is far enough outside the megacity to avoid its dizzying costs but close enough to be attractive to the highly skilled workers high-tech firms are trying to woo. But less well-known is Kunshan's clever manipulation of policies governing labor mobility. China has a national household registration system under which many citizenship rights (including education) are linked to one's household registration, or *hukou*. Most Chinese are registered in the place where they (or their parents) were born. Localities decide the terms on which they will grant resident status and which privileges they will reserve for registered residents. That means a local government can make itself attractive to migrants—or not.

Kunshan has one of the most generous residency policies in China. It is relatively easy to gain resident status in the city, and it provides generous benefits to migrants (those who do not have resident status but live in Kunshan) as well. This policy facilitates labor recruitment for all the city's businesses—even, interestingly, the city itself. During a visit to Kunshan City Hall, I met a mid-ranking official in the department responsible for business recruitment. He told me how fortunate he was to have a job in the Kunshan government. He was born in a different province, and he explained that it normally would be impossible for him to get a job in a local government outside his home area. Kunshan, he said, was uniquely open to hiring "outsiders." His enthusiasm and commitment were a strong demonstration that Kunshan's generous workforce policies enhance the quality and loyalty of workers in the city.

One of the most surprising findings in studies of foreign investment in China is that until very recently, the policies put in place by the PRC government actually benefited foreign companies *at the expense of* China's domestic firms. It is hard enough for PRC-based start-ups to assemble the capital, technology, and market they need to compete with foreign-invested firms, but to make matters worse, they were for many years subject to more regulation and higher taxes than their foreign competitors. Governments at all levels—from the central government down to individual counties and cities—adopted measures that gave foreign investors special treatment and incentives. For example, in the early 2000s, SOEs and TVEs in Jiangsu province, where Kunshan is located, paid an income tax of 55 percent, while Taiwanese firms paid only 15 percent—with a five-year tax holiday for new entrants. The goal of these policies was to jump-start China's economic development by bringing in capital and know-how from abroad, and that goal eventually came to fruition. But would-be Chinese entrepreneurs waited a long time for their turn to come.

So far, I've told a story of how China worked to attract foreign investment *in general*, in a book about Taiwanese investors *in particular*. It is true that the PRC welcomes investment from around the world. Nonetheless, Taiwanese play a special role, for economic, political, and social reasons.

Taiwanese were able to have an outsized role in China's economic takeoff in large part because of serendipitous timing. At the moment China opened to foreign investment, the two economies happened to be perfectly complementary. Taiwan's traditional manufacturing sector was dominated by SMEs located mostly in small towns and cities that knew how to make and sell goods that consumers around the world wanted to buy. They weren't trying to grow huge; they didn't expect to be babied by bureaucrats hoping to nurture them into "national champions." They were used to hard work and competition. What they needed was to lower their costs. In a way, Taiwan's early investors in the mainland were a supercharged, privatized version of China's own TVEs, so they fit both China's economic needs and its institutional setup. These early arrivals paved a smooth path for subsequent waves of investors.

Chun-Yi Lee makes a persuasive case that China favored investors from Taiwan for political reasons as well.[7] At first, she argues, Beijing saw *Taishang* as one of many sources of investment that local governments could cultivate as they wished. Around 1994, however, China's central government began to recognize the potential for Taiwanese investment to advance its strategic goal of unification, and it began to encourage localities to give preferential treatment to Taiwan-owned firms. For the locals, this meant attracting *Taishang* investment was not only an economic plus but also a way of currying favor with the center. After 2000, when Taiwan elected the Sino-skeptical president Chen Shui-bian, Beijing stepped up its efforts to recruit *Taishang* as political allies. By giving them opportunities to influence policy making at the local level, Beijing hoped to win their support for its unificationist policy agenda.

Lee says Beijing lost faith in this approach after 2005; its efforts to enlist *Taishang* as agents to influence Taiwan's cross-Strait policies seemed to have failed. At the local level, however, *Taishang* continued to be an important economic factor, and many localities continued to provide favorable treatment.

Socially, too, *Taishang* were a good fit with the PRC economy. Compared to investors from nations that emphasize legal norms, Taiwanese were more comfortable with China's schmoozy approach to business. For many foreign investors, the absence of legal guidance and clear lines of authority made doing business in China a daunting prospect. Despite the cottage industry in how-to-do-business-in-China books detailing complex rules for interacting with Chinese ("never put a Chinese person's business card in a paper clip," "assign one member of your party to do most of the drinking," "pay careful attention to the seating arrangement at dinner"), many foreign investors were so intimidated that they chose to work through local (or Taiwanese) agents rather than risk transgressing some mysterious, unwritten Chinese rule.

Taiwanese didn't find doing business in the mainland easy, but they did have some advantages over investors from other countries. To begin with, they spoke the same language as their Chinese associates and they knew the rules about drinking and eating. More importantly, though, they were comfortable using personal relationships—*guanxi*—to solve problems in business. They did not expect the law to be clear; they were used to ambiguity, and they had a long history of asking forgiveness instead of permission. While large multinational corporations were accustomed to working with target countries' national bureaucracies to guide their investments, Taiwan's SME bosses were used to getting things done without government help. Taiwan's developmental model—create the conditions for SMEs, then step back—meant *Taishang* were used to operating in flexible, informal settings. Indeed, they were delighted to avoid contact with China's central government altogether.

China in the 1980s was like the Wild West—unpredictable, exciting, and more than a little dangerous. But there were sheriffs, and if you wanted to succeed in China, you needed to figure out who the sheriff was and make him your friend. The *Taishang* pioneers quickly came to realize that local officials—especially Communist Party secretaries—had enormous discretion in making decisions for their localities, including on the economic front. With their support, almost anything was possible. Without it, nothing was. Cultivating local officials—giving them gifts, sponsoring lavish banquets for them, agreeing to "fees" that everyone knew would wind up in their pockets—was a necessary part of doing business in China.

Local governments' extraordinary flexibility to implement rules and regulations is a boon to investors much of the time, but it can be a two-edged sword. The same local official who offers an irresistible incentive package to a business looking to relocate may turn around two years later and demand huge fees that were never mentioned in the original deal. The arbitrary power that seemed so appealing during the matchmaking phase of the relationship can become predatory once the factory is built and the foreign investor is locked in. These perils apply to all investors—plenty of western entrepreneurs have lost their shirts in China—but Taiwanese were especially vulnerable, for the same reason they have been especially successful. By burrowing more deeply into local Chinese economies, by playing the game of *guanxi* and gift exchange, *Taishang* opened themselves to its abuses.

All too often, *Taishang* found themselves on the wrong side of a local patron or partner. In 2003, a group of frustrated *Taishang* founded the Association of Taiwanese Businessmen Who Suffered Unfair Treatment from Investing in China; their goal was to inform their countrymen of the risks of cross-Strait investing. A *Taiwan Today* article about the group's founding offered several cautionary tales, including the story of a plastics manufacturer who lost half a million dollars when his company's Chinese vice president absconded with its assets, including its machinery. One disappointed *Taishang* told *Taiwan Today*, "My only regret in life is investing in China." Reported cases, the magazine intoned, "are just the tip of the iceberg."

Investors from many countries report being abused in China, but Taiwanese are especially vulnerable. There is no embassy or consulate for Taiwanese to turn to in the mainland, and the Taiwan authorities' leverage with Chinese localities has never been more than minimal. The situation was worst in the early years. It improved after *Taishang* founded the Taiwanese Business Association (TBA) as a way to work around their lack of official status. In addition to local-level TBAs, there are provincial and national TBAs in China. At each level, the TBA is linked to its counterpart organization in the Chinese government, the Taiwan Affairs Office (TAO).

While TBAs began as a way to provide a modicum of protection for *Taishang*, they soon morphed into something quite different—a collective voice that allowed *Taishang* to influence policy and enhance their status. When other foreign investors ran into difficulties, they sought assistance from China's Commission on Foreign Economic Relations and Trade (CFERT). *Taishang* were eligible to use the CFERT channel, but they also could turn to TBAs and to a special agency set up specifically for them: the TAO. From the central TAO in Beijing to the local Taiwan Affairs Offices in counties and towns, TAOs have two functions: promoting positive interactions between Taiwanese and Chinese (including attracting Taiwanese investment) and implementing the PRC's policies on cross-Strait relations. The TBAs are an important target for both kinds of work, and as Chun-Yi Lee details in her book *Taiwanese Business or Chinese Security Asset?* China's changing thinking about cross-Strait relations created new opportunities for TBAs to serve their members.

Taishang first started thinking about organizing to protect their common interests soon after they arrived in the mainland, but local governments there were reluctant to endorse collective action by *Taishang*. They preferred to cultivate *guanxi* with individual *Taishang* rather than dealing with them as a group. But as the number of *Taishang* increased, the need for a more efficient mode of communication and management also grew.

Dongguan was the first locality to approve the creation of a TBA. The local government decided that allowing *Taishang* to create a formal organization would give the local Taiwan Affairs Office a point of access—even influence—in the Taiwanese community. Also, as Lee has shown, in the early 1990s, China's central government began to regard *Taishang* as a strategically important group, a potential bridge to Taiwan that could help the PRC advance its interests there. Beijing encouraged localities to institutionalize their relationships with *Taishang* in the hope of activating that potential. Taiwan's government, too, finds TBAs useful because they allow Taipei to communicate with *Taishang* more efficiently. When cross-Strait relations are good, TBAs coordinate with Taiwan's quasi-governmental organ responsible for the working-level management of cross-Strait issues, the Straits Exchange Foundation (SEF). When relations between Taipei and Beijing are strained, the SEF channel can be cut off. That's what happened after Taiwan president Tsai Ing-wen took office in 2016. In those periods, the TBAs become even more important.

TBAs serve many purposes, but the two most important ones are helping *Taishang* navigate business challenges and building collective *guanxi* with local officials. Even before they decide to invest, Taiwanese entrepreneurs benefit from the information TBAs provide. For newly arrived *Taishang*, the TBA is a good source of advice and consultation—a club whose members have decades of combined experience. And when a Taiwanese gets into trouble in the mainland—anything from a traffic accident to a regulatory problem—the TBA can use its connections to negotiate a good outcome.

The Dongguan TBA became something of a legend among *Taishang* under the leadership of furniture maker Kuo Shan-hui. Kuo was a master of the (allegedly nonexistent) win-win deal: his special genius was finding opportunities for both *Taishang* and the Dongguan city government to prosper. For example, he persuaded the Dongguan city government to sell land to the TBA for its headquarters at a below-market price. He financed the construction with an assessment on local *Taishang* that entitled them to shares in the building. Once it was finished, the shares were sold at a profit. The *Taishang* got their money back, and Dongguan got a nice downtown office building. Kuo's connections with local officials and his strong reputation among *Taishang* were what made the project work. Kuo also was instrumental in bringing a branch of one of Taiwan's leading hospitals to Dongguan, and he helped China-based furniture makers fend off anti-dumping charges leveled by the US government by hiring a prominent American trade expert to represent them.

As the TBAs grew stronger, both *Taishang* and PRC local officials discovered their value. To China's local governments, they were a useful ally in recruiting and retaining Taiwanese businesses. The TBAs, with help from SEF, became a key source of information for potential investors, hosting regular events in the mainland and on Taiwan and maintaining websites and libraries. They helped *Taishang* navigate the regulations and requirements and gave them confidence that they would not be left defenseless if something went wrong. The net result was an increase in overall investment. Meanwhile, the *Taishang* were able to formalize interactions with local officials that had previously been entirely informal.

Another example of TBAs' ability to create win-win outcomes is in the area of taxation. In 2004, Beijing cracked down on companies that had understated the size of their workforce in order to avoid income taxes. Fearing punishment, some TBAs sat down with their friends in the local governments to determine a "fair" amount of tax for *Taishang* to pay. The local officials agreed the tax rate set in Beijing was too high, and they didn't want to lose the benefits of investment (including local taxes). Ultimately, sources say, the *Taishang* agreed to pay a "reasonable" amount of tax, and the local governments agreed not to look into the matter too closely. One Taiwanese *Taishang*-watcher explained, "You paid more than before, but you paid a lot less than you were supposed to. *And it's all legal!*"

TBAs were in their heyday from the mid-1990s to around 2005. They were an effective tool for Taiwanese investors and PRC local governments to resolve conflicts and promote mutually beneficial activities. Not all *Taishang* were impressed with their performance—I've been told more than once that TBAs are just talking shops for *Taishang* with too much time on their hands—but the groups did have concrete accomplishments, such as helping Kunshan City officials establish an export-processing zone based on Taiwanese models. Perhaps the TBAs' greatest success was establishing schools in a handful of cities for the children of Taiwanese working in the mainland. Both Taiwan and the PRC use exam-based university admissions processes, which makes it difficult for a student to attend school on one side and university on the other. As a result, many *Taishang* families were separated—mother and children in Taiwan, father in the mainland. The creation of *Taishang* Dependents Schools (*Taishang Zidi Xuexiao*) meant that families in some cities, at least, did not have to make this difficult choice.

Even during TBAs' heyday, the TAO never lost sight of its political goals. Providing an ever-more-advantageous investment environment, upgrading infrastructure, allowing *Taishang* to manage their affairs collectively—Beijing did these things out of self-interest. Economics was important, but the long-term goal never changed. China's leadership hoped that by linking Taiwan and the mainland economically, by providing a welcoming and profitable base for Taiwanese businesses to grow and thrive, it would be able to advance the cause of political unification. Meanwhile, the local governments were happy to follow a policy that brought them huge amounts of high-quality investment. Even though other foreign investors sometimes complained about the favorable treatment *Taishang* received, Chinese authorities at all levels prioritized good relations with Taiwanese investors.

Of course, the relationship between Beijing and *Taishang* was not all positive reinforcement all the time, and in some cases, China's actions crossed the line into active political interference. After Chen Shui-bian was elected president in 2000, Beijing lashed out at *Taishang* who had supported the DPP candidate. China's official Xinhua News Agency issued a strong threat:

"Some people in Taiwan's industrial and commercial fields openly clamor for 'Taiwan independence.' . . . Meanwhile they scrabble for profits by engaging in business and economic operations on the mainland. . . . Such a situation will not be allowed to continue."[8] This rebuke apparently was aimed at a number of well-known *Taishang* who had been supporters or advisors to Chen, including some of Taiwan's leading entrepreneurs: Acer computer's Stan Shih, Shi Wen-long of plastics giant Chi Mei, and the Evergreen shipping magnate Chang Yung-fa. While none of their companies suffered major damage, journalists documented many incidents of harassment against these and other firms.

An even more direct form of intervention takes place at election time in Taiwan. In the past several election cycles, local TAOs have encouraged TBAs to charter planes to take *Taishang* home to vote (Taiwan does not have absentee voting). Still, although both the mainland government and many DPP supporters believe the *Taishang* are a significant source of votes for the KMT, no one knows for sure how they vote. And even if they do support the KMT disproportionately, the number of *Taishang* who return to vote is rarely enough to swing an election.

During Chen's first term in office, Beijing ramped up interactions between TBAs and TAOs. Beijing cut its channels of communication with Taipei in 1999 after Chen's predecessor, Lee Teng-hui, characterized cross-Strait relations as a "special state-to-state relationship." Chen's election confirmed PRC leaders' conviction that *Taishang* were its best option for influencing Taiwan. Senior PRC officials visited some of the largest TBAs, and in 2002, *Taishang* were even invited to participate in local-level People's Congresses and People's Political Consultative Conferences, which are official representative bodies. While the SEF channel reopened and even blossomed during Ma Ying-jeou's presidency (2008–2016), Beijing cut it off again when Tsai Ing-wen took office in May 2016. Semiofficial relations can wax and wane, but the TBAs continue to function, working in conjunction with their TAO partners.

When the first Taiwanese visited the mainland in the late 1980s, they found a society in desperate need of economic opportunity. They found an eager workforce, undervalued resources, and entrepreneurial local governments. They brought capital, technology, business-process know-how, and orders from global companies. They clustered together, building "fortresses in the air" that were largely autonomous from the communities in which they were located. They paid wages and taxes, and they negotiated with local officials for better treatment. As the scale of their participation in the PRC economy expanded, *Taishang* banded together in formal organizations to promote their interests beyond individual localities.

PRC officials played an integral role in this process, and they were keen to learn the secrets of *Taishang* success. Growing numbers of PRC citizens went to work in *Taishang* enterprises as managers and partners. Some set up their own businesses modeled on Taiwanese companies, sometimes using technology acquired (with or without a license) from those same companies. Some moved into supply chains with *Taishang* firms. Others formed their own clusters and supply chains adjacent to the *Taishang*, often producing for the domestic market the same types of goods produced for export in *Taishang*-dominated supply chains.

The PRC economy today is a hybrid of hybrids, but its resemblance to Taiwan's economy circa 1980 is hard to miss. Most of the big, globally competitive native-born Chinese companies are state-owned enterprises: of the top five Chinese companies in the global Fortune 500 firms, three are SOEs and two are public/SOE hybrids. As in Taiwan during the developmental state era, China's big SOEs are concentrated in upstream industries—energy, construction, banking, insurance. The top manufacturing firm is SAIC Motor, a state-owned automaker that barely breaks the Fortune 500 top forty. But the PRC also has a robust private sector, filled with small and medium-sized companies that dominate consumer manufacturing and services. Those firms have benefited most from the opportunity to observe, learn from, and collaborate with foreign-invested companies, especially Taiwanese. Like Taiwan's SMEs, China's private firms outperform SOEs on many indicators. But just as in Taiwan in the 1970s and '80s, the PRC state is using SOEs strategically to build up bigger, more successful domestic firms and to create opportunities for SMEs to grow into large companies.

NOTES

1. Jason Dedrick, Greg Linden, and Kenneth L. Kraemer, "China Makes $8.46 from an iPhone and That's Why a U.S. Trade War Is Futile," CBS News, 2018, accessed December 15, 2020, https://www.cbsnews.com/news/china-makes-8-46-from-an-iphone-and-thats-why-u-s-trade-war-is-futile/.

2. Ming-chi Chen, "Fortress in the Air: The Organization Model of Taiwanese Export-Manufacturing Transplants in China," *Issues and Studies* 48, no. 4 (2012): 73–112.

3. Terence K. Hopkins and Immanuel Wallerstein, "Commodity Chains in the World-Economy Prior to 1800," *Review (Fernand Braudel Center)* 10, no. 1 (1986): 157–170.

4. G. Gereffi, "The Organisation of Buyer-Driven Global Commodity Chains: How US Retailers Shape Overseas Production Networks," in *Commodity Chains and Global Capitalism*, edited by G. Gereffi and M. Korzeniewicz (Westport, CT: Praeger, 1994).

5. This history is detailed in Yasheng Huang's book *Capitalism with Chinese Characteristics: Entrepreneurship and the State* (Cambridge: Cambridge University Press, 2008).

6. John Q. Tian, *Government, Business, and the Politics of Interdependence and Conflict across the Taiwan Strait* (New York: Palgrave-Macmillan, 2006), 128.

7. Chun-Yi Lee, *Taiwanese Business or Chinese Security Asset: A Changing Pattern of Interaction between Taiwanese Businesses and Chinese Governments* (London: Routledge, 2011).

8. Xinhua, quoted in James Kynge and Mure Dickie, "China Warns Taiwan Businessmen," *Financial Times*, April 10, 2000.

8

Affordable Luxury

Changing the Way China Eats (and More)

Taipei's Grand Hyatt is the very image of a luxury hotel. Its massive glass doors hold back the city's racketing bustle and enfold visitors in serenity. Its soaring lobby is filled with the glow of sunlight, the trickling of fountains, the fragrance of flowers. Its surfaces are shiny, but its seats are inviting; it manages somehow to be comfortable and thrilling, welcoming and impressive, all at the same time.

And, like most luxurious things, the Grand Hyatt is very expensive.

It was while he was eating a very expensive pastry in the very expensive Grand Hyatt in 2003 that Wu Cheng-hsueh had a brainstorm: What if you could provide the essence of luxury—the comfort, the elegance, the feeling of stepping out of the urban cacophony—at an affordable price? What would it look like to reproduce the products, service, and atmosphere of a five-star hotel at a two-star price?

Taiwanese call Wu's concept *pingjia shenhua*, or fair-price luxury. Fair-price luxury, or affordable luxury, as it's known in the West, is a critical ingredient in the success of Taiwanese companies seeking to sell their products in mainland China. While most international consumer product brands have found the PRC market hard to crack, some Taiwanese entrepreneurs have leveraged their island's reputation for modernity, cosmopolitanism, and high-quality leisure experiences to build brands mainland consumers love.

Wu Cheng-hsueh's version of affordable luxury is 85° C Café—a coffee shop chain that first took Taiwan by storm, then moved to the mainland, then upgraded to meet Chinese consumers' rising standards (and incomes). Other companies have activated mainland consumers' stereotypes of the "Taiwanese lifestyle" to sell packaged foods, restaurant meals, and even bridal photography. Selling Taiwanese lifestyles and affordable luxury are the keys to success for Taiwan-based firms that see the mainland as a market rather than just a production platform.

Everyone knows the PRC market is huge: a billion consumers just waiting to buy! But foreign companies that have tried to sell things to those billion-plus consumers will tell you: it's not that easy. Some of the challenges facing foreign companies are related to policy—the PRC government isn't always welcoming to competition—but most are related to price, distribution, and branding. The Taiwanese firms that have had the most success in the mainland are those that have overcome these three obstacles—often by borrowing business strategies from *Taishang* friends in the manufacturing sector and by adjusting their management practices for the mainland context.

Only a small percentage of PRC citizens can afford to pay what shoppers in Europe and North America pay for consumer goods, but in China, a small percentage is a large number, and super-luxury brands count China among their top markets—especially when we add in purchases of luxury goods Chinese tourists make overseas. Nonetheless, the vast majority of Chinese consumers are poor by developed-world standards. In nominal terms, China's gross domestic product per capita is about ten thousand dollars (the US figure is sixty-five thousand; Taiwan's is twenty-seven thousand) and income is distributed unequally. Recent estimates of China's Gini Coefficient (a measure of inequality on a scale of zero [perfectly equal] to 1 [perfectly unequal]) is around .46. That's compared to a US Gini Coefficient of about .43 (Taiwan's is .34). What that means is that there are plenty of people in China, but relatively few of them have the resources to buy consumer products at global prices.

Given the average Chinese citizen's limited purchasing power, even though well-known foreign brands can charge a premium for their reputation as high-status, high-quality companies, brands that are not in the super-luxury category need to find a China-friendly price. And even when the price is right, challenges remain. China's distribution networks are not easy to navigate, and widespread counterfeiting has undermined the power of many brands. Counterfeit cosmetics are everywhere in China; in early 2017, Chinese police seized over one hundred million dollars' worth of counterfeit luxury cosmetics in a single raid. Widespread counterfeiting makes customers wary—even those who would be willing to pay for the real thing—since they can't be sure the real thing is what they're getting.

In short, selling into the China market is a lot harder than manufacturing for export, but Taiwanese companies have long recognized the mainland's potential as a market as well as a manufacturing platform. Through years of careful planning, reckless abandon, and a few happy accidents, *Taishang* have made significant inroads in the Chinese consumer market. By serving and developing that market with an emphasis on affordable luxury and lifestyle-oriented brands, Taiwanese companies have brought new products, services, and experiences to Chinese consumers, subtly reshaping everyday life in urban China.

COFFEE WARS

If there is one product that says "modern" in China, it's coffee. China is a tea-drinking nation, and tea consumption still dwarfs its caffeinated competition. But coffee consumption has been growing fast, thanks to coffee's image as the preferred drink of the modern global citizen. According to a Brazilian study, China's coffee consumption grew by 1,000 percent between 2008 and 2018.[1] The Swiss firm Nestlé was the first big coffee player to enter China, in 1990. Its "all-in-one" instant packets, which include creamer and sugar as well as coffee powder, are an inexpensive and appealing introduction to coffee for many Chinese consumers, not least because they allow people to enjoy coffee without any special equipment. Instant coffee dominated the China market until the early 2010s, when sales of brewed coffee and espresso drinks began to accelerate.

In 1999, Starbucks arrived in China, bringing its star-power branding to urban Chinese who were excited to be part of a massive global trend. For many Chinese, however, Starbucks was about the experience more than the coffee. They cared more about good service, comfortable chairs, and fancy pastries than a well-roasted bean. Starbucks was not the first foreign chain to encounter this reaction. Fast-food restaurants, led by McDonald's and KFC, were among the first foreign retailers to gain a strong following in China.

Customers may have stayed for the food, but they came for the chance to have a novel experience that connected them with people around the world. The American fast-food giants, for their part, quickly learned that Chinese customers were not attracted by the "fast" in "fast food"—they wanted to savor the experience. Multistory McDonald's restaurants where customers linger over their meals are the norm in China (and throughout East Asia).

A widely quoted coffee blog, Crop to Cup, lamented the state of Shanghai's coffee culture in 2011. After encountering a carefully crafted cappuccino that nonetheless tasted terrible, the blogger wrote, "I started thinking that perhaps the main issues here are the quality of beans and a focus on image over quality. . . . Café owners concentrated on the romantic origin of the beans instead of their quality or flavor. Many cafes have some sign in the window telling you that the beans came from some supposedly famous company roasting coffee in Europe since some long-ago year. It all plays into a romantic image of the old-world European roaster. China loves it. They love the Kopi Luwak too, and the Jamaica Blue Mountain or anything else with a famous name or an 'extra big' bean."[2] The blogger's disappointment only deepened with the realization that reviews of cafés in the city "focused on ambiance, wi-fi, cuteness, food, and cats"—not delicious coffee.

The Crop to Cup blogger's disappointment is understandable, but it misses the point. For Chinese, coffee is about an experience; the connection to romantic European locales and exotic tropical coffee-producing regions, the ambiance and Wi-Fi, the comfy chairs and cats—this *is* coffee culture in China. (On the menu, those exotic regions are spelled out, painfully, one sound at a time, in Chinese characters: ge-lun-bi-ya [Colombian], ye-jia-li-fu [Yirgacheffe]. Thankfully, Blue Mountain is typically translated, Lan Shan, making it one of the few varieties a foreigner just learning Chinese can order.)

Starbucks has capitalized on the lifestyle dimension of China's coffee market, building a brand that is considerably more upscale than its American sibling—drinks cost about half again what they do in the US. Starbucks in China also pays close attention to food, and many items are adjusted to Chinese tastes (try the green tea tiramisu!). With drinks, the focus is on coffee and espresso cut with milk, sweeteners, and flavorings. In fact, it can be hard to get a simple cup of brewed coffee ("today's coffee") in a Chinese Starbucks. So few people actually drink plain coffee that some stores don't brew it unless a customer requests it.

There is no question that Starbucks has "Sinified" itself by adding much more seating and adjusting its products to suit Chinese tastes. But it remains pricey, and it's a *coffee* place. As such, its market niche leaves space for other companies. And that's where 85° C Café comes in.

When Wu Cheng-hsueh had his pricey pastry epiphany in 2003, he was already an experienced entrepreneur in Taiwan's second-largest city, Taichung. After the idea for an affordable luxury-style coffee chain came to him in the Grand Hyatt, he began researching the coffee business. During his studies, he learned that 85 degrees centigrade (185° Fahrenheit) is the ideal temperature for brewing coffee, so he named his company 85° C Café.

The name 85° C Café—which rolls off the tongue nicely in Chinese—telegraphs the company's attention to quality. From the beginning, Wu insisted on using high-grade Arabica beans from Guatemala, and he hired chefs from five-star restaurants to develop recipes and oversee the production of breads and cakes. In 2014, the company's top chef won a global pastry competition in Norway.

The first 85° C Café opened in a Taipei suburb in 2003, and the chain expanded to eighty shops within its first two years. Wu's previous business, a personal pizza chain, had taught him two important lessons. First, franchising is the best way to expand rapidly. Second, competitors and copycats are always on your tail. If you want to preserve your market advantage, you have to keep strict control over your brand and your products. Keeping those two, somewhat contradictory, imperatives in balance was challenging. Among Wu's smartest decisions were setting up a central development and manufacturing facility and keeping a tight rein on distribution.

The first 85° C Café opened on the mainland in 2007, in Shanghai, following six months of intensive research in which Wu and his team studied the market to figure out how best to reach mainland customers. The chain caught on quickly, and expansion soon followed. Within two years, revenue from the mainland operations exceeded the company's Taiwanese revenue. In 2010, 85° C Café's parent company was listed on the Taiwan Stock Exchange in an initial public offering that raised more than sixty-six million dollars. By 2016, the company had more than five hundred locations in mainland China, as well as four hundred in Taiwan and another forty in the US, Hong Kong, and Australia.

CHAPTER 8

85° C Café's expansion to China was a huge success, but that success was the result of careful planning, attention to detail, and smart management. Company founder Wu reportedly dislikes the comparison, but the chain is often referred to as an "affordable Starbucks." With Starbucks defining luxury for many Chinese consumers—and pricing its products accordingly—85° C Café has an opening to welcome a much broader market segment, bringing them a great product and pleasant ambiance at prices well below Starbucks.

Another key to Wu's success is his attention to Chinese preferences. Starbucks is an American company—that's its appeal, even if it adjusts its products to suit Chinese tastes. 85° C Café is rooted in culturally Chinese society; from the very beginning, its food and drink items were designed by and for Chinese palates. While the name says "coffee," the shops offer a much wider range of food items than Starbucks, including bread baked on-site. 85° C Café also targets a younger demographic with lower prices, stronger food options, and an emphasis on takeout. Another decision Wu made that helped his company stand out was to keep 85° C Cafés open twenty-four hours to accommodate China's hardworking (and in some neighborhoods hard-partying) youth.

The copycats (e.g., 80° C Café) didn't disappear when Wu moved to the mainland, forcing him to adjust his business model. The greatest threat facing the company was losing its reputation for high quality and good service. In the mainland, Wu discovered, franchisees tended to cut corners, so instead of franchising, Wu kept his PRC stores under centralized management. To keep the brand healthy, 85° C Café built a centralized kitchen in Kunshan, the "Little Taiwan" just west of Shanghai, which ensures consistent quality. The chain also pays above-market wages to retain and motivate staff, and it has invested heavily in marketing aimed at cementing its reputation for affordable luxury. The company slogan is "Sweeten your life."

In the first ten years 85° C Café was in the mainland, the Chinese economy grew rapidly, and so did its customers' wealth. A higher level of luxury had become affordable, and the company upgraded the 85° C Café experience accordingly. Adding deluxe seating, free Wi-Fi, and more sophisticated décor helped customers view 85° C Café as a leisure experience. At the same time, the company doubled down on its commitment to quality. It introduced imported specialty coffees and ingredients and introduced a line of higher-priced premium products alongside its lower-priced standbys. The new items included nutrition-forward varieties with "fiber" and "multigrain" in their names. As Chinese consumers' incomes grow, they are more interested than ever in finding healthy products. 85° C Café has the answer.

85° C Café flourished in the mainland by creating a brand that gave Chinese consumers products they enjoyed and made them feel as if they were part of a bigger world. Another Taiwanese lifestyle brand that succeeded by translating the West for Chinese tastes is UBC Coffee (known in Chinese as Shangdao Kafei). UBC calls itself a coffeehouse—that's what the name means—but it's really a restaurant. In the 1990s, UBC was hugely successful in Taiwan, but it fell out of fashion. Like many Taiwanese manufacturing firms, UBC found a "second spring" in the mainland, where its mellow, slightly louche atmosphere and varied menu of Chinese and Western dishes (the latter tailored to Chinese tastes) encouraged newly rich Chinese to conduct long business meetings over set meals and elaborate juice drinks or thumb their phones for hours sprawled on enormous banquettes. Food blogger Fiona Reilly described UBC as "vaguely Western style," which is just right: the chain plays to stereotypes of the West and invites Chinese to see themselves as modern and international, but with all the comforts of home.[3]

NOODLE KINGS

It's easy to think of the coffee competition as the Taiwanese David, 85° C Café, going up against the American Goliath, Starbucks. But the truth is Wu Cheng-hsueh's competition is closer to home than it seems: in China, Starbucks retail stores are operated under a licensing agreement between the Seattle-based giant and a Taiwanese food-processing colossus, Uni-President Enterprises.

Uni-President, Want Want, and Master Kong are Taiwanese companies that grew to massive size selling processed foods to convenience-starved Chinese when China's consumer economy was in its infancy. Master Kong (the name means "Master Healthy," and it's a subsidiary of Tingyi foods, which also owns the intriguingly named Sour Smell Family and Asian Hot Picks brands) is the biggest of the three, with strong market share in instant noodles, beverages, and baked goods. It also partners with international beverage companies Pepsi, Asahi, and Starbucks (for which it makes ready-to-drink beverages). A SWOT analysis in a company profile sums up Master Kong's position: its strengths are food safety and strong business process; its threats are growing competition, regulation, and rising wages. And those threats are serious: Master Kong's profit margins have declined precipitously since 2012.

In many ways, Master Kong is a familiar *Taishang* tale but with one big twist: the company started its core business in the mainland, then brought it back to Taiwan. The company's roots are in a classic Taiwanese SME, a cooking oil processor founded in 1958 and run by the founder, Wei Hede, and his four sons. After the Wei sons inherited their father's estate, they scraped together a small investment stake from friends and relatives and sent the youngest brother to the mainland to look for opportunities. They explored a couple of businesses that failed to thrive, and in 1991, the Weis were teeing up yet another new product, cookies, when fate intervened.

They were traveling by train when the passengers around them took an unexpected interest in the Wei brothers' snack: instant noodles they had brought with them from Taiwan. What they discovered in the course of that trip—and confirmed with market research—was that the Chinese instant noodle market had a big hole in it. There were cheap noodles, and there were high-end imported noodles for tourists, but ordinary Chinese didn't have a good option for tasty, hygienic instant noodles at an affordable price—especially ones that hit the spot for Northerners, who liked thick wheat noodles with a strong flavor. So the Weis launched Master Kong in 1992 to make just that kind of noodles for Chinese consumers.

Master Kong took advantage of the fashion for all things Taiwanese in the 1990s to hike the brand. The company advertised heavily on television, often buying ad spots during popular Taiwanese programs to help viewers associate Master Kong with Taiwan. With a strong product pitched to a clear market niche and aggressive advertising, the business grew quickly and soon went nationwide. By late 1994, Master Kong was pumping out three million packages of instant noodles every day; twenty years later, 90 percent of Chinese households were buying Master Kong products each year. The company soon expanded into ready-to-drink beverages, including Taiwanese favorites like lemon tea, chrysanthemum tea, and oolong tea, and brought on Taiwanese celebrities with a strong mainland following as brand representatives.

When Master Kong began selling instant noodles in the mainland, the Taiwan market was dominated by the Uni-President brand. Uni-President entered the mainland market around the same time as Master Kong. Unlike Master Kong, which developed its flavors with an eye to pleasing specific segments of the China market, Uni-President sold the same products in the mainland as it did in Taiwan. When Master Kong decided to make the leap (back) to Taiwan, it positioned itself as a lower-priced alternative to Uni-President noodles. Meanwhile, Uni-President leveraged its familiarity with the Chinese business world to win contracts to operate the China branches of international retailers such as 7-Eleven, Starbucks, and Cold Stone Creamery, an Arizona-based premium ice cream company.

Ironically, "Master Healthy" has suffered in recent years from the new health consciousness of Chinese consumers. Like many foreign brands, Master Kong has a good reputation for safety and quality, an important asset in a country where food safety scares are common. The company imports some ingredients, and its factories have won international quality certifications, but today's wealthy Chinese consumers are looking for products that are more nutritious than instant noodles. Affordable, high-quality prepared food, which is available in supermarkets and by delivery, also is cutting into the market for instant noodles. Master Kong is working to develop healthy alternatives, but instant noodles are its core business. Meanwhile, competition continues to intensify, further driving down Master Kong's profit margins.

The third big player in Taiwan's processed food space is Want Want. Want Want's story is unusual because unlike the majority of *Taishang*, who avoid political entanglements, its founder has expanded into a business with political implications—and paid the price. Want Want specializes in rice crackers and other snacks as well as children's milk drinks. The company head, Tsai Eng-meng, was nineteen years old when he went to Japan to learn to make rice crackers in the late 1970s. The businessman he hoped would be his teacher initially rebuffed him as too young, but Tsai eventually won him over and his rice cracker business took off. One especially creative marketing strategy was to promote rice crackers as an offering in temples. (Taiwanese typically leave fruit and flowers on a table in the temple as an offering to the gods.)

When the company began selling crackers in the mainland in the late 1980s, Tsai had to find a new strategy: religious rituals were not something middle-class Chinese spent money on. Instead, Tsai told *Forbes* in a 2009 interview, he targeted kids, something middle-class Chinese *do* spend money on. Want Want claims to be the first Taiwanese company to seek the PRC government's approval for a trademark; its logo, a spiky-haired boy with a wide grin and heart-shaped tongue called Hot Kid, is a particularly memorable specimen of the species.

While Master Kong and Uni-President have expanded their businesses from food processing to retail, Want Want's ambitions are considerably bigger. In 2008, Tsai Eng-meng purchased the *China Times*, one of Taiwan's leading newspapers. A year later he bought two cable TV news stations. But that was not enough: the newly formed Want Want China Times Media Group then went after one of Taiwan's top cable companies and Hong Kong–based Next Media's Taiwan operations. Both deals were eventually blocked by regulators, but if they had succeeded, Tsai's empire would have included more than half of Taiwan's media market.

The regulators acted against the backdrop of a massive public uprising aimed at stopping Tsai's company from acquiring a dominant position in the island's news media. The activists could not accept an entrepreneur with such broad and deep business interests in the mainland controlling a large share of the nation's media. For Taiwanese, the PRC is a source of opportunity, but it also poses a profound threat to their political system and personal freedom; in 2012, many went to the streets to say they did not want their media controlled by a man with deep financial interests in the PRC. That year's Anti-Media Monopolization Movement called attention to the trend of concentrating ownership in Taiwan's media, and it may have influenced the regulators' decision. But it gave ammunition to those who claimed Taiwanese society was sacrificing economic opportunity to political paranoia. Above all, the incident was a stark reminder that while Taiwanese celebrate local companies' success in the mainland, they expect *Taishang* to keep their business interests out of politics.

DINING TAIWAN STYLE

Nothing says luxury like your own personal hot pot. For centuries, Chinese have gathered to share food cooked fondue-style in broth boiling around a coal-burning chimney. Until a couple of decades ago, the main innovation in hot pot technology was to replace the smoky coal with a cleaner-burning heat source. After all, part of the fun of hot pot is the communal pleasure of circling the pot and adding ingredients that flavor the soup for everyone. But not everyone likes the same thing. Some people are vegetarians. Others eat meat but hate the taste of lamb. And then, of course, there's the spicy/not spicy debate. Enter Xiabu Xiabu, a fast-food chain specializing in individual hot pots so all the guests can have exactly what they want.

Xiabu Xiabu's founder, He Guanqi, headed to China more than twenty years ago. He started out running jewelry factories but quickly saw potential in the restaurant biz. As he explained in an interview, "At that time, people in China just wanted to eat." But He recognized that while some people just want to eat, others are looking for something more, something that combines daily sustenance with a touch of luxury. To satisfy that customer, he said, "the facility needs to be nice, the service good, and the quality of the food also needs to be good and consistent." And so he decided to "create a new model, one that would combine the desire for fast food and the leisure experience."

When he first began exploring the restaurant business, KFC and McDonald's dominated China's fast-food market. And despite their down-market image outside China, they led the way in bringing leisure and even luxury to the industry. "Even KFC and McDonalds, in mainland China, no longer look like student cafeterias, with the tables and chairs bolted to the floor. Now they have story after story of comfortable, moveable furniture, suspended lighting, that sort of thing. They are more like Starbucks. Their original food doesn't always fit the new environment, but that's okay," says He.

Individual hot pots, called shabu shabu, have been popular in Japan and Taiwan for decades. The setup is a usually a bar with a heated stainless-steel bowl set into the counter at each seat. The waiter fills your bowl with your choice of broth, and you select from a menu or buffet of meats, vegetables, seafood, noodles, and dumplings, which you cook to your taste. For Mr. He, bringing consistently delicious, well-prepared ingredients to every bowl is the key to success; it's what made Xiabu Xiabu the leading individual hot pot brand—and China's third-largest fast-food chain, after (you guessed it) KFC and McDonald's.

You might expect that Xiabu Xiabu has done well in China because it offers a familiar product, but Mr. He doesn't buy that explanation.

> The theory of taste doesn't really work. Plenty of foreign products are popular there, including food and restaurants. Lots of Korean restaurants do well there. Objectively speaking, China is a strange nation. For so long they suffered from foreign bullying, so they have some anti-foreign elements. . . . But at the same time, they worship foreign things. Taiwan products, ideas, standards—they

believe these are higher than theirs. Not everyone thinks like this, of course, but most people do. Twenty years ago, when I first went to China, anything foreign was easy to sell. . . . Our success comes from getting there early. . . . But now they are getting more and more brand conscious. In Taiwan we don't care that much about labels—if the quality is good, we'll buy it—but the Chinese do care about brands, and they don't have many of their own. So if Chinese want to eat individual hot pot, they eat ours because we have the brand.

To build and protect a brand requires consistent quality, and here is where management processes become critical. Taiwanese brands get the benefit of the doubt when it comes to quality, but if they don't do a good job, they can lose that privilege in a hurry. To avoid that fate, Mr. He adapted the industrial model he learned in the jewelry business to standardize Xiabu Xiabu's operation: "Everything in our business is done to a particular standard. This is a new business model; without a strong model you can't fight successfully in the China market. It's just like a factory: you need to know how many units you produced today. We pay close attention to how much business we did each day. If we have five hundred stores, we want each store to serve five hundred customers—that's twenty-five thousand customers per day. And we will keep opening more."

Xiabu Xiabu is one of the top Taiwanese restaurant chains in the mainland—but it has no presence in Taiwan at all. According to Mr. He, the Taiwanese market is too competitive and too small for his business to flourish. He prefers to keep his affordable luxury offering in the mainland cities where customers are hungry for it.

Even with excellent quality and careful attention to detail, no company will thrive without tackling an even bigger challenge: marketing. Says Mr. He, "I'll tell you something: Production is easy. Marketing is hard." Xiabu Xiabu used expansion to drive its marketing effort. The company took care of facilities and supplies, but individual stores were responsible for local marketing. With a well-managed corporate operation behind them, individual outlets were able to build their own sales and promote the brand at the same time, making Xiabu Xiabu one of the top three Taiwanese IPOs in mainland China in 2014.

Marketing may be hard, but production and quality control turned out to be more difficult than Mr. He realized. In 2018, a couple of years after I interviewed him in Taipei, the chain lost almost two hundred million dollars in market value after a customer pulled a well-done rat out of her hot pot in a Shandong province Xiabu Xiabu. The photogenic rodent was an Internet sensation, and Xiabu Xiabu's business was hit hard. The incident proved fatal only to the rat, however, and within about six months, the company's stock price had rebounded to 85 percent of its peak value. Nonetheless, it was a hard lesson: when your competitive advantage is your reputation for quality and safety, one mistake can bring disaster.

MANUFACTURING JOY

The first time I saw a bride standing up to her knees in muddy water with the train of her gown tangling in a cluster of lotus flowers, I was flummoxed. Since then I have seen brides striking poses in the doorways of collapsing farmhouses, batting artificial eyelashes in the jungle, lounging on the sand as ocean waves wash over them, even smiling gamely next to the sulfur-steaming mouth of a fumarole, or volcanic vent.

What could possibly possess a grown woman to put on a dress worth several months' salary and climb into a volcano?

Wedding photos, that's what.

Documenting a new marriage with a photograph is a long-standing Chinese tradition, but as Taiwan prospered in the decades after World War II, Taiwanese took bridal photography into uncharted territory. Together, couples and photo studios created a wholly new industry, one that now takes in a few hundred million dollars a year and has become an indispensable component of the marriage rituals practiced by ethnically Chinese couples the world over. Noodles have been around for centuries; individual hot pot is just a twist on a familiar dish; coffee didn't originate in Taiwan. But Taiwanese-style bridal photography is a true original, and it has taken mainland China by storm. It is the ultimate example of how Taiwanese investors have transformed PRC lifestyles by putting fantasy and luxury within reach of China's fast-growing middle class.

In the early 1970s, technology and economics aligned to produce a new cultural practice in Taiwan. Improvements in color photography and photo editing, as well as rapid increases in family incomes, allowed couples to purchase whole albums of high-quality wedding photographs. While the traditional wedding photo had been a somber affair, with bride and groom posed amid family members whose serious expressions reflected the weight of the moment, buying multiple photos allowed for individual shots that highlighted the romantic hopes of the young couple—and the bride's resplendent beauty.

Until the 1970s, Taiwanese photography studios took pictures for all occasions. Brides rented their wedding attire from specialty shops, then hired a photo studio to take a picture, usually on the wedding day. Improvements in technology allowed photographers to focus more on taking pictures than developing them, and the two businesses—clothes rental and photography—gradually merged. Soon the studios added backdrops, hair styling, and makeup artistry to the services they provided. The result was a whole new industry, one dedicated to creating images that highlighted the bride's beauty and suggested a romantic connection between bride and groom. As Lee Yu Ying has written, bridal photographers became experts in "manufacturing joy."[4]

By the 1990s, bridal photography was a huge industry in Taiwan. Photo production was getting cheaper just as Taiwanese incomes were rising, and that meant families could afford more, and more elaborate, photo shoots. The "traditional" white wedding gown was still the centerpiece of a bridal portfolio, but studios invested in a splendid array of gowns and costumes. From 1920s Shanghai retro looks to elaborate Japanese kimono to Hello Kitty–themed pink tulle confections to Miss America–style evening gowns, if a bride could dream it, she could find it somewhere on Chungshan North Road, Taipei's bridal photography miracle mile. These rented dresses rarely appear at the actual wedding, which typically takes place weeks or months after the photo shoot, so they don't need to fit perfectly. With ingenious application of clips and pins, the same dress can fit brides of many sizes.

To showcase these looks, which include elaborate hairdos and astonishing makeovers, photographers began offering on-location shoots. Bride, groom, photographer, assistants, stylists—the whole entourage troops out to some dramatic locale to capture the couple at the pinnacle of their beauty, crafting an image of idealized romance. The anthropologist Bonnie Adrian wrote a wonderful book on Taiwanese bridal photography in which she argues that the cultural purpose of bridal photography is to create the fantasy of marriage based on romantic love, free of the pragmatic considerations that shape most real marriages.[5] Truly: the photographer's job is to manufacture joy.

As was true of many other industries, the market for bridal photography in Taiwan was saturated by the late 1980s. Adding new products and services (wedding planning, printed invitations and place cards, renting clothing for the wedding banquet and limousines for the wedding party) kept the studios humming, but when mainland China opened to Taiwanese investment, photography studios quickly followed manufacturing into what was, at that time, a bridal photography *terra nullius*.

According to Gao Zhirong, owner of the Best Romance bridal photography studio, director of the Taipei Wedding Photography Trade Association, and a thirty-year veteran of the industry, bridal photography was one of the first retail-oriented businesses to enter the mainland from Taiwan. Studios' experience mirrored that of other industries in another way: local governments on the mainland actively courted them and provided cut-rate facilities to attract them. The underlying rationale for their actions, Mr. Gao explained in a 2016 interview, was to allow Chinese workers to learn the skills of the trade and open their own businesses.

Bridal photography was an instant hit among mainland China's nascent middle class. After decades of being punished for displays of vanity and femininity, Chinese women were primed for an industry that allowed them to look beautiful and enjoy fashion from Taiwan, the trendsetter and embodiment of modernized Chinese culture. Said Mr. Gao, "As soon as those Taiwanese businesses went to China, they immediately became popular. Because, regardless of whether it was formal wear or makeup, they were market leaders. So as soon as they went, they immediately started to make money." At first, wedding photos were a luxury item. A few Taiwanese companies opened in Beijing and Shanghai. The photos they took were superior to anything Chinese couples could acquire locally, so "friends [of the couple] would see the pictures, and that is how it started to become popular—everyone liked to go to a Taiwanese wedding photo store."

By the mid-2000s, Taiwanese studios had lost their advantage over their local competitors as local employees acquired the skills to open their own studios. Like *Taishang* in other industries, Taiwanese studio owners lacked the connections they needed to outcompete locals. China also swiftly upgraded its technical capacities, so Taiwanese no longer had an advantage in printing quality. In fact, the flow of innovation was partially reversed, as Taiwanese began embracing a pared-down version of the bridal photography studio that first developed in the PRC. According to Mr. Gao, most of the Taiwanese-owned studios have sold out to PRC buyers; by 2016, Taiwanese-owned chains continued to operate only in big cities such as Beijing and Shanghai. "In other cities," he said, "they have all been beaten."

Bridal photography also shares some similarities with other retail businesses. According to Mr. Gao, most of the large chains that once dominated the business in Taiwan broke up after entering the mainland: "Because chain stores are quite a bit harder to control, it's very difficult to ensure the same quality. It's a lot like cooking food. . . . One cook might like spicy food, and make a certain dish very well, but if another cook has a lighter taste, then he might make it poorly. So it's very difficult to control chain stores. Every store has its own personality." That personality is critical in an industry based on convincing a young couple that their photographer will be able to make their love for one another visible in a photograph.

On the whole, Mr. Gao observed, "the wedding photo industry is a microcosm. Based on the wedding photo industry model of entering China, you can examine other industries' experiences. . . . I often speak with other people in other industries, and they all think that this is true. There is no way of competing with the locals." While the localization of the bridal photography industry has meant a loss of business for *Taishang*, it also proves that Chinese consumers have adopted the Taiwanese practice of buying bridal photographs—and the romantic, love-and-beauty-based aesthetic that infuses the industry.

CHANGING CHINA, ONE CUSTOMER AT A TIME

Xiabu Xiabu founder He Guanqi compares doing business in a China to a war in which "the final determiner of victory and defeat is your product." If it's a war, some Taiwanese companies are winning, and in the process, they are changing the environment for Chinese consumers. Taiwanese have brands, and "Taiwanese" *is* a brand. And despite all the negative politics surrounding the relationship between Beijing and Taipei, PRC consumers like the "Taiwan" brand.

Many of the most successful Taiwanese companies entered the PRC in the early 1990s, when consumer goods still were not widely available and things like comfort, luxury, quality, and service were hard to find in an economy just emerging from socialism. Taiwanese companies brought all of these but without the high cost of goods imported from the West. They allowed Chinese to enjoy foreign flavors and styles without paying foreign prices and often in adapted forms that made them less alien. The Taiwanese brand represented modernity, sophistication, novelty, variety, internationalism, relaxation, quality, and beauty—all at a price mainlanders just entering the consumer class could afford. Affordable luxury is more than a product category; in China, it's a lifestyle.

It is precisely the fact that these brands are *not* local that gives them their appeal: the Shanghai-born, Taiwanese-owned bakery chain Christine ran into trouble because it was perceived as "too local." Other international companies, including the Korean-owned BreadTalk and Singapore's Paris Baguette, took market share from Christine because their presentation was more "foreign."

One reason it is so valuable to be perceived as foreign is that "foreign" means more than "fun and exotic." It also means "made outside China's compromised food system." In recent years, China has suffered a series of high-profile food safety failures, from melamine-laced milk powder that killed six infants and sickened thousands more in 2008 to fake meat scandals and cadmium-contaminated rice. Many consumers in the PRC will pay a premium for foods they believe are safe, which usually means foods with a foreign source. Even if the raw materials are produced in the mainland, companies can benefit from this image by foregrounding their foreign origins and emphasizing health and quality in their marketing.

Marketing is important, but it's not enough. Companies actually need to deliver on their quality assurances, which requires a strong supply chain and smart management practices. I asked Xiabu Xiabu's Mr. He about dealing with Chinese regulators and he replied, "The regulators are not bad, but if customers complain, you'll hear from them. You need to be able to meet the regulatory standards. If your internal controls are okay, you're fine. Anyway, you hear the same message from your insurance company!" Mr. He makes it sound easy, but those internal controls are critical, and Taiwanese companies excel in this area, in part because they have learned from their colleagues in the manufacturing world. And, as Mr. He learned from that rat, even the best companies can make mistakes.

As previous chapters make clear, Taiwanese manufacturers are masters of supply chain management—their value as suppliers to international companies comes from their ability to deliver a high-quality product consistently at a competitive price. Other *Taishang* attributes also help consumer-facing companies succeed in the mainland. For example, Taiwanese manufacturers are well-known for their ability to adapt technologies and products to serve new markets. We see this among the Taiwanese who sell into the mainland market, too. Their products are different enough to have the cachet of foreignness yet familiar enough to please Chinese tastes: there's less coffee in the coffee drink, and you can buy a dozen different flavors of mooncakes at Christine.

In short, Taiwanese companies are a bridge between Western and Chinese lifestyles. Western versions of a product tend to be expensive and to require more adjustment to appeal to Chinese tastes. That is not to say they can't succeed—Xiabu Xiabu's competition is KFC and McDonald's, after all—but the Taiwanese have carved out a niche that works. The average American or European might not recognize all the pastries at a Shanghai Christine or 85° C Café (is that a *hot dog* in that croissant??), but the alteration is something that makes the product more appealing to Chinese.

Finally, Taiwanese companies benefit from their ability to leverage China's political idiosyncrasies. A big restaurant or fashionable café counts as economic development just as a factory does. As in any business, *Taishang* who sell into the Chinese market place a high value on maintaining good relations with local officials. And local officials value those relationships, too. According to Mr. He, local governments count restaurants toward their economic development goals, and he's been solicited by many localities to open a store in their area. In fact, he said, "Whether we are in a city or not is a marker of its development. People check to see who's there: do you have KFC, McDonald's, Xiabu Xiabu? If we're not there yet, it means the market is not fully developed."

As with other types of business, *Taishang* no longer enjoy the strong advantages they once did. Many of the assets that made them successful and desirable in the mainland—their focus on quality and service, their management systems, their business models—have been adopted by PRC-originated companies. Meanwhile, competition is growing, both from local companies and from other international firms, and the cost of doing business is rising rapidly. To succeed, it's not enough to have a good product and be well-managed; you need to have a truly novel product, a great business plan, and deep pockets. The dedicated manufacturing and distribution systems that allow chains like 85° C Café and Xiabu Xiabu to provide consistent quality are expensive; they require a large number of retail outlets to pay for themselves. Mr. He summed it up: "The whole world is going the same way: the big are getting bigger, and it's nearly impossible for the small to grow."

NOTES

1. "Coffee Consumption in China Has Risen by Over 1,000% in the Last 10 Years," International Comunicaffe, 2018, accessed December 15, 2020, https://www.comunicaffe.com/coffee-consumption-in-china-has-risen-by-over-1000-in-the-last-10-years/.

2. "Coffee in China: A Few Observations," Crop to Cup Coffee Blog, 2011, accessed December 15, 2020, https://croptocup.wordpress.com/2011/10/07/coffee-in-china-a-few-observations/.

3. Quoted in LiAnne Yu, *Consumption in China: How China's New Consumer Ideology is Shaping the Nation* (Cambridge: Polity, 2014).

4. Yu Ying Lee, "Zhangban Xinniang: dangdai Taiwan hunshaye de xingqi yu fazhan lishi" [Dressing up the bride: The historical rise and development of Taiwan's bridal industry], *Feng Chia Journal of Humanities and Social Sciences*, no. 8 (2004): 183–217.

5. Bonnie Adrian, *Framing the Bride: Globalizing Beauty and Romance in Taiwan's Bridal Industry* (Berkeley: University of California Press, 2003).

9

Beyond Business

How Taiwanese Are Reshaping Chinese Society

If you met him on the street, at one of the exquisite Japanese restaurants he loves, or in the airport waiting for a flight out to Guangzhou, you would never guess that Mr. Cheng founded a successful ODM manufacturing company. He is attentive, down-to-earth, and generous. Just how generous? Read on.

Mr. Cheng started a manufacturing business in the 1980s. The company's original factory was in Dongguan, wedged alongside hundreds of other *Taishang*. Over the years, the firm has developed a reputation for high-quality manufacturing. What makes Mr. Cheng's company even more distinctive is his emphasis on corporate social responsibility (CSR). Even before it established a CSR department in 2008, the firm won recognition for its CSR work from Disney and Walmart. The firm takes pride in the working conditions in its factories, which Mr. Cheng calls campuses, and it has been honored several times by local governments and citizens for its contributions to the communities where its factories are located.

When Mr. Cheng's second child was born profoundly deaf, he and his wife researched how deaf people communicate in Chinese. Spoken Chinese is tonal—whether a word means "numb" or "curse" depends on whether the word is pronounced with a rise at the end, like a question, or with a falling tone, like a command. Tonality makes it extremely difficult for the hard-of-hearing to learn Chinese; in fact, many people once believed it was impossible. When the Chengs' daughter was born, Taiwan and the PRC were tough places to grow up deaf.

As they navigated through the challenges of raising a deaf child, the Chengs decided to share what they were learning with others. In 1996, they founded the Children's Hearing Foundation (CHF) to help other Taiwanese families who were facing the same challenge. CHF developed techniques for teaching Mandarin Chinese to children with limited hearing—overcoming the long-held belief that Chinese was beyond the reach of the hard-of-hearing. CHF built centers in Taipei and Kaohsiung where deaf children from around the island are tested, fitted with assistive devices, and taught to understand and speak using a method called Auditory Verbal Training (AVT). Successfully teaching Chinese to deaf children takes many hours every week, so CHF also trains parents in techniques they can use to teach their children at home.

The Children's Hearing Foundation has had a huge impact on Taiwan's deaf community, enabling thousands of deaf people to participate in the hearing world. But helping deaf children in Taiwan was not enough for Mr. Cheng. After his wife passed away in 2001, he decided to use his skills as an entrepreneur to expand the foundation's reach. The CHF began publishing teaching materials and textbooks to allow others to use AVT to assist Chinese-speaking deaf children. In 2008, Mr. Cheng stated, "We hope to realize the goal of making a CHF resource center for AVT in every Mandarin-speaking region." In other words, Mr. Cheng decided that his philanthropy would follow his business to mainland China.

As it turns out, it's a lot easier to do well in the mainland than to do good. The PRC still does not have a well-developed system of private organizations that provide direct services to people in need. In Taiwan, the nonprofit sector blossomed as the country grew richer; today, there are organizations for every imaginable purpose, from advocating for political change to caring for the needy. Such organizations are on the rise in the PRC, too, but they are still relatively rare, and their activities are closely scrutinized and limited by the state.

In Taiwan, the Children's Hearing Foundation operates out of freestanding facilities where its audiologists test and treat deaf children and teach them to understand and speak Chinese. Instead of building its own facilities in the mainland, CHF established partnerships with Chinese clinics that care for people with disabilities. They trained Chinese staff to use the CHF's tech-

niques and curriculum to help their patients. As is true for so many Taiwanese undertakings in the mainland, quality control is a challenge. The clinics
CHF worked with in the mainland are responsible for people with disabilities
of all kinds, and they tend to be highly bureaucratic, which can make it hard
for them to adopt new ideas. But Mr. Cheng and his foundation were determined to help as many deaf children as they can, so they persevered through
the challenges.

The Children's Hearing Foundation is making a difference to thousands of
Chinese children who are gaining access to the world of spoken language. It
is also part of a wave of Taiwanese organizations that are changing China by
bringing new ideas—and reviving old ones—about how society can accomplish important shared tasks.

This nonprofit social service ethic is a novelty in the PRC. After 1949, the
Chinese Communist Party centralized the organization of economic, political, and social life under the party-state umbrella, leaving no room for an independent civil society. Since Deng Xiaoping opened the country in the late
1970s, the private sector has returned in the economy, but Chinese citizens
still rely on the party-state to manage most other aspects of life—an expectation that taxes the capacity of China's institutions.

China's changing society and its people's rising expectations are making it
increasingly difficult for the PRC state to meet their complex needs. Some social tasks need to be moved into the private sphere, and here again, practices
and institutions transferred from Taiwan are having a significant influence
on China's development. Philanthropy, religion, law, popular culture—these
are among the "soft" contributions Taiwanese have made to the PRC. In the
long run, they may prove even more consequential than "hard" contributions
such as investment, trade relationships, technology, and business know-how.

BRINGING THE GODDESS HOME: TAIWANESE
IN CHINA'S RELIGIOUS REVIVAL

Lin Moniang was born in Putian, Fujian, in 960, during the Song dynasty. In
her twenty-nine years on earth, she accomplished many miracles, and when
she left this earth—reportedly ascending into the heavens from a mountain
on Meizhou Island—she gained the status of a goddess. As a goddess, she is
known by the title Heavenly Mother and the name Mazu. Villages across Fujian built temples to honor her; the oldest extant Mazu temple is on Meizhou

Island, near where she lived. The Song court recognized Mazu with an official title, enabling her cult to spread. By the early 1200s, there were Mazu temples throughout coastal China. By the time China's last dynasty ended in 1911, at least 150 temples were dedicated to Mazu, the patron goddess of fisher-folk and other seafaring Chinese.

As Fujianese migrated away from the mainland, they carried the goddess with them. She protected their passage first to the Penghu Islands midway between Taiwan and Fujian and then, in the mid-1600s, to Taiwan itself. As a patron and protector of sailors, she was especially important to Taiwan's Fujianese settlers; her cult became the most important of the many interwoven religious belief systems on the island, and she remains popular today, with an estimated eight hundred to one thousand temples dedicated to her in Taiwan. Nor did Taiwanese forget their goddess's origins. They believe the "mother temple" in Meizhou is an especially potent source of divine power, a place where Mazu's presence on earth is strong, and they have been making pilgrimages to Fujian to visit the places Mazu lived and where she performed her miracles for centuries.

The Chinese civil war cut Taiwan off from Fujian and ended regular interactions between Mazu faithful on the two sides of the Strait. While the Mazu cult thrived on Taiwan, the Chinese Communist Party's attitude toward traditional religious practices stigmatized all such cults as "feudal superstition." In the 1950s, the CCP tolerated religion, although it discouraged and disparaged it, but during the Cultural Revolution in the mid-1960s Mao Zedong instructed his followers to destroy "the Four Olds"—old thinking, old culture, old practices, and old habits. The Red Guards, young Chinese eager to prove their devotion to Mao, violently attacked religious practitioners and demolished temples, monasteries, mosques, churches, and other religious sites.

The Red Guards destroyed many Mazu temples; the rest were stripped of their ritual items, the buildings converted to secular uses. The Maoist state banned traditional religious practices, but when Deng Xiaoping came to power in the late 1970s, he led the CCP in relaxing the prohibition on religion. The state issued regulations that legalized private belief in five religions: Buddhism, Daoism, Islam, Protestantism, and Catholicism. Although faith traditions like the Mazu cult do not really fit into any of those categories, resourceful believers throughout China affiliated their temples with Daoism in order to obtain legal status and a measure of protection.

In 1983, the Chinese government allowed residents of Quanzhou, a city near Mazu's birthplace, to repair a temple dedicated to one of Mazu's fellow deities, Guan Gong the Protector. The leadership of the restored temple labeled it a historic site at which research on Daoism would be conducted; under the guise of "cultural preservation" and "academic research," the temple resumed ritual activities. To fund the restoration, the Quanzhou temple committee activated long-dormant ties between the Guan Gong faithful in Fujian and Taiwan.

The anthropologist Murray Rubinstein visited the temple in the early 1990s and saw the names of Taiwanese donors inscribed on the walls.[1] The PRC government permitted—even encouraged, at least at the local level—Taiwanese contributions for "historic preservation." The temples' fundraising activities were clearly oriented toward donors from outside China, including ethnic Chinese living in Southeast Asia as well as Taiwan: Rubinstein noted that the Guan Gong temple's official history was written in the traditional characters used in Taiwan and Hong Kong, not the simplified version normally used in the PRC. In the plaza outside the temple, he met a shopkeeper who sold ritual objects in both Quanzhou and Taipei—an early example of a cross-Strait retail chain.

Quanzhou is home to an important Mazu temple as well as the Guan Gong temple. It suffered devastating damage in the Cultural Revolution but was rebuilt in the 1980s and reopened in 1988. As with the Guan Gong temple, the Mazu temple committee relied on contributions from Taiwanese faithful to finance the project. Fujian's Mazu temples have a unique claim on Taiwanese believers: because they are older and closer to the sites of Mazu's life and apotheosis, Taiwanese believe that connections to these "mother temples" are a source of potency for the "branch temples" in their own villages and towns. The closer the relationship between a Taiwanese temple and the mother temple, the more powerful the Taiwanese branch can become and the more effective it will be in answering prayers.

The idea that connections to the Meizhou mother temple enhance a temple's spiritual potency and efficacy sparked fierce competition among some of Taiwan's oldest Mazu temples, each of which tried to establish its primacy in the Mazu cult by showing that it was the closest to the mother temple on Meizhou Island. To access the spiritual power in the Meizhou temple, Taiwanese revived the old pilgrimage tradition. The pilgrims brought money, of course, which flowed to both the Fujian temples and the local tourism industry, but they also brought ritual objects and practices. And they came in large numbers: it is estimated that in the first fifteen years of cross-Strait travel, more than a million Taiwanese visited Meizhou. By the early 1990s, the PRC-government-run China Travel Service was advertising "Mazu Pilgrimage Tours," and in 2002, the Meizhou tourist bureau reported more than one hundred thousand Taiwanese visitors to the island.

The desire to reach Meizhou made Mazu pilgrims an important force behind policy changes that eased restrictions on cross-Strait travel. Businessmen grumbled about the inconvenience of having to fly though Hong Kong to reach the mainland, but Mazu devotees actually *did* something about it. In 1987, the leaders of Taiwan's Zhenlan Mazu Temple decided to make a pilgrimage to Meizhou Island's mother temple. At that time, such visits were technically illegal, but the group traveled to Fujian via Japan, returning with ritual objects from the mother temple—items that elevated the status of their temple on Taiwan.

Thirteen years later, just after Chen Shui-bian's presidential inauguration, Zhenlan Temple officials decided to test Chen's campaign promise to open direct transportation links with the mainland. In a divination session that was broadcast throughout the island, Mazu selected July 16 as the date for the pilgrims to cross the Strait by boat, sailing directly to Meizhou. Chen's administration did not approve the trip in time for the goddess's deadline, so the pilgrims—more than two thousand of them—flew to Meizhou via Hong Kong and Macao, accompanied by a small army of Taiwanese journalists. The pilgrims didn't succeed in forcing open direct transport links, but their attempts highlighted the government's failure. One of Ma Ying-jeou's first acts as president in 2008 was to open the links.

Since 2008, pilgrims no longer need to detour through non-Chinese ports and airports to visit the mainland, but their journeys still involve some unusual hardships. They often stop at many sacred sites, traveling by plane, train, boat, and bus—and sometimes even on foot. Their luggage is unique— it includes special palanquins for carrying statues of the goddess, elaborate costumes, ritual weapons with which spirit mediums beat themselves when they are in a trance state. Mazu statues make the journey with the pilgrims, too, carried on devotees' chests in red slings and belted into airplane seats with special restraints. At the Meizhou temple, visiting statues recharge by bathing in the mother temple's incense and communing with one another overnight. For Taiwanese pilgrims, these events are powerful spiritual experiences. For Fujianese, they reinvigorate religious practice and introduce new modes of worship.

PRC efforts to promote cross-Strait engagement through religious exchanges don't always work. Anthropologist Robert Weller describes a Mazu ceremony in Nanjing that was sponsored, planned, and carried out by the Nanjing Metropolitan Tourism Bureau.[2] The ritual was conducted in a rebuilt Mazu temple, the reconstruction of which was motivated by local authorities' desire to make the city more appealing to Taiwanese. Although the CCP officials who conducted the ritual were able to report having carried out an act of "cultural preservation," Weller found the ceremony lacking in the cultural content that would have made it appealing—or even recognizable—to Taiwanese Mazu devotees. The nadir of the event, he writes, was when the people carrying Mazu's sedan chair set it down on the ground—unthinkable to true Mazu devotees. Weller learned that no one from Taiwan even showed up for the event, for such a poorly done ritual risked bringing bad luck on those in attendance. In the end, far from cultivating a sense of shared identity, the event reaffirmed for Taiwanese residents just how different the two sides' cultures really are.

The Singaporean scholar J. J. Zhang has observed numerous pilgrimages. His work describes how Taiwanese believers helped bring traditional religion, including the Mazu cult, back to life in the mainland. Under the PRC's religious restrictions, mainland Chinese lost the knowledge of how to practice the Mazu cult. Many of the rituals for worshipping the goddess were reintroduced by Taiwanese on pilgrimages. Zhang describes the Taiwanese temple organizations as "big brothers" to the temples in the PRC. One of his informants, a Mazu temple official from Taiwan, said of the Fujianese, "They have lost those traditions . . . propitiation to the goddess . . . recital of religious scriptures. . . . The recital team in the Meizhou ancestral temple was trained by us. They had no idea of food offerings too. When I brought apples there, they thought they were fake! Haha! Joss sticks and incense paper were also re-introduced by us. Now on Meizhou Island, there are proper rituals commemorating Mazu's birthday, and the day she ascended to heaven. At her birthplace at Xianliang Gang, there is even a sea prayer event. We have re-introduced them to those rituals performed by our ancestors."[3]

Zhang notes the irony of this situation: the Taiwanese playing the role of elder brother to the mainland devotees. Indeed, for centuries, the Mazu cult was rooted in Fujian, and Taiwanese crossed the Strait to pay homage and to learn from those closest to the heartland of the faith. Even today, the Meizhou temple is the most powerful spiritual force in the Mazu religion. But while the goddess may be firmly planted in Meizhou, her human followers have switched places: the pilgrims from afar are grafting the rituals and beliefs of Mazu religious practice back onto its withered root. Now that mainlanders can travel to Taiwan, many include temples on their itineraries. At first glance, this feels like a reversal, but if we consider the overall pattern of Taiwanese participation in the mainland, the idea that Taiwanese would provide leadership, guidance, and material help to their PRC counterparts is hardly surprising.

Religious activity parallels business in other ways, too. As we have seen, PRC leaders promoted cross-Strait economic opening in part because they hoped *Taishang* and their mainland business contacts would become a linkage community that would help pull the two sides together politically. They see religious connections, too, as something that helps Taiwanese feel connected to China. That feeling of connection is a step toward breaking down their view that Taiwan has an identity of its own, distinct from China.

According to researchers who study Mazu pilgrimages, interacting with believers on the other side of the Strait affects Taiwanese pilgrims in complex ways, only some of which align with Beijing's goals. It definitely helps build a sense of community with mainland believers, but those emotions don't translate automatically into support for unification. Mazu devotees on both sides feel a bond when they are worshipping the goddess together, but the Mazu cult is very temple-centered (even competitive), which reinforces local identities and exposes differences, not only between mainlanders and Taiwanese but even among the Taiwanese faithful. Taiwanese pilgrims say they value the opportunity to forge relationships with co-religionists across the Strait, but they are not interested in promoting the CCP's political agenda.

Using cross-Strait religious pilgrimages to cultivate emotional connections is a soft form of pro-unification work. In recent years, Taiwanese temple organizations have also become targets for a harder type of unificationist mobilization. PRC money is flowing into local temple committees through local political networks, organized crime gangs, and *Taishang* looking to curry favor on the mainland. Temples have always existed in a financial gray area—they deal in cash (large amounts) and are shielded from legal scrutiny. Meanwhile, the procedures they use to select their leaders are anything but transparent. They have proven an easy target for groups like the China Unification Promotion Party (CUPP), an organization that works to cultivate pro-PRC sentiment in Taiwan. The CUPP—which is led by a convicted gangster known as "White Wolf"—scatters money and opportunity in Taiwan's rural areas, including helping temples set up pilgrimages to the mainland. In 2019, White Wolf claimed that thirty temple heads were formal members of the CUPP. The CUPP's goal is to develop loyal followers who will take pro-unification positions, not out of ideology but out of gratitude. Many Taiwanese regard it as a threat, a subversive fifth column that is weakening Taiwan from within and softening it up for a PRC takeover.

It's hardly surprising that Beijing would use religion to pursue its political goals. Until the early 2010s, when President Xi Jinping began touting traditional Chinese religions as a solution to some of China's social problems, the Communist Party leadership in Beijing was ambivalent about religion. On the one hand, the party wanted to move away from the violent extremism and tight control of the Mao era; it was no longer interested in controlling every aspect of its citizens' daily lives. On the other hand, as an atheist organization, the party was skeptical of religion, especially when people from outside the PRC were involved. In recent years, the PRC has tightened restrictions on religious practices even more.

Local officials, in contrast to the central government, embraced Taiwanese religious visitors with the same enthusiasm as they welcomed Taiwanese investors. For them, the Taiwanese pilgrims were a source of revenue and local pride. Building and restoring temples, bringing in tourists flush with cash—these were the first-order benefits, and they are substantial. Between the late 1980s and 2000, Taiwanese are estimated to have contributed more than three hundred million dollars to restore temples in the mainland. Having vibrant religious sites attracted even more pilgrims—and other tourists, including many from within the PRC. Meanwhile, some Taiwanese religious pilgrims became business investors, bringing even more economic benefits to the locality. As with business, local officials courted Taiwanese religious groups actively, although they were careful to cloak the religious revival in the guise of "historic preservation" and "academic research." As T. J. Cheng and

Deborah Brown have observed, the PRC government is happy to see religious *buildings* constructed, but it is not so enthusiastic about religious belief and activity.[4]

Taiwanese are active in the revival of Buddhism on the mainland as well as the Mazu and Guan Gong cults. The island is home to a thriving Buddhist community, including several organizations with global reach. Taiwan's most influential Buddhist groups are associated with an approach to the faith known as Engaged or Humanistic Buddhism. While individual self-cultivation is central to their practice, these groups also focus on humanitarian activities and promote the religion as a path to shared peace and mutual understanding. They also concern themselves with social issues, encouraging followers to cultivate an active compassion for others. Several of Taiwan's large Buddhist sects circulate publications and videos that are distributed widely in the mainland. One, the Buddhist Compassion Relief Tzu Chi (Ciji) Foundation, typically referred to as Tzu Chi, is one of the largest fully independent organizations offering direct services to the needy in the PRC. Taiwanese Buddhist sects also are central players in the World Buddhist Forums, one of which, in 2009, was held partially in the mainland and partially in Taiwan.

Because it falls neatly within the CCP's five-official-religion framework, China's Buddhist community is more cohesive than its local temple cults, and it has a direct line to officialdom via the state-sponsored Buddhist Association of China. As a result, it is less dependent on Taiwanese believers for financial support and spiritual guidance. Nonetheless, several Taiwanese Buddhist movements are influential on the mainland. Two of the most interesting and important of these are Fo Guang Shan (the Light of Buddha Mountain), led by the monk Hsing Yun, and Tzu Chi, led by its founder, Master Cheng Yen, a Taiwanese nun. The challenges they have encountered as they expand their reach into the mainland suggest the limitations as well as the potential for Taiwanese institutions to influence the PRC.

Hsing Yun was born in mainland China in 1927; he became a monk at the age of ten. He moved to Taiwan with the Nationalist government in the 1940s, and in 1967, he founded the Fo Guang Shan temple complex in southern Taiwan. His approach to Buddhism was shaped by the engaged Buddhism he encountered as a youth. As a leader, he sought to extend his teachings and the benefits of a Buddhist life as widely as possible. As a 2017 *New York Times* article put it, his teaching style "owed more to Billy Graham than the sound of one hand clapping."[5] Today, Fo Guang Shan claims more than a million adherents around the world, including many in mainland China. (A Fo Guang Shan–linked temple in Los Angeles had a moment of notoriety in 2000 when a visit from presidential candidate Al Gore was linked to illegal campaign donations from non-US citizens.) Hsing Yun's version of Buddhism also has overtones of the "prosperity gospel": rather than disdaining wealth as some Buddhists do, he has encouraged followers to accumulate wealth honestly and to use it to help others.

In Taiwan, Hsing Yun is known as a "political monk" (the description is not meant as a compliment). He has long-standing ties with the Kuomintang, even accepting a seat on the party's central committee. He has played an important role in electoral politics, too, mediating disputes within the KMT and endorsing KMT candidates. To justify his political activity, Hsing Yun cites both tradition (Buddhist monks advised Chinese emperors for centuries) and doctrine (humanistic Buddhism advocates actively caring for the world). Many Taiwanese have criticized Hsing Yun's political involvement, especially his support for unification. At a press conference at the 2009 World Buddhist Forum, he reportedly said, "Both sides of the Taiwan Strait belong to one family. There are no Taiwanese in Taiwan and Taiwanese are all Chinese. Which Taiwanese is not Chinese?" he asked. "They are Chinese just like you are. . . . We are all brothers and sisters." And "The more [cross-strait] exchange we have, the more mixed we will be. Then we won't be able to distinguish who's Mainland and who's Taiwanese—and we will naturally become unified."[6]

Hsing Yun's enthusiasm for unification is welcome on the mainland, where he has been allowed to build a large religious movement. Since his first visit in 2003, Hsing Yun has built, among other things, a library with two million volumes, a 150-million-dollar temple complex, and cultural centers in four of China's largest cities. He has met with China's president Xi Jinping on several occasions, and Xi claims to have read Hsing Yun's books. Yet the political engagement that is the hallmark of Fo Guang Shan in Taiwan is nowhere to be found on the mainland. Hsing Yun even downplays the religious significance of his movement, preferring to describe his work as "advancing Chinese culture" rather than promoting Buddhism. As for the Communist Party, Hsing Yun, the former KMT central committee member, told the *New*

York Times, "We Buddhists uphold whoever is in charge. Buddhists don't get involved in politics."

Indeed, disengagement from politics seems to be a requirement for Fo Guang Shan to remain active in the mainland. As a Taiwanese scholar told the *Times,* "The mainland continues the ideology of ancient emperors—you can only operate there when you are firmly under its control. Fo Guang Shan can never be its own boss in the mainland."[7] Even direct service to the needy is off-limits to Fo Guang Shan.

While Fo Guang Shan emphasizes Buddhist worship and education and downplays social activism, Tzu Chi takes the opposite tack. Tzu Chi *is* allowed to provide service to people in need in the mainland, in part because it downplays its religious element and presents itself as a charity with religious inspirations rather than a religious group with charitable aspirations—even though in Taiwan, religion is at the heart of Tzu Chi.

Tzu Chi's founder, Master Cheng Yen, comes from the same engaged, humanistic Buddhist tradition as Hsing Yun, but she has interpreted its ideas somewhat differently. Her focus is on "great/universal love," and her core teaching is that practicing active compassion for suffering people is the key to finding spiritual happiness. That principle is embodied in the Tzu Chi custom of thanking recipients for the opportunity to serve them. Tzu Chi's original social base is Taiwan's middle class; many of Cheng Yen's followers are professionals and managers. The typical Tzu Chi adherent has succeeded in business and comes to Tzu Chi seeking a fulfillment material wealth alone cannot provide. Master Cheng Yen provides a structure in which her followers can find that fulfillment by using the skills they developed in their business careers to provide for others.

Master Cheng Yen's teaching diverges from Buddhist tradition in an important way: unlike the many Buddhists who believe that charity is an end in itself, she believes that to be meaningful, charity must genuinely benefit the recipient. It must meet a real need, it must meet that need efficiently, and it must be done directly: it is not enough to provide assistance through a third party. True compassion means confronting suffering directly and abiding with it. This conviction is a far cry from Buddhist practices such as releasing birds and fish that have been caught for the sole purpose of being released; it directs Tzu Chi's charities to engage in means testing and rigorous self-evaluation. They also pay attention to how their donations are affecting the recipients. The Taiwanese director of a Tzu Chi facility in mainland China explained to me that she had recently stopped providing cash assistance to a needy family because she learned that the father was using the money to buy alcohol, which was making his family's situation even worse.

The group's pragmatism reflects the socio-economic environment in which Tzu Chi was born and raised: the decades from 1965 to the early 2000s, when entrepreneurship and hard work drove double-digit GDP growth. The master's economic ideas even apply to Tzu Chi's nuns. Unlike most Buddhist religious, Tzu Chi's monastic community does not rely on alms but supports itself by selling items produced by the nuns. All donations collected by the order go directly to its charitable activities. Tzu Chi differs from Buddhist groups like Fo Guang Shan in yet another important way: Master Cheng Yen forbids her followers to participate in politics. She also forbids them to proselytize their religious faith (although critics have argued Tzu Chi's commitment to provide only vegetarian food imposes its religious preference on the needy).

Tzu Chi's focus on effective philanthropy, skilled personnel, and self-assessment have made it an extraordinarily effective service provider. With operations in more than a hundred countries and volunteers numbering in the millions, Tzu Chi can respond to a range of needs almost anywhere, and it places special emphasis on frontline disaster relief. Whether it's a natural disaster—the devastating Southeast Asian tsunami in 2004, Hurricane Katrina, the Nepal earthquake of 2015—or a man-made catastrophe like 9-11, Tzu Chi's blue-and-white clad volunteers are often among the first on the scene, working to stabilize and comfort victims and assist with rescue, recovery, and rebuilding. Tzu Chi also has more mundane projects: feeding the hungry, assisting the poor, providing medical care in underserved communities. It has a particular commitment to medical research and education; one of Tzu Chi's earliest initiatives was the construction of a charity hospital in one of the island's most underserved regions. Tzu Chi also promotes the donation of human remains for research and bone marrow and organs for transplantation. Both practices are frowned upon in traditional Chinese culture, but Master Cheng Yen's advocacy has helped Taiwan attain the highest rate of organ donation in Asia.

Tzu Chi was Taiwan's largest philanthropic organization when it sent its first shipment of blankets, clothing, and money destined for flood victims to mainland China in 1991. By 2008, when it became the first foreign foundation approved to operate throughout the PRC, Tzu Chi volunteers had responded to emergencies in every Chinese province. But its biggest challenge came on May 12, 2008, when Sichuan province was hit by one of the deadliest earthquakes in history. It killed about ninety thousand people, injured almost half a million, and left five million homeless. Its economic cost was second only to the 2011 Tohoku earthquake in Japan, which included a devastating tsunami and nuclear meltdown. There was a massive need for the disaster relief expertise Tzu Chi had spent decades developing.

The PRC government accepted Tzu Chi's offer of assistance the day after the earthquake, and on May 14, a chartered cargo jet loaded with supplies set off from Taipei to Sichuan. The first Tzu Chi volunteers arrived on May 15, just three days after the quake. The Tzu Chi foundation remained in Sichuan for months, providing meals, shelter, and medical assistance and building temporary housing and schools. It also raised more than sixty million dollars from donors around the world for the earthquake relief effort. Later that year, the PRC permitted Tzu Chi to set up offices in the PRC on a long-term basis.

Tzu Chi is unique in its ability to provide direct service to needy people in the PRC. It protects that privilege by downplaying its religious orientation and by studiously avoiding political involvement, in Taiwan as well as in the PRC. Even those efforts are not always enough. Despite their extraordinary work after the 2008 Sichuan temblor, when an earthquake rocked a politically sensitive Tibetan region in Qinghai province two years later, Tzu Chi was not allowed to participate in relief efforts. According to Cheng and Brown, the only Taiwanese relief association the PRC authorities permitted to respond was the Red Cross.

Tzu Chi doesn't just respond to emergencies in the mainland—it has put down roots there. While the higher-ups in Tzu Chi's mainland operations are Taiwanese (often *Taishang* or their family members), mainlanders are permitted to volunteer and participate in its activities. The Tzu Chi headquarters in one major mainland city occupies an enormous office suite. In addition to staging areas for social service efforts, the complex includes information about Master Cheng Yen's spiritual teachings and the organization's charitable works. There is also a large room set up for religious teachings where volunteers prepare their minds before going into the community to work. Staff conducting a tour of the headquarters were careful to avoid language that might suggest volunteers are proselytized, but the space itself incorporates plenty of information that invites spiritual seekers to learn about Tzu Chi's religious teaching while they're taking care of the needy.

Whether secular, like the Children's Hearing Foundation, or religious, like Tzu Chi, externally sponsored charitable activity is sensitive in mainland China. Anna High's research suggests that Christian missionaries who operate orphanages in the PRC face similar challenges to the Taiwanese philanthropists.[8] On the one hand, charities based outside China can provide important services that PRC local governments just can't afford. On the other hand, Beijing is determined to prevent outsiders from setting up institutions that might become a base for unsanctioned mobilization of people and resources. That's why the PRC government limits the scope of activity foreign charities can engage in. It also denies them official recognition in most cases, forcing them to operate in a gray zone of, in High's words, "uncertainty and vulnerability." Meanwhile, the PRC state also requires charities to eschew political involvement. Even the pro-unification Buddhist Master Hsing Yun avoids politics when he's in the mainland.

FROM TERESA DENG TO JAY CHOU:
TAIWANESE POP CULTURE INVADES CHINA

In 1992, Thomas Gold, a UC Berkeley sociology professor, traveled through Shanghai, Hangzhou, and Xiamen.[9] Along the way he made an astonishing discovery: Taiwanese and Hong Kong popular culture had taken over China!

Gold knew Taiwanese popular culture when he saw it: he had spent years in Taiwan researching a pathbreaking study of Taiwan's economic development. He had also lived in the PRC in the waning years of the Maoist era, so he was familiar enough with the "before" picture to recognize the changes in the "after" shot. He chronicled his discoveries in *China Quarterly*, enumerating in delicious detail a huge variety of pop culture influences:

- Literature and film: "Works of contemporary fiction by Taiwan and Hong Kong writers . . . are widely published by mainland presses." "Films from Taiwan and Hong Kong play in theatres and on television. . . . Pirated video cassettes of Taiwan and Hong Kong films are sold quite openly on the street."

- Advertising: "Television advertisements have the same rough jerky quality and off-time voice dubbing as Taiwan's. The stylishly dressed actors inhabit a world of consumption and interior decoration clearly reflecting the middle-class tastes of Taiwan and Hong Kong."
- Interior decoration: "With their gleaming chrome columns, aquariums full of live and struggling seafood, well-stocked bars, brightly lit interiors, polished linoleum or marble floors and costumed service personnel, restaurants resemble the same establishments one sees in Hong Kong and Taiwan."
- Urban design: "Shenzhen's architecture and cityscape are a mirror image of Kowloon, and Xiamen is filling up with town-houses and apartment buildings with names such as 'Taiwan Village' which duplicate the style of the burgeoning suburbs of Taipei."

The most ubiquitous and unmistakably Taiwanese cultural import Gold observed was pop music, traveling with its sidekick, karaoke. Gold wrote, "Fan magazines of Hong Kong and Taiwan singers and actors, referred to as giant stars and idols, are published and sold on the mainland. Staid publications . . . run puff pieces about visiting Taiwan and Hong Kong celebrities with concert photos of them. . . . China's own concerts . . . on television increasingly resemble those seen in Hong Kong and Taiwan: elaborately outfitted singers backed up by dancers, 'mood' created by strobe lights and dry ice." Meanwhile, "cities are densely packed with karaoke bars."

Contemporary Chinese pop culture has many influences; it incorporates global (rock and roll music), regional (karaoke), and indigenous features. But for Tom Gold, comparing Chinese pop culture in 1979 and 1992, the importance of Taiwanese and Hong Kong was undeniable. Everywhere he looked, China was absorbing, reproducing, and adapting pop culture from Taiwan and Hong Kong. That trend continued through the 1990s and 2000s, although, like many other "invasions," it began to recede in the early 2010s, especially after Xi Jinping came to power in 2012.

Since its founding, the Chinese Communist Party has viewed popular culture as a political tool. During the Mao era, music, visual art, and theater were harnessed to the party-state project of building a socialist China. By the time Deng Xiaoping introduced reform and opening in the late 1970s, there was a huge pent-up demand for music intended solely for enjoyment—no political agenda required. Taiwanese musicians were poised to meet that demand, and the very first to win mainlanders' hearts was Teresa Teng (Deng Lijun).

As a student in Shanghai in 1979, Gold heard his classmates listening to samizdat recordings by the Taiwanese superstar. Teng's romantic, nostalgic singing style (think Karen Carpenter—another huge favorite in Taiwan) and her facility in multiple languages and musical styles made her a massive sensation in Taiwan, Hong Kong, Japan, mainland China, and beyond. Born into a military family in 1953, Teng began singing professionally as a teenager, and her songs remained at the top of the charts throughout East Asia until her death in 1995. Her songs show the through line of Taiwanese pop music from Japanese-era *enka* to Minnan songs to the distinctive combination of melodies, themes, and language that has come to be called Mandopop.

The comments on dozens of YouTube videos of her music testify to Teresa Teng's enduring popularity more than two decades after her death. (Search for "The Moon Represents My Heart" to hear one of her most beloved numbers.) As her fame spread throughout the Chinese-speaking world, PRC leaders initially tried to keep her music out, but her sweet siren songs were irresistible. By the late 1970s, it was said, "Old Deng [Deng Xiaoping] rules during the daytime, but Little Deng [Teresa Teng] rules at night."

Teresa Teng was the first, and maybe the biggest, but her popularity opened the door for an influx of Taiwanese music into the PRC so large that it came to be called a "counter invasion." In the 1980s and '90s, much of the most interesting new Taiwanese music focused on the island's democratic transformation and deepening sense of national identity, but apolitical pop singers were also an important part of the scene, both in Taiwan and in the mainland. One Taiwanese singer, Hou Dejian, took mainland youth by storm in the late 1980s with his patriotic anthem "Descendants of the Dragon." Hou's career on the mainland was derailed, however, when he joined student protesters in Tiananmen Square in 1989.

In the 1980s, Mandopop artists from Taiwan shared the mainland market with their Hong Kong equivalents, the so-called Cantopop stars. But the audience for Cantopop was limited since most mainland Chinese preferred Mandarin lyrics, and Mandopop took the lead in the 1990s. According to Marc Moskowitz, an anthropologist who authored a book on Taiwanese Mandopop in the PRC, between 2002 and 2010, Taiwanese Mandopop titles held an 80 percent share of the PRC's Chinese-language music market.

Moskowitz's observations came twenty years after Gold's, but his conclusion was the same. According to Moskowitz, between 1989 and 2010, visible (and audible) Taiwanese influences in PRC pop culture increased by "almost Twilight Zone proportions." His book, *Cries of Joy, Songs of Sorrow*, mentions many of the same themes as Gold—Taiwanese influences on advertising, design, literature, and music—but he is especially interested in the ways Mandopop was affecting mainlanders' thinking about gender, identity, and consumption.

Mandopop, Moskowitz argues, is not just Western-style pop music sung in Mandarin. The most successful artists blend elements from East Asian and Western traditions to create something that is wholly new and uniquely appealing to Chinese-speaking listeners in the PRC, Taiwan, and the global Sinophone diaspora. The most successful practitioner of this style is the Taiwanese Mandopop megastar Jay Chou (Zhou Jielun).

By any measure, Jay Chou—Jay to his fans—has had an extraordinary career as a musician. He has managed to navigate the tricky terrain of cross-Strait relations to become an icon on both sides and beyond. In the process, he has stretched the boundaries of acceptable masculinity while embodying what Anthony Y. H. Fung calls "'safe' Chineseness."[10] Most of Jay's oeuvre are R&B-inflected love songs. His music videos are full of long, lingering shots of his handsome face. He also has a more up-tempo side that mixes hip-hop vocals and dance moves with traditional Chinese instruments and martial arts. The music video "Nunchucks" is an extended fight scene: Jay rescues women and beats back a stream of assailants while rapping "What's my favorite weapon? Nunchucks, they're supple and tough." Jay's presentation is modern and global as well as proudly Chinese. He embodies a Chinese masculinity that—like his favorite weapon—is both supple and tough. The skillful merging of all these elements won him a massive following on both sides of the Taiwan Strait.

Taiwanese pop culture influenced speech as well as song. On both sides of the Strait, Mandarin is the official language. Although people in different localities continue to speak their local dialects (which are really more like languages; they're often unintelligible to Mandarin speakers), most people—and nearly all youngsters—understand and speak Mandarin. That's not to say, though, that the Mandarin they speak is the same everywhere. There are pronounced differences between the Mandarin spoken in Taiwan and that spoken in the mainland—starting with "Mandarin" itself, which is *Guoyu* (the national language) in Taiwan and *Putonghua* (the common speech) in the mainland.

What Taiwanese call *Taiwan Guoyu*, or Taiwan-style Mandarin, differs from the Mandarin spoken on the mainland in pronunciation, syntax, vocabulary, and vocal quality. The differences are comparable to differences in British and American English: we can understand each other, but we have no trouble differentiating who's who. Taiwanese pronunciation, syntax, and word choice reflect the influence of *Minnanyu*, the dialect of Chinese spoken in Fujian, the Chinese province where most Taiwanese families originated. Until 1945, Minnanyu was the lingua franca of Taiwan, although Japanese was the official language from 1895 to 1945. After its arrival in 1945, the KMT-led government pressured Minnanyu speakers (as well as Hakka speakers and speakers of indigenous languages) to adopt Mandarin, but elements of Minnanyu and Japanese lingered in their speech.

As for vocal quality, many Mandarin speakers describe Taiwanese speech as softer and friendlier, more feminine and enthusiastic than standard mainland Mandarin. Linguists suggest this may be because Taiwanese tend to speak more slowly than mainlanders and because they tend to end sentences with softening words—little exhalations of "aw," "la," and "ma." Another attribute many mainlanders associate with Taiwanese speech is *dia*, a way of speaking that is childish, coquettish, cutesy—even a little whiny.

In the ears of many mainlanders, Taiwan's vocal style resembles the American practice of "uptalk," and it has a similar love-it-or-hate-it effect on listeners. Studies find that PRC listeners have at times considered Taiwan-style Mandarin trendy and friendly; in the early days of Taiwanese investment in the mainland, it was associated with wealth and modernity. In the early 2000s, PRC pop culture personalities, including singers, actors, and TV announcers, began copying Taiwanese speech, adding softeners to their sentences and adopting a *dia* lilt. The trend became pronounced enough that it alarmed the PRC government. In 2005, the State Administration for Radio, Film, and Television released a directive that broadcasters should not use "non-standard" Mandarin. It singled out the "imitation of the *Gang-Tai* [Hong Kong and Taiwan] accent" as something that must be avoided in order to preserve the purity of standard Mandarin.

The accent is not the only feature of how Taiwanese talk that has crossed the Strait. Vocabulary, too, has made the trip. My favorite example is the word *tongzhi*, which has not only traveled from the PRC to Taiwan and back again, changing its meaning in the middle, but has helped propel an entire social movement. *Tongzhi* is the word the Chinese Communist Party uses for the communist honorific "comrade." Throughout the Mao era, Chinese people eschewed specific titles—Mister, Miss, Doctor, Teacher—in favor of the all-purpose, nonhierarchical, gender-free *tongzhi*.

A new use of the term first appeared in Hong Kong, where a magazine columnist used *tongzhi* to refer to LGBTQ people. The 1989 Hong Kong Lesbian and Gay Film Festival adopted the terminology, which quickly took hold in Hong Kong and jumped to Taiwan. Since the 1990s, LGBTQ people in Taiwan have called themselves *tongzhi*, fully aware of (in fact delighting in) the irony of redirecting a CCP term to such a subversive purpose. Taipei's annual LGBTQ Pride Parade, the largest in Asia, is technically the Taiwan *Tongzhi* Parade. From Taiwan and Hong Kong, *tongzhi*'s new meaning made it back into the PRC, where many LGBTQ people and organizations have adopted it, including the Beijing Tongzhi Center, whose website explains its goals as "creating a pluralistic, welcoming social environment in which the *tongzhi* community can enjoy equal rights and attain a lifestyle that is healthy, self-determining, and respected." The wholehearted adoption of *tongzhi* by LGBTQ communities across the Sinophone world is actually a bit of a problem for the Communist Party, which in 2016 launched a campaign to restore the term to its original use.

BUILDING INSTITUTIONS FOR A TWENTY-FIRST-CENTURY ECONOMY

Taiwanese have influenced the PRC's institutions as well its cultural environment. One little-known, but very important, arena in which Taiwanese have shaped the mainland's development is law. During the Maoist period, the PRC twice tried and failed to draft and implement a civil code. After Deng Xiaoping introduced his reform and opening program in the late 1970s, Beijing tried again. And once again, it failed. The problem during the Mao era was politics; during the Deng era, the obstacle was a mismatch between the available legal expertise and the needs of the rapidly changing Chinese economy. China's legal scholars were the products of a socialist political and economic system; most were trained in Soviet or traditional Chinese law, neither of which provided good models for the direction Deng Xiaoping wanted his country to go. The top priority was to create a legal framework for contracts, but it was hard to bend socialist legal concepts to fit an economy in which private ownership and market-driven transactions were playing an ever-more-important role.

In the mid-1980s, Beijing suspended its effort to develop a comprehensive civil code in favor of an à la carte model in which individual laws were written for specific purposes. Civil law in China limped along until the 1990s, when the PRC finally broke out of the socialist legal mode and adopted a unified contract law. For the first time, Chinese law was influenced, not by Soviet or other socialist models, but by legal concepts from capitalist countries— especially Germany.

One reason the legal drafting was so hard was that few Chinese legal specialists were able to read legal texts from outside the socialist bloc. Importing new models required finding consultants who could translate complicated documents and unfamiliar concepts into Chinese. Who better for the job than Taiwanese legal scholars? Taiwan's legal framework is influenced by both Germany and Japan, putting it firmly in the continental camp, which is where the PRC wanted to be. Taiwanese legal minds were happy to work as consultants and teachers to PRC officials and scholars who wanted to build a stable, predictable legal environment. Chu Yun-han, one of Taiwan's leading political scientists, wrote in 2012 that "Taiwanese legal scholarship has been the greatest overseas source of ideas in China's recent efforts to overhaul its civil and criminal codes, litigation and bankruptcy procedures, and regulatory frameworks."[11] Chu listed numerous forms of collaboration, from legal education to scholarly exchanges "in the fields of finance and banking, public administration, management science, local governance, and survey research."

Taiwan was a logical place to turn for expertise in building out the legal and institutional infrastructure for a twenty-first-century, globalized economy. Using Taiwanese consultants accelerated and eased the PRC's integration into international norms and practices, and it also helped Taiwanese working in the mainland. There was no getting around the need to adjust to the political practices on the mainland, but at least the civil and commercial codes were familiar. That familiarity was yet another advantage for Taiwanese investors.

It's interesting that the PRC was willing to take advice from Taiwan on commercial law, given the political tensions between the two sides. It shows that for Beijing, developing a legal framework for its new economic practices was a pragmatic consideration, not one freighted with political risk. But opening the mainland to Taiwanese ideas inevitably introduced some more sensitive topics, including ideas about democracy.

In 2006, I lived in Shanghai, and my landlord was a great fan of the (unfortunately named) Taiwanese cable news station TVBS. In fact, he loved all manner of Taiwanese cable TV news shows, so he bought a satellite dish and mounted it outside his apartment and turned it to face Taiwan so it would catch the broadcasts. What he enjoyed about the shows was not so much the specifics of the debates but the performance of unfettered political disagreement. While many Taiwanese roll their eyes at the very mention of these programs, my landlord told me he longed for the day when China's staid state-run media would show people shouting at each other about political topics. He saw Taiwan's raucous democracy on TVBS, and he wanted it.

At one time, the question of how Taiwan's democracy might affect political development in the mainland sparked hopeful anticipation.

Chu Yun-han, the political scientist who wrote about Taiwan's role in developing China's legal institutions, also noted that Beijing's Ministry of Civil Affairs consulted Taiwanese experts in developing procedures for village elections; I participated in one such consultation in the mid-1990s, traveling with an official from Beijing from village to village peddling democratic elections to local Communist Party officials. As many observers have noted, Taiwan stands as proof that democracy is possible in a culturally Chinese society. Many mainlanders who dream of a democratic future for the PRC look to Taiwan for inspiration.

For now though, those dreams are on hold. Under Xi Jinping, the PRC has become less, not more, likely to move toward political liberalization. Today, Taiwan's democracy is often characterized as a problem for China because it has allowed pro-independence voices to emerge more forcefully. Also, Taiwan's recent elections have brought to power leaders who show little interest in pursuing unification—especially not on Beijing's terms. Chinese nationalists in the mainland have come to view Taiwan's democracy not as an inspiration but as an obstacle. Still, for a few years, the PRC allowed itself to absorb Taiwanese legal and political institutions and ideas. That legacy remains in the legal realm, if not, for the moment, in politics.

CONCLUSION

In pop culture, as in business and technology, the PRC has caught up with—and in some ways overtaken—Taiwan in recent years. Not so long ago many mainlanders viewed Taiwan as a center of sophistication and modernity—distant enough to be an aspiration but similar enough to feel attainable. As mainland cities like Shanghai and Shenzhen have grown into international hubs, Taiwan has faded in the PRC imagination. Visitors from China's first-tier cities often comment on how old-fashioned, even shabby, Taipei seems compared to their hometowns. And while Teresa Teng may have opened Chinese ears to pop music, there is no shortage of PRC-born musicians they can listen to today.

Nor is Taiwan's diminishing cultural influence solely the result of market forces. Under Xi Jinping, the PRC state is actively limiting Taiwan's influence. Instead of allowing Taiwanese culture and ideas to influence mainland values and fashions, the Chinese leadership increasingly seeks to use its market power to shape Taiwan. The China Unification Promotion Party's efforts to turn temple committees into advocates for Beijing's interests are just one example. The PRC also has taken to forcing Taiwanese artists to choose between expressing their political views and accessing mainland audiences. The most famous of these is an artist who has transformed herself from the Queen of Mandopop to an indigenous Taiwanese feminist avenger.

For the first phase of her career, this artist was known as A-Mei. She never hid her indigenous heritage—her 1996 album, *Sisters*, features her mother and sisters singing with her in Puyuma, their mother tongue—but she positioned herself as a mainstream Mandarin pop singer under the stage name A-Mei (her Mandarin name is Chang Hui-Mei). In the late 1990s, A-Mei toured widely, including successful concerts in Beijing and Shanghai. In 1998, *Billboard* magazine proclaimed her Asia's most popular singer; her 1999 song, "Give Me Feelings," is the best-selling single in Taiwanese pop music history. Her regional star power won her a gig as the Asia spokesperson for the Coca-Cola brand Sprite, and a 1999 concert tour took her to mainland China as well as Hong Kong, Singapore, and Malaysia.

In May 2000, A-Mei performed the ROC national anthem at Chen Shui-bian's presidential inauguration ceremony. Beijing was furious; overnight, A-Mei's voice and image disappeared from the mainland. According to a PRC government spokesperson, "All her songs, advertisements and programs have been cancelled. . . . If a singer behaves like this, how can we allow her to still appear on the mainland?" A spokesperson for Coca-Cola told the BBC that an edict had come down from Beijing the night before the inauguration demanding the immediate termination of the Sprite ad campaign, including erasing A-Mei's image from billboards in China.

A-Mei herself was shocked by the backlash; no one at her record label had raised any alarms. A few days before the ceremony, a reporter asked whether her appearance might hurt her career in the mainland, but she laughed off the question. Not long after, a crestfallen A-Mei told a reporter, "The president felt I could represent so many people, and I would never have another chance. I had sung the national anthem since I was a girl. I never expected anything to come of it." A January 2001 article in *Newsweek* added a bit more context to the story. According to a music producer interviewed for the story, it was Beijing that had politicized A-Mei by trying to use her identity as an indigenous Taiwanese who was willing to be seen, as the *Financial Times* put it, as "a symbol of cross-straits goodwill" to reinforce its claim to Taiwan as its own territory. According to her producer, the PRC promoters latched onto A-Mei's identity, describing her as an "ethnic minority" singer—the same designation they would use for a singer of Uighur or Mongol descent. A-Mei's appearance at the inauguration of a president who rejected Beijing's claim that Taiwan was part of the PRC was not part of their plan.

A fascinating article by Nancy Guy in the journal *Ethnomusicology* details the story of A-Mei's inauguration performance and shows how it was received by different audiences. There were many different responses to and interpretations of the incident; Guy concludes that "A-mei can be read as representing a vision of Taiwan that is modern and global, and at the same time quintessentially 'of Taiwan.'"[12] Indeed, it was to her Taiwanese roots that A-Mei eventually returned.

The blacklisting drastically reduced A-Mei's access to the lucrative PRC market, but it did not end her career. She spent some time overseas; resting her voice, it was said. She produced a musical, recorded a duet with Andrea Bocelli, appeared in a Japanese remake of Puccini's *Turandot*, and became a tourism promoter for Taiwan. She continued to release albums, tour, and win awards. She even returned to China, but the reception was not the same. In 2004, she was forced to cancel a performance when students at Zhejiang University protested her appearance, calling her an independence supporter.

A few months later, she tried again; this time, supporters clashed with pro-testers outside the concert venue, and A-Mei reportedly cried on stage from the pressure. Returning to Taiwan, she tried to pacify the PRC nationalists, telling reporters, "I'm a Chinese person, and I sing Chinese people's songs," a statement that infuriated *Taiwanese* nationalists. It seemed the space for a cross-Strait musical career was all but gone.

In 2009, A-Mei changed both her sound and her name. She had always been more of a rocker than Teresa Teng, but her new sound was even more distant from the sweet—almost saccharine—vocal quality that made Teresa so beloved. The eponymous album *Amit* introduced fans to A-Mei's Puyuma name, Kulilay Amit, and to a new style, one best described in Cello Kan's review on the website Taiwan Beats:

> Amit is different from A-mei in both music and lyrics. The themes of the lyrics are quite rare among Chinese songs, conveying a sense of darkness and Goth, even a little bit of morbidity. "Amit" released A-mei from her former self, reviv-ing her, taking her to a new field and also, leading her fans to accept a brand-new her and a brand-new type of music. This time, she's being even more ambitious and more drastic. This album is an epic. It's hard to find an album these days with so many different music elements in one. It's a combination of hard rock, classical music, opera, reggae, dancehall, world music, electro, dub step and electronic music. Every year, we hope there will be an album to represent that very year. I believe "Amit" will be the album of the year and it is no easy task for others to overtake it. If you're going to buy only one album this year, "Amit" will definitely be your best choice.

Amit foregrounded the singer's identity as an indigenous Taiwanese. The title song is a rock medley of Puyuma songs sung in the original language. The cover art and music videos use indigenous imagery. *Amit* and *Amit 2*, which was released in 2015, both blend indigenous references with a strong feminist element. Music videos for songs like "Double Cross" and "Matri-archy" depict women's violent rejection of submission to male authority. In both of her incarnations—as A-Mei and as Amit—she is enormously popular with LGBTQ audiences in the Sinophone world. At a concert she organized to celebrate a pro-same-sex-marriage decision by Taiwan's high court, she referred to her song "Rainbow" as the gay movement's "theme song." Meanwhile, videos from a concert in buttoned-up Singapore show the crowd

roaring with delight as same-sex couples kiss for the jumbotron camera during a performance of "Rainbow."

Chang Hui-Mei/A-Mei/Amit has come a long way from her days as the
regional spokeswoman for a sparkling, sugary beverage to gay icon and proud
indigenous feminist. I don't claim to know what prompted her reinvention,
but her decision to stop trying to please everyone—including conservatives
in the PRC—feels a lot like Taiwan society's trajectory in the past decade. If
singing the ROC national anthem makes A-Mei a warrior for independence,
what's the point in trying to mollify Chinese nationalists? She might as well go
ahead and be her true self, whether Chinese nationalists like it or not.

NOTES

1. Murray Rubinstein, *The Revival of the Mazu Cult and Taiwanese Pilgrimage to
Fujian*, Working Papers Issue 5 (Cambridge, MA: Fairbank Center, 1994).

2. Robert P. Weller, "Cosmologies in the Remaking: Variation and Time in Chinese
Temple Religion," in *It Happens among People: Resonances and Extensions of
the Work of Fredrik Barth*, edited by Keping Wu and Robert Weller (New York:
Berghahn Books, 2019).

3. J. J. Zhang, "Paying Homage to the 'Heavenly Mother': Cultural-Geopolitics of
the Mazu Pilgrimage and Its Implications on Rapprochement between China and
Taiwan." *Geoforum* 84 (2017): 38.

4. Deborah A. Brown and Tun-jen Cheng, "Religious Relations across the Taiwan
Strait: Patterns, Alignments, and Political Effects," *Orbis* 56, no. 1 (2012): 60–81.

5. Ian Johnson, "Is a Buddhist Group Changing China? Or is China Changing It?"
New York Times, June 24, 2017.

6. Loa Lok-sin, "Taiwan Buddhist Master: 'No Taiwanese,'" *Taipei Times*, March
31, 2009.

7. Johnson, "Is a Buddhist Group?"

8. Anna High, "'It's Grace and Favor: It's Not Law': Extra-legal Regulation of
Foreign Foster Homes in China," *University of Pennsylvania Asian Law Review* 12
(2017): 357–405.

9. Thomas B. Gold, "Go with Your Feelings: Hong Kong and Taiwan Popular Culture in Greater China," *China Quarterly* 136 (1993): 907–925.

10. Anthony Y. H. Fung, "The Emerging (National) Popular Music Culture in China," *Inter-Asia Cultural Studies* 8, no. 3 (2007): 435.

11. Yun-han Chu, "China and the Taiwan Factor," in *Democracy in East Asia: A New Century*, edited by Larry Diamond, Mark Plattner, and Yun-han Chu (Baltimore, MD: Johns Hopkins University Press, 2012), 92.

12. Nancy Guy, "'Republic of China National Anthem' on Taiwan: One Anthem, One Performance, Multiple Realities," *Ethnomusicology* 46, no. 1 (2002): 112.

10

The End of an Era?

In 1987, Taiwanese travelers were permitted to travel to mainland China for the first time in almost forty years; when they arrived, they must have felt they had traveled through time as well as space. The China they found at the end of their journey was only just turning outward after decades of isolation. Its economy was far behind Taiwan's; it had few manufactured exports, and its domestic markets were starved for consumer goods. But those early travelers saw potential and opportunity in China's arid economic landscape, and in five years' time, they had turned parts of southern and eastern China into manufacturing hotspots pumping out shoes, clothing, and toys for global markets. Within a decade, they had made China a key link in the global IT manufacturing chain and, before long, the world's leading source of electronic devices. Taiwanese investors were uniquely successful in connecting China's abundant workforce to the global brands that dominated—and continue to dominate—the world market for manufactured goods. In the process, they reshaped not only the Chinese economy but the economy of Taiwan—and, in very real ways, the global economy itself.

Now, however, the picture has changed. After three decades of explosive growth, investment by Taiwanese firms is no longer the driving force in the PRC economy that it once was. The *quantity* continues to rise, but the *quality* of Taiwanese investors' contribution has changed. Perhaps most importantly, Taiwanese investment is no longer transformational to the PRC economy as it once was. That change has important consequences for Taiwanese individuals and firms, for the PRC economy, for cross-Strait relations, and for the world.

Most economies take off like a Boeing 747: they lumber down the runway for ages before finally lurching into the air, engines screaming (or, unlike 747s, crashing back to earth). China's takeoff was more like a fighter jet catapulting off the deck of an aircraft carrier. A more gradual takeoff might have been less stressful for China; like a fighter pilot pulling Gs on takeoff, China's economy endured enormous pressures during its rapid acceleration, including a persistent imbalance in the share of China's GDP that is devoted to investment versus consumption. The decision to focus on export-oriented manufacturing exacerbated the stresses of its high-speed takeoff, but China's leaders forged ahead, confident in their ability to manage the tensions and determined to foster development and prosperity in their nation.

When the PRC emerged from the enforced economic isolation of the Mao era, it had massive pent-up economic potential. Its hardworking, ambitious people deserve much credit for its successes, as does a generation of creative, pragmatic leaders. But the industries that have positioned China at the leading edge of global manufacturing are not the ones that have thrived under the Chinese government's patronage. Exports are key to China's economy; without them, China's domestic economy would not have reached takeoff velocity. Its major exports—mechanical, electrical, and high-tech products; labor-intensive light consumer goods; and integrated circuits—all fall into categories in which foreign investors played a critical role in bringing China into the global production chain. Among those foreign investors, Taiwanese have played the leading role.

Without Taiwanese investors to bring export manufacturing to the mainland, China's rise would have been much slower. Exports enabled China's lightning-fast GDP growth. They generated the foreign exchange Beijing uses to support its currency and upgrade its technology. They have brought enormous wealth to the PRC state, driving a cycle that enables China to enlarge its military and expand its diplomatic relationships and economic influence around the world. Export-oriented industrialization also helped make many PRC individuals incredibly wealthy, and it has provided employment to millions of Chinese, helping them pull themselves out of poverty.

One of the strengths of China's development model was its leaders' decision to allow new economic forms to grow up alongside China's existing economic institutions. If we imagine the Chinese economy as a forest, in the 1970s, that forest was crowded with large trees—state-owned enterprises—many of which were overgrown and unhealthy. When Deng Xiaoping came to power, he decided not to cut down those trees but to plant new ones, small and large, in among them. The forest became populated by many different species: TVEs, private companies, SOEs, foreign-invested firms. The plants in the forest competed for space and resources, but they formed an ecosystem. Some thrived; others died. Over time, Beijing allowed some of the SOEs to be cut down.

In this forest, Taiwanese-invested firms were some of the most tenacious and fast-growing. Of course, many withered and died, and some of the survivors remained small. Nonetheless, many Taiwanese-invested firms grew into huge trees. Between 1995 and 2008, the Taiwan transplants stood out. Some, like Foxconn and shoemaker Feng Tay, towered over their neighbors. Others were not as tall, but they were unusually healthy, producing ample crops of fruit and seeding new ventures.

Since 2008, the ecology of the forest has changed again. There are still many healthy Taiwanese transplants in the forest, but they no longer stand out as they once did, and they are less important to the forest's overall health. In fact, some observers are worried that the Taiwanese "trees" are being crowded out. Meanwhile, the PRC's position as the "factory to the world" is also in doubt. The PRC government aspires to upgrade its economy to be more of a technology leader, one that relies on indigenous technology and local companies for its success. Meanwhile, rising production costs and growing tensions with China's trade partners, especially the United States, are undermining its competitiveness in manufacturing. In August 2020, Foxconn chairman Young Liu told investors that China's "days as the world's factory are done."[1]

When the first wave of Taiwanese investors arrived in the mainland in the late 1980s and early 1990s, the PRC's private sector was in its infancy. Or, more accurately, the domestic private sector had been driven into an infantile state. Instead of allowing local entrepreneurs to lead the nation's move into consumer manufacturing, the PRC's economic bureaucrats restructured the SOE sector and liberalized China's policies on foreign direct investment. At the same time, they created a reward structure for local officials that created strong incentives to attract economic activity from outside. Their goal was to accelerate the growth process by leveraging external capital and demand rather than waiting for the domestic economy to get big enough to absorb its own output and power its own growth.

These policy decisions created an ideal environment for Taiwanese traditional manufacturers looking to invest in the mainland. In the late 1980s, the PRC state simultaneously cut off credit to rural entrepreneurs and encouraged local officials to stimulate economic activity. That left foreign investors as the obvious target for localities' efforts to attract business.[2] Liberalized rules on FDI gave officials confidence to engage with foreign partners, and those foreign partners were happy to take advantage of the opportunity. Taiwanese investors were especially eager, both because they were facing tight cost constraints at home (wages, regulatory burdens, and currency appreciation had put the squeeze on Taiwan's traditional manufacturers) and because they found themselves more comfortable in the mainland than in other potential low-wage investment destinations, thanks to the low language barrier and hospitable regulatory environment.

By the time the second wave of Taiwanese investors—those in the high-tech sector, including both device manufacturing and semiconductors—began making their way across the Strait in the mid-1990s, Taiwanese firms had established a large, even dominant, presence in several mainland regions. In the early 2010s, however, evidence began to pile up that the growth trend that had been so powerful in the '90s was losing momentum.

Since 2001, and especially since 2008, China's domestic private and non-private businesses have developed at an ever-accelerating pace. If the Chinese economy is a forest, the Taiwanese-invested firms were some of the first newly planted trees to mature in the 1990s and early 2000s. Because they were transplanted from Taiwan as established businesses, they were among the larger trees in the forest. What has happened since 2000, however, is that many of China's domestic species have overgrown the Taiwanese transplants.

The year 2008 was a turning point. As the global financial crisis crashed consumer spending in China's major export markets, export-oriented firms suffered. Taiwanese-invested companies were leaders in some of the most vulnerable sectors—electronic devices, branded apparel and footwear, and so on. In effect, the recession pruned the Taiwanese trees in China's economic forest—some of them quite dramatically. Meanwhile, the PRC government poured stimulus—water and fertilizer—on other sectors of its economy, especially those connected with infrastructure and construction, areas in which Taiwanese-invested companies had little or no presence.

The result of this simultaneous pruning of the Taiwanese-invested sectors and fertilizing of PRC-originated firms, mainly SOEs but also some nonstate companies, was to leave the Taiwanese firms much less important, *relative to* firms founded in the PRC, than had been the case before 2008. These events undermined the perception of Taiwanese firms as leaders in the Chinese economy, as somehow uniquely able to thrive and grow. PRC firms—especially well-financed SOEs—also began to reveal their export-manufacturing might. Companies like Haier stand as proof that Chinese domestic firms can complete in branded global manufacturing, and the size of these firms (as compared to Taiwanese firms in the same sectors, such as Haier competitor Tatung) allows them to exploit economies of scale that are available only to the very largest Taiwanese companies.

In short, even though many Taiwanese firms continued to do well in China, the 2008 recession and stimulus changed the way they are viewed in Taiwan and in the PRC. These events, combined with other negative perceptions of the PRC's economic policies, led many Taiwanese to fear that *Taishang* firms would be squeezed out of the mainland altogether or lose their profitability. While on the surface, that perception seems at odds with the reality of successful companies like Foxconn, Want Want, and TSMC, the high sensitivity of many Taiwanese to any sign of decline or vulnerability relative to the PRC makes it understandable.

As the Chinese economy has grown, the size of individual Taiwanese firms and the Taiwan-invested sector as a whole have declined, relative to individual PRC firms and the overall Chinese economy. But it is not only their size that has declined; Taiwanese firms' importance and influence have also diminished in recent years. A principal reason for that diminution is that the "low-hanging fruit" the early Taiwanese investors harvested has largely been exhausted. To remain relevant and influential in the PRC economy today, Taiwanese firms need to upgrade their skills, technology, and connections. They need to perform at a higher level to outpace domestic PRC competitors, and not all Taiwanese firms are able to meet the new standard. It doesn't help that many of their competitors are getting PRC government help.

The first Taiwanese investors who moved to the mainland were able to dominate export-oriented manufacturing in a wide range of industries. Their superior performance rested to a significant extent on their long experience as contract manufacturers doing original equipment manufacturing (OEM) for international brands. While Taiwan had a handful of branded manufacturers in the 1980s, no Taiwanese brand had a global reach, and even the Taiwanese brands that were known within East Asia also did OEM for international brands.

When rising production costs challenged Taiwan's contract manufacturing in the 1980s, instead of losing out to competitors in less expensive locations, Taiwanese firms were able to take advantage of the mainland's low-wage, low-regulation environment to reinvigorate their contracting relationships. From the branded firms' point of view, this was an ideal outcome: they could lower the prices they paid without changing suppliers, and those suppliers would bear the cost of adapting to the lower-cost platform. As an added bonus, international firms got access to China without having to set up their own operations there.

Meanwhile, mainland-originated companies, whether private, TVE, or SOE, had virtually no experience in manufacturing consumer goods for export—or even for a domestic consumer market. That meant Taiwanese and other foreign investors had the opportunity to introduce export-oriented manufacturing to China as well as many types of retail and service businesses. Foreign investors from the West and Japan tended to use joint ventures to enter the Chinese market, which entailed sharing management techniques, technology, and marketing channels with PRC partners. Taiwanese investors, in contrast, preferred to set up WOFEs—wholly owned foreign enterprises. As a result, the Taiwanese firms' technology, know-how, and contracting relationships remained locked up within the Taiwanese investor community. Most Taiwanese firms set up their operations in clusters with other Taiwanese companies in the same industry—the so-called fortresses in the air.

In sum, Taiwanese succeeded in the mainland because they were ahead of PRC domestic firms, and they were able to leverage that lead to give themselves a "second spring." They used the mainland as a platform to shift from OEM to original design manufacturing (ODM), a form of contracting that provides higher value-added to the client and returns higher profits to the firm. While they started the 1990s with superior technology, management practices, and marketing relationships, Taiwanese companies did not enjoy some kind of magical superiority over all competitors. As PRC firms have overtaken them, *Taishang* are facing the "three trans- (*san zhuan*)" dilemma: *zhuanxing* (transform through upgrading), *zhuanyi* (transfer to another location), or *zhuanhang* (transition to another career).[3]

Taiwanese firms have achieved impressive results in upgrading (Taiwanese companies have driven process-technology innovation in a number of fields), but they do not have a magic upgrading wand; transformation is just as hard for them as it is for firms from other countries. The Taiwan government has provided assistance for upgrading, but it remains a tough slog. Some Taiwanese firms have succeeded, but many have failed—or simply cashed out and gone home when the going got too tough (the *zhuanhang*/"transition to another career" group). The barriers to entry have risen in many industries and the overall climate for doing business on the mainland has become more competitive as more firms—Taiwanese, domestic PRC, and others—have matured.

Not all Taiwanese manufacturing firms adopted upgrading as their strategy. Some chose instead to cut costs by moving to less expensive parts of China. As wages in the coastal provinces rose, traditional manufacturers moved inland—pushed along, in some cases, by local governments hoping to "empty the cages and swap out the birds" (*tenglong huanniao*)—expel less desirable industries to make room for more desirable ones. This was a deliberate strategy, promoted by China's central government, to encourage industrial upgrading.

Many of the investors that chose the "Go West" strategy (*zhuanyi*/"transition to a new location") discovered it was not the remedy they had hoped. While inland provinces do offer tax incentives and cheaper production costs, labor conditions in the west are very different from the places where Taiwanese investors thrived in the early 1990s. Jian-bang Deng's research on Taiwanese-invested firms in western China discovered that they faced significant challenges in the new environment.[4] Labor rights activists may not like it, but the classic Pearl River delta factory of the 1990s—thousands of young women from the countryside working long hours and living on-site in company dormitories—is an ideal arrangement for manufacturers. The "military style" management described by You-tien Hsing in her 1997 study of Taiwanese shoe manufacturers entitled *Making Capitalism in China* produced strong profits for Taiwanese companies—and their foreign customers.

Moving inland, Deng found, requires major adjustments to that model. The workforce in inland China may be less expensive, but it is also less pliable, more demanding, and ultimately more privileged than the migrant-based labor force in the coastal provinces. One simple reason: unlike migrant workers in Guangdong or Jiangsu, many industrial workers in Sichuan or Hubei have their household registration where they work. They are not subject to exploitation by virtue of their second-class citizenship, as migrants are. They live at home; they are responsible for family members and farmland. They expect to go home at night. In some places, Deng found, they even receive time off during the agricultural busy seasons. To succeed in this environment, Taiwanese managers have found it necessary to tether their "floating fortresses" to particular communities and to hire local managers.

Another strategy adopted by some Taiwanese firms to maintain their position in the mainland was to treat China not only as a manufacturing platform but as a market. That is a logical response to the diminishing role of exports in China's economy, which peaked in 2006 at 35 percent of GDP. Since then, exports as share of GDP has declined steady, falling to less than 20 percent in 2019. That leaves the domestic market as a more appealing target. Some of the early Taiwanese entrants—especially food processors like Uni-President and Want Want—have done well, but China's consumer market is highly competitive, with domestic, Taiwanese, and other foreign firms all vying for consumers' *renminbi*. Except where their familiarity with Chinese products and tastes gives them a leg up, Taiwanese enjoy few structural advantages in the PRC market. Where they do have a lead on Chinese domestic firms is in the service sector (Taiwan's service sector is much better developed than the PRC's), but the Cross-Strait Services Trade Agreement (CSSTA) negotiated with Beijing during Ma's administration has been stuck in limbo since its opponents occupied Taiwan's legislative chamber in the spring of 2014.

Frankly speaking, from 1987 until the early 2000s, Taiwanese investors were harvesting low-hanging fruit. In the early 2000s, they were able to extend their era of predominance by streamlining production methods and realizing efficiencies. But eventually they exhausted the opportunities that were within reach. The quick fixes—moving to less expensive regions of China, selling into the PRC market—were not a panacea. To retain a leading position required transformation and upgrading beyond the capacity of many—although by no means all—firms.

As the PRC's domestic firms thrive, Taiwanese investment becomes less important to localities in the PRC, and the special treatment and privileges Taiwanese firms enjoyed in the 1990s and 2000s are disappearing. Individual Taiwanese workers, too, find themselves less competitive than before: Chinese have improved their skills to match. Not long ago, Taiwanese youth thought of looking for work on the mainland as a "second best" option—something to explore if the right job didn't come through on Taiwan or you wanted an adventure. Then, for a while, Taiwanese youth counted themselves lucky to find a job in the PRC. Today, working on the mainland is rapidly losing its appeal, both because the bonuses and "hardship pay" have largely disappeared and because the tightening political controls on the mainland are unappealing, even frightening.

Chun-Yi Lee summed up the challenges of rising competition from domestic PRC firms in a 2016 blog post:

> Taiwan has to face the reality that China's supply chain in the coming years may no longer include Taiwanese factories. . . . One interviewee from the HSP [Hsinchu Science Park—Taiwan's high-tech incubator] informed me in 2015 that Chinese companies offer highly competitive compensation packages and promised to settle Taiwanese employees' families in China. "Few of my colleagues could resist such temptation," my interviewee confessed. This is the main and most acute problem that the new government [of Tsai Ing-wen] will have to face.[5]

In this climate of declining profitability and rising competition, many Taiwanese are reassessing the opportunities and threats in cross-Strait economic relations. That said, the news is not all bad for Taiwan. Many scholars who follow cross-Strait economics closely believe that allowing PRC firms to enlarge their role in high-tech manufacturing could actually improve Taiwan firms' competitiveness. In a study of integrated circuit design houses, for example, Jenn-hwan Wang and Sheng-wen Tseng argue that Taiwanese firms are using the Red Supply Chain to escape their traditional role as contract manufacturers and become lead firms with technology of their own.[6]

According to a 2020 Brookings Institution report, the PRC's chip-making capacity has almost overtaken Taiwan's. But when the report's authors adjusted the data to reflect the chips' technological sophistication, Taiwan's share of global output shot up to 43 percent, with the PRC capturing only 3 percent.[7] The political economist Douglas Fuller has written a number of papers detailing the obstacles facing PRC tech firms in their effort to overtake Taiwan's industry leaders. According to Fuller, "Despite massive expansion and strong government backing, domestic state-owned firms have generally failed to generate the technological dynamism that official policy seeks."[8] Some Taiwanese firms have been pushed out by the intensified competition, but many others have been pushed up; the pressure to upgrade has made them stronger. If their development doesn't resonate back to Taiwan in a way that gives confidence to job seekers, that is less a statement about the quality of Taiwanese firms and technology than it is about contemporary economies' tendency to create jobless growth.

Even if the rapid, state-supported expansion of PRC firms does not drive the Taiwanese out of business, however, Taiwanese are unlikely to ever again enjoy the massive advantages they once took for granted in the mainland. The economics have changed, and so have the politics. For many years, China's leaders believed that the Taiwanese business community in the PRC was their best ally for promoting their agenda of unification with Taiwan. After eight years of the Ma presidency—a period in which Taiwanese enjoyed virtually unfettered access to the PRC economy—unification is no closer than it was before 2008. Indeed, it is hard not to conclude that it is even more distant. Using Taiwanese businesses to promote unification hasn't worked. If that is how Beijing sees it, there is little chance it will continue to extend privileges to Taiwanese firms.

Although the PRC government is no longer confident that favoring Taiwanese firms is the way to advance unification, its basic policy hasn't changed, and it hasn't given up on using cross-Strait economic relations to promote its interests. For example, in February 2018, Beijing's Taiwan Affairs Office announced thirty-one measures designed to entice more Taiwanese investors and professionals to the mainland. According to the TAO spokesman, the goal was to create a level playing field for Taiwanese and mainland-born firms. The incentive package allowed Taiwanese companies to participate in the Made in China 2025 program and to bid for infrastructure projects. It also included tax benefits and made it easier for Taiwanese books, TV shows, and movies to reach PRC consumers. Taiwanese were invited to join professional associations on the mainland and apply for professional qualifications.

Beijing followed up the thirty-one measures with another twenty-six in November 2019, many of which were aimed at institutionalizing ties between Taiwanese individuals and the PRC state. They offered Taiwanese access to PRC consulates abroad as well as temporary passports. In a separate move, Beijing offered Taiwanese residence permits. Like the thirty-one measures, the twenty-six measures eased some investment restrictions for Taiwanese companies, allowing *Taishang* to take part in high-value industries such as 5G and civil aviation.

The thirty-one plus twenty-six measures were carrots extended from Beijing to Taiwanese firms and individuals, and the response to them was mixed. An estimated hundred thousand Taiwanese accepted residence permits, but demand for the passport was limited, not least because Taiwan's passport is widely accepted internationally, offering visa-free entry to twice as many countries as a PRC passport. According to Taiwan's Mainland Affairs Council, the various measures were not enough to reverse the negative trends in mainland-bound investment, which decreased for four consecutive years, from 2016 to 2019. Taiwanese investment in the mainland has been declining since 2010, when 83 percent of the capital leaving the island went to the PRC. In 2017, that percentage was only 44 percent.[9] Meanwhile, Taiwan's Ministry of Labor also shows the number of Taiwanese working in the PRC declining since its peak in 2013–2014. The US-PRC trade war in 2019 only accelerated those trends.

Even more paradoxically, at the same time Beijing was working to shrink the role of *Taishang* in the PRC economy writ large, it also was creating a Pilot Free Trade Zone (PFTZ) in Fujian aimed at promoting cross-Strait trade and investment. The PFTZ was approved in 2014 and officially launched in 2015. According to an official announcement, the goals of the PFTZ are to explore a new model of Fujian/Taiwan economic cooperation, innovate new mechanisms for cross-Strait cooperation, and promote the free flow of goods, services, financial capital, and personnel.[10] The Fujian PFTZ may be a return to the early days of cross-Strait investment: after decades of inviting local governments throughout the mainland to recruit Taiwanese firms to their localities, Beijing is using the PFTZ to attract Taiwanese investment and personnel to a specific location for specific, limited purposes.

Pilot Free Trade Zones and double-digit incentive packages notwithstanding, Taiwanese firms are just not that special anymore. They sink and swim based on their competitive advantages and performance. And they choose which pool to jump in based on their own calculations and business logic. Meanwhile, many Taiwanese companies are strong swimmers; it would not be wise to count them out. To change the metaphor, Taiwanese-owned trees will not disappear from China's economic forest. Nor, however, will they continue to stand taller or grow faster than those around them. From 1987 until around 2010, Taiwanese played a central role in China's economic development, driving globalization, manufacturing growth, consumer trends, and popular culture. For most *Taishang* and their mainland partners, those interactions were a win-win. But we were warned: in the long run, there is no such thing as a win-win in the PRC business world. Taiwanese learned how this lesson applied to individual firms back in the 1990s; today, they are learning how it works for *Taishang* collectively.

THE CHANGING BUSINESS CLIMATE UNDER XI JINPING

Taiwanese firms could not expect to retain their special status forever; it was inevitable that Chinese companies would catch up eventually. That process has accelerated under the leadership of Xi Jinping, an economic nationalist who has prioritized domestic firms—especially state-owned enterprises—over foreign investors. The preference for SOEs is strong; even though foreign firms no longer enjoy the privileges they once did, China's domestic private firms continue to face policy challenges. Private firms—domestic, foreign-invested, and *Taishang*—are hobbled by rising taxes, stepped-up regulatory enforcement, and limited access to credit.

Economic nationalism and competition from the Red Supply Chain are not the only challenges facing *Taishang* in the mainland. Taiwanese popular culture and brands are less popular than they once were, a trend fed by popular nationalism and an anti-Taiwan narrative that claims Taiwanese are disloyal to the Chinese nation. Meanwhile, Xi is tightening controls on information, communication, and organizations. Nongovernmental organizations face increasing restrictions, including a 2017 law regulating foreign NGOs, which also applies to Taiwanese groups. Religious organizations, too, are facing increased surveillance and interference in the Xi Jinping era, while popular entertainers are at pains to avoid any action that might put them at odds with the PRC state.

If the opportunities for turbo-charged growth in mainland China are largely exhausted, what's next for Taiwanese companies? Economically, Taiwanese companies are rethinking their reliance on the PRC as their main manufacturing platform and looking for opportunities to diversify their supply chains and operations to new locations. Between 2010 and 2020, China's share of Taiwan's outbound investment fell by half.[11] The US-PRC trade war accelerated that process, as US tariffs on Chinese imports cut into *Taishang* profits. Taiwan's government responded strategically to these developments, rolling out policies aimed at diversifying Taiwan's economic partnerships and reshoring manufacturing.

First, President Tsai Ing-wen's New Southbound Policy (NSP), which she enacted after taking office in 2016, helps Taiwanese firms build relationships with suppliers and other partners in South Asia and Southeast Asia. Investors have been cagey—political motivations are no substitute for profit, after all—but rising production costs in the PRC and the trade war altered their economic calculus. Taiwanese investment in NSP countries increased by more than 16 percent in 2019. Meanwhile, the number of Southeast Asian tourists and students in Taiwan has been rising quickly, as has the number of Southeast Asian workers.

A second policy development is a package of incentives aimed at attracting Taiwanese firms to return to the island. The program helps companies that find themselves squeezed by the US-PRC trade war manage the costs of relocation through tax breaks, interest rate cuts, and relaxed rules for hiring foreign workers. In the first half of 2019, *Taishang* applied for incentives to repatriate twenty-seven billion dollars through inbound investment. Some of Taiwan's biggest tech names are part of the trend. Quanta Computer, the world's third-largest electronics manufacturing services company, committed five hundred million dollars to building capacity in Taiwan, including a huge new factory in Taoyuan. Unimicron Technology, a leading supplier of printed circuit boards, said 80 percent of its capital spending in 2020 would be in Taiwan.[12]

Repatriation has been a boon to Taiwan—and to its president, who cruised to reelection in January 2020 thanks in part to the surge in investment. Still, the trade war is not an unmixed blessing. Many Taiwanese firms have extensive operations on the mainland that are not easily unraveled. Washington's biggest target is Huawei, which also happens to be a huge customer for TSMC, the world's largest pure-play foundry and Taiwan's single most important firm.

THE RISE AND FALL OF THE CROSS-STRAIT ECONOMIC MIRACLE: POLITICAL IMPLICATIONS

Taiwan's contributions to the PRC's economic and social development have received surprisingly little attention from scholars and policy makers. Most of the articles and reports that have been written about cross-Strait economic relations focus on their political implications. And most of those center on this question: will the integration of the two economies narrow the political gap between the two sides and eventually lead to unification?

I find this question a little odd, to be honest. Why would we expect two self-governing polities to merge just because they have a lot of trade and investment with each other? Admittedly, Taiwan and the PRC have more in common than that: they were once ruled by the same empire (the Manchu Qing Empire); they speak the same language, by and large; they share cultural roots; and many citizens on both sides of the Strait are connected by ancestors a few generations ago. But if those circumstances, plus close economic ties, are enough to bring about political unification, why haven't the United States and Canada overcome the historical differences of the eighteenth century and reunified?

Of course, there is a big difference between these two cases. It's been a long time since a Canadian or US politician called for reunification of British North America, while the PRC government is still advocating unification of Taiwan with the mainland today. And for much of the postwar period, a significant number of Taiwanese also believed that unification was Taiwan's destiny. Chinese nationalists in Taiwan believed the two sides should unify under the Republic of China, the successor to the Qing Empire, while Chinese nationalists in the mainland believe they should unify under the PRC. It is this claim—which is upheld much more strongly on the mainland side than in Taiwan today—that prompted the speculation as to whether economic interactions would ease the road to unification.

Thirty-plus years into the era of economic engagement, the answer is clear: when it comes to politics, economic interactions have not changed the situation much. It has produced a great deal of wealth on both sides, it has enabled cooperation on a vast range of projects and topics, and it has subdued enthusiasm for militant action—whether for independence or unification—on both sides. But economic engagement has not moved Taiwan closer to accepting Beijing's version of unification, and it has not tempered Beijing's determination to bring Taiwan under its control, on its terms.

Beijing's approach has changed very little. Its expectation that cross-Strait economic ties will pull Taiwan toward China is still its main focus; PRC officials rarely acknowledge how much Taiwanese investors contributed to the PRC's economic development. As for Taiwanese, they have spent thirty-five years finding out what cross-Strait economic ties could accomplish. Where they've ended up is pretty much right where they started—albeit older, wiser, and richer.

In the aptly titled volume *Taiwan and China: Fitful Embrace*, political scientist Chih-hsian Liou explains why the next phase of cross-Strait economic integration will be more difficult than the previous ones.[13] Like businesses and policy makers in the US, Taiwanese view the PRC government's statist economic policies as a threat to market competition that leaves Taiwan at a disadvantage. Taiwanese, she points out, were especially nervous about measures adopted during the Ma Ying-jeou era aimed at legalizing PRC investment in Taiwan. The fear of unfair competition was a major driver of the 2014 Sunflower Movement and other acts of resistance to Ma's initiatives. Liou also points out that—whether it's true or not—many Taiwanese believe cross-Strait economic integration has driven inequality in Taiwan. As Liou put it, "The new pattern of economic growth is different from what Taiwanese people ever experienced under Taiwan's state capitalism, which emphasized both high economic growth and low income inequality."[14] Finally, Liou observes that economic engagement "stimulates popular awareness of Taiwan's sovereign status"—and the PRC's desire to undermine it.[15]

Another important reason for the waning excitement about mainland opportunities is the global business climate. For both economic and political reasons, mainland China is no longer the indispensable business location it once was. Labor-intensive manufacturing is moving to Southeast Asia and other destinations, while technology companies are looking to automate production and move it back to Taiwan. Intellectual property rights are one motive for the change, but increasing economic tensions between China and the US (and other Western countries) is another. *Taishang* went to the mainland in part because their customers demanded it; now their customers want to source technology products from less politically sensitive markets, and the *Taishang* will follow.

From the beginning, Taiwanese investment in the PRC has been driven by economic considerations. A chapter by Chung-min Tsai in *Taiwan and China: Fitful Embrace* shows that the pattern of Taiwanese investment in the mainland tracks much more closely with economic factors than with political developments.[16] In other words, whether Taiwan's president is Lee Teng-hui, Chen Shui-Bian, Ma Ying-jeou, or Tsai Ing-wen matters very little in how the economic relationship unfolds. The fact that *Taishang* followed economic cues makes it hard for Taipei to control the relationship, but it also limits Beijing's influence as well. For example, as the political scientist Leng Tse-Kang wrote in the same volume, Foxconn's success has nothing to do with state assistance from either side—it's wholly a product of economic drivers.[17] Despite the hopes and fears about how the economic relationship would reshape political ties in the Taiwan Strait, the truth is it's all about the economy.

Taiwanese people's enthusiasm for cross-Strait interactions has been cooling since at least 2014, but events in 2019 and 2020 turbocharged that trend. In 1979, Deng Xiaoping unveiled a plan for Taiwan's political integration into the PRC using the "One Country, Two Systems" formula. Under this concept, Taiwan was to enjoy a "high degree of autonomy" after it accepted PRC sovereignty. In 1981, PRC official Ye Jianying detailed Beijing's plans: "After China is reunified, Taiwan may become a special administrative region. It may enjoy a high degree of autonomy and may keep its military forces. The national government will not intervene in the local affairs of Taiwan. Taiwan's current social and economic systems will remain unchanged, its way of life will not change, and its economic and cultural ties with foreign countries will not change."[18]

One Country, Two Systems has never been popular in Taiwan. Even the KMT, the historical advocate for unification in Taiwan, has never endorsed it. The KMT's position is that unification should occur but under the ROC's democratic constitution, not the PRC's communist system. Nonetheless, Beijing has made the formula a centerpiece of its Taiwan policy. In order to demonstrate its positive potential for Taiwan, Beijing decided to use One Country, Two Systems as the institutional framework for Hong Kong's absorption into the PRC in 1997. Thus, Hong Kong became a kind of canary in the One Country, Two Systems coal mine. By respecting its commitment to preserve Hong Kong's autonomy, Beijing hoped to persuade Taiwanese that unification under the same formula would allow the two sides to merge without changing Taiwan's most valued attributes.

Until recently, Taiwanese paid little attention to Hong Kong. Because most Taiwanese were unimpressed with One Country, Two Systems to begin with, they didn't spend much time noticing how it was working in Hong Kong. That inattention began to change in 2014 when demonstrations broke out in both places—Taiwan's Sunflower Movement, followed a few months later by Hong Kong's Umbrella Movement. The protests had similar aims—they both reflected rising concern about the extent of mainland influence in the two places—and they were both led by Sino-skeptical activist youth.

After the two movements subsided, activists continued to support one another and coordinate some of their activities. Thus, it was a big deal in Taiwan when Hong Kong citizens rose up to protest a proposed extradition law that many feared would allow Beijing to try and punish Hong Kong political dissidents in the mainland. The Hong Kong protests that began in March 2019 and continued for more than a year were a sensation in Taiwan. Hong Kong activists who visited Taiwan to drum up support attracted big crowds; young Taiwanese created "Lennon Walls"—huge displays made up of posters and sticky notes with messages of encouragement—to show their feelings. When police violence took center stage in the Hong Kong demonstrations, Taiwanese youth ramped up their support even more. They shouted the protesters' Cantonese slogan "Free Hong Kong, Revolution of Our Times" in Mandarin: *Guangfu Xianggang; Shidai Geming*.

The escalating violence even became an issue in Taiwan's January 2020 presidential election. The DPP incumbent, Tsai Ing-wen, expressed her support for the protesters, while her KMT opponent, Han Kuo-yu, at first failed to take a clear stance. Han's foot-dragging hurt him with young voters. Hong Kong was by no means the only, or even the most important, issue in the campaign, but it was striking how much attention voters and the media gave to the protests, especially in comparison to previous election years. Tsai won the election with 57 percent of the vote, a huge margin in an election with the highest turnout in over a decade.

The election had just wrapped up when news came from the mainland that an unknown illness was spreading in the central city of Wuhan. Unlike other governments, many of which waited for the World Health Organization to raise the alarm, Tsai kicked her country's epidemic response mechanisms into operation at the first sign of trouble. On December 31, Taiwan implemented screening measures for flights arriving from Wuhan. On January 20, Tsai activated the Central Epidemic Command Center. Taiwan's first novel coronavirus patient—a Taiwanese woman who had been teaching in Wuhan—arrived by plane on January 21.

Taiwan's response to the COVID catastrophe was swift and effective. The government took over the production and distribution of masks and mandated face coverings in public places. It implemented widespread testing and contact tracing, which kept the number of local transmissions low. The Lunar New Year school vacation was extended while officials figured out how to open schools safely. Travelers from abroad were required to quarantine for fourteen days, and arrivals from hard-hit areas were forbidden. Six months after the first case was reported, Taiwan had a total of 455 cases (about fifty of which were contracted locally) and seven deaths, in a total population of twenty-four million. It was among the best COVID-19 records in the world.

In June 2020, China's National People's Congress passed a national security law governing Hong Kong. In Taiwan—and much of the world—the law was interpreted as Beijing abandoning the One Country, Two Systems formula and imposing direct rule in Hong Kong. The idea of peaceful unification with a high degree of autonomy for Taiwan seemed farther away than ever. Combined with the conviction that Taiwan had barely avoided a catastrophic encounter with a mainland-originated pandemic, the collapse of the One Country, Two Systems promise sparked a surge in support for Taiwanese identity and sovereignty. The percentage of Taiwanese claiming a Taiwanese-only identity (as opposed to Chinese or both Chinese and Taiwanese) reached a historical high of 67 percent in spring 2020. At the same time, support for eventual independence reached an all-time high of 28 percent.[19]

The negative consequences of Beijing's actions in Hong Kong and the COVID epidemic wiped out any positive effects of cross-Strait economic cooperation. As the PRC's image and reputation sunk to new lows, even the KMT was forced to revise its policies on cross-Strait relations.

If the PRC hasn't had much luck changing Taiwan's political context, Taiwan hasn't done any better at changing the PRC. If Taiwanese don't see the mainland as a source of productive ideas for Taiwan's political development, neither do leaders in the PRC look to Taiwan for political inspiration. There are individuals within the PRC—people like my Shanghai landlord—who may view Taiwan as a model, but there is little room in the public sphere for that kind of thinking during the Xi Jinping era.

So where does this leave us? After almost thirty-five years of economic cooperation and engagement, Taiwan and the PRC are, it seems, drifting apart. The mainland has learned all that it needs to from its Taiwanese teachers, and Taiwanese firms are no longer enthusiastic about expanding their activity on the mainland. That's not to say they are decoupling—like the US and China, the two sides of the Taiwan Strait are too tangled up economically to sever their ties completely—but the era of breakneck integration and mutual benefit has come to an end.

NOTES

1. Quoted in Debby Wu, "China's Days as World's Factory Are Over, iPhone Maker Says," Bloomberg, August 12, 2020, https://www.bloomberg.com/news /articles/2020-08-12/hon-hai-beats-profit-estimates-after-pandemic-spurs-apple -demand.

2. Huang Yasheng, *Capitalism with Chinese Characteristics: Entrepreneurship and the State* (Cambridge: Cambridge University Press, 2008).

3. Chih-peng Cheng, "Embedded Trust and Beyond: The Organizational Network Transformation of Taishang's Shoe Industry in China," in *Border Crossing in Greater China: Production, Community and Identity*, edited by Jenn-hwan Wang (London: Routledge, 2015), 48.

4. Jian-bang Deng, "Marginal Mobilities: Taiwanese Manufacturing Companies' Migration to Inner China," in *Border Crossing in Greater China: Production, Community and Identity*, edited by Jenn-hwan Wang (London: Routledge, 2015).

5. Chun-Yi Lee, "Green Taiwan vis-à-vis China's the Red Supply China," University of Nottingham Asia Research Institute Blog, January 22, 2016, accessed December 15, 2020, https://theasiadialogue.com/2016/01/22/green-taiwan-vis-a-vis-chinas-the -red-supply-chain/.

6. Jenn-hwan Wang and Sheng-wen Tseng, "Managing Cross-Border Innovation Networks: Taiwan's IC Design Industry," in *Border Crossing in Greater China: Production, Community and Identity*, edited by Jenn-hwan Wang (London: Routledge, 2015).

7. Saif M. Khan and Carrick Flynn, "Maintaining China's Dependence on Democracies for Advanced Computer Chips," *Global China: Assessing China's Growing Role in the World*, Brookings Institution, April 2020, accessed December 15, 2020, https://www.brookings.edu/wp-content/uploads/2020/04/FP_20200427 _computer_chips_khan_flynn.pdf.

8. Douglas B. Fuller, "Growth, Upgrading, and Limited Catch-up in China's Semiconductor Industry," in *Policy, Regulation, and Innovation in China's Electricity and Telecom Industries*, edited by Loren Brandt and Thomas G. Rawski (Cambridge: Cambridge University Press, 2019), 263.

9. Sophia Yang, "China's Pro-Unification 31 Measures for Taiwan Have Failed: Academia Sinica Scholar," *Taiwan News*, January 26, 2019, accessed November 19, 2020, https://www.taiwannews.com.tw/en/news/3625988.

10. "Guowuyuan guanyu yinfa Zhongguo (Fujian) ziyou maoyi shiyanqu zongti fang'an de tongzhi" [Announcement of the State Council on the overall plan for the China (Fujian) Pilot Free Trade Zone], accessed November 19, 2020, http://www.gov.cn/zhengce/content/2015-04/20/content_9633.htm.

11. Min-Hua Chiang, "Taiwan's Growth Up, Despite Trade War Hit," *East Asia Forum*, January 11, 2020, accessed November 20, 2020, https://www.eastasiaforum .org/2020/01/11/taiwans-economic-resilience/.

12. Kensaku Ihara, "Taiwan Tech Companies' China Exit Fuels $25bn Investment Drive," *Nikkei Asia*, May 28, 2020, accessed November 20, 2020, https://asia.nikkei .com/Business/Business-trends/Taiwan-tech-companies-China-exit-fuels-25bn -investment-drive.

13. Chih-hsian Liou, "Varieties of State Capitalism across the Taiwan Strait: A Comparison and Its Implications," in Lowell Dittmer, Ed. *Taiwan and China: Fitful Embrace*, edited by Lowell Dittmer (Berkeley: University of California Press, 2017).

14. Liou, "Varieties of State Capitalism," 128.

15. Liou, "Varieties of State Capitalism," 129.

16. Chung-min Tsai, "The Nature and Trend of Taiwanese Investment in China (1991–2014): Business Orientation, Profit-Making and Depoliticization," in *Taiwan and China: Fitful Embrace*, edited by Lowell Dittmer (Berkeley: University of California Press, 2017).

17. Tse-Kang Leng, "Cross-Strait Economic Relations and China's Rise: The Case of the IT Sector," in *Taiwan and China: Fitful Embrace*, edited by Lowell Dittmer (Berkeley: University of California Press, 2017).

18. "A Policy of 'One Country, Two Systems' on Taiwan," Ministry of Foreign Affairs of the People's Republic of China, accessed November 24, 2020, https://www.fmprc.gov.cn/mfa_eng/ziliao_665539/3602_665543/3604_665547/t18027.shtml.

19. Election Study Center, National Chengchi University, accessed November 24, 2020, https://esc.nccu.edu.tw.

References

"1992 Consensus Beneficial to Taiwan." Xinhua News Agency. January 14, 2012. Accessed November 25, 2020. http://www.china.org.cn/china/2012-01/14/content_24405190.htm.

Adrian, Bonnie. *Framing the Bride: Globalizing Beauty and Romance in Taiwan's Bridal Industry*. Berkeley: University of California Press, 2003.

Biggs, Tyler S. "Heterogeneous Firms and Efficient Financial Intermediation in Taiwan." In *Markets in Developing Countries: Parallel, Fragmented, and Black*, edited by Michael Roemer and Christine Jones. San Francisco, CA: ICS Press, 1991.

Brown, Deborah A., and Tun-jen Cheng. "Religious Relations across the Taiwan Strait: Patterns, Alignments, and Political Effects." *Orbis* 56, no. 1 (2012): 60–81.

Brown, Kerry, Justin Hempson-Jones, and Jessica Pennisi. "Investment across the Taiwan Strait: How Taiwan's Relationship with China Affects Its Position in the Global Economy." Chatham House. November 2010. https://www.chathamhouse.org/sites/default/files/public/Research/Asia/1110pp_taiwan.pdf.

Chang P. C. *Taishang Zhuanxing Shengji yu Inying Celue Sikao* [Strategic responses to Taishang transformational upgrading]. Unpublished paper presented to the Conference on Mainland-Based Taishang's Transformational Upgrading: Strategy, Cases, and Prospects, Taipei, 2012.

Chen Ming-chi. "Fortress in the Air: The Organization Model of Taiwanese Export-Manufacturing Transplants in China." *Issues and Studies* 48, no. 4 (2012): 73–112.

Chen Ming-chi and Tao Yi-feng. 2010. "Quanqiu ziben zhuyi, Taishang yu Zhongguo jingji fazhan" [Global capitalism, Taishang and China's economic development]. In *Taishang yu Zhongguo Jingji Fazhan* [Taishang and China's economic development], edited by Tien Hung-mao and Gao Wei-feng, 51–65. Taipei: Institute for National Policy Research, 2010.

Chen Tain-Jy and Ku Ying-Hua. "Quanqiuhua xia Taiwan dui dalu touzi celue" [Taiwan's mainland investment strategy under globalization]. In *Jingji quanqiuhua yu Taishang dalu touzi* [Economic globalization and Taishang investment on the mainland], edited by Chen Te-sheng. Taipei: Ink Publishing, 2008.

Cheng Chih-peng. "Embedded Trust and Beyond: The Organizational Network Transformation of Taishang's Shoe Industry in China." In *Border Crossing in Greater China: Production, Community and Identity*, edited by Jenn-hwan Wang. London: Routledge, 2015.

Cheng Lu-lin. *Embedded Competitiveness: Taiwan's Shifting Role in International Footwear Sourcing Networks*. Unpublished PhD thesis, Department of Sociology, Duke University, 1996.

Chiang Min-Hua. "Taiwan's Growth Up, Despite Trade War Hit." *East Asia Forum*. January 11, 2020. Accessed November 20, 2020. https://www.eastasiaforum.org/2020/01/11/taiwans-economic-resilience/.

Chin Chung. "Division of Labor across the Taiwan Strait: Macro Overview and Analysis of the Electronics Industry." In *The China Circle: Economics and Electronics in the PRC, Taiwan, and Hong Kong*, edited by Barry Naughton. Washington, DC: Brookings Institution Press, 1997.

Choudhury, Saheli Roy. "Apple Denies Claims It Broke Chinese Labor Laws in iPhone Factory." CNBC. September 8, 2019. https://www.cnbc.com/2019/09/09/apple-appl-claims-it-broke-china-labor-laws-at-iphone-factory-mostly-false.html.

Chu, Wan-wen. "Industrial Growth and Small and Medium-sized Enterprises: The Case of Taiwan." Academia Sinica. 2003. Accessed November 24, 2020. http://idv.sinica.edu.tw/wwchu/SME%20TW.pdf.

Chu Yun-han. "China and the Taiwan Factor." In *Democracy in East Asia: A New Century*, edited by Larry Diamond, Mark Plattner, and Yun-han Chu. Baltimore, MD: Johns Hopkins University Press, 2012.

Clarke, Peter. "Global Top 50 Ranking of EMS Providers for 2019." eeNews Analog. April 19, 2020. https://www.eenewsanalog.com/news/global-top-50-ranking -ems-providers-2019.

"Coffee Consumption in China Has Risen by Over 1,000% in the Last 10 Years." International Comunicaffe. 2018. Accessed December 15, 2020. https://www .comunicaffe.com/coffee-consumption-in-china-has-risen-by-over-1000-in -the-last-10-years/.

"Coffee in China: A Few Observations." Crop to Cup Coffee Blog. 2011. Accessed December 15, 2020. https://croptocup.wordpress.com/2011/10/07/coffee-in -china-a-few-observations/.

Dedrick, Jason, Greg Linden, and Kenneth L. Kraemer. "China Makes $8.46 from an iPhone and That's Why a U.S. Trade War Is Futile." CBS News. 2018. Accessed December 15, 2020. https://www.cbsnews.com/news/china-makes-8-46-from -an-iphone-and-thats-why-u-s-trade-war-is-futile/.

Deng Jian-Bang. "Marginal Mobilities: Taiwanese Manufacturing Companies' Migration to Inner China." In *Border Crossing in Greater China: Production, Community and Identity*, edited by Jenn-hwan Wang. London: Routledge, 2015.

"Editorial: PNTR Won't Cure All China's Woes." *Taipei Times*. May 26, 2000. https://www.taipeitimes.com/News/editorials/archives/2000/05/26/0000037548.

Election Study Center, National Chengchi University. Accessed November 24, 2020. https://esc.nccu.edu.tw.

Ernst, Dieter, and B. Naughton *China's Emerging Industrial Economy—Insights from the IT Industry*. Paper prepared for the East-West Center Conference on China's Emerging Capitalist System, Honolulu, Hawaii, August 10–12, 2005.

Fuller, Douglas B. "Growth, Upgrading, and Limited Catch-up in China's Semiconductor Industry." In *Policy, Regulation, and Innovation in China's Electricity and Telecom Industries*, edited by Loren Brandt and Thomas G. Rawski. Cambridge: Cambridge University Press, 2019.

Fung, Anthony Y. H. "The Emerging (National) Popular Music Culture in China." *Inter-Asia Cultural Studies* 8, no. 3 (2007): 435.

Gereffi, G. "The Organisation of Buyer-Driven Global Commodity Chains: How US Retailers Shape Overseas Production Networks." In *Commodity Chains and Global Capitalism*, edited by G. Gereffi and M. Korzeniewicz. Westport, CT: Praeger, 1994.

Gold, Thomas B. "Go with Your Feelings: Hong Kong and Taiwan Popular Culture in Greater China." *China Quarterly* 136 (1993): 907–925.

———. *State and Society in the Taiwan Miracle*. Armonk, NY: M. E. Sharpe, 1986.

"Guowuyuan guanyu yinfa Zhongguo (Fujian) ziyou maoyi shiyanqu zongti fang'an de tongzhi" [Announcement of the State Council on the overall plan for the China (Fujian) Pilot Free Trade Zone]. Accessed November 19, 2020. http://www .gov.cn/zhengce/content/2015-04/20/content_9633.htm.

Guy, Nancy. "'Republic of China National Anthem' on Taiwan: One Anthem, One Performance, Multiple Realities." *Ethnomusicology* 46, no. 1 (2002): 112.

Haggard, Stephan, and Chien-Kuo Pang. "The Transition to Export-Led Growth in Taiwan." In *The Role of the State in Taiwan's Development*, edited by Joel D. Aberbach, David Dollar, and Kenneth L. Sokoloff. Armonk, NY: M. E. Sharpe, 1994.

Hamilton, Gary G. "Organization and Market Processes in Taiwan's Capitalist Economy." In *The Economic Organization of East Asian Capitalism*, edited by M. Orru, N. Biggart, and G. Hamilton. Thousand Oaks, CA: SAGE, 1996.

———. *Patterns of Asian Capitalism: The Cases of Taiwan and South Korea*. Working Paper Series no. 28, Program in East Asian Culture and Development Research. Davis: University of California, Institute of Governmental Affairs, 1990.

Hamilton, Gary G., and Cheng-shu Kao. "The Asian Miracle and the Rise of Demand-Responsive Economies." In *The Market Makers: How Retailers Are Reshaping the Global Economy*, edited by Gary G. Hamilton, Benjamin Senauer, and Misha Petrovic. Oxford: Oxford University Press, 2011.

High, Anna. "'It's Grace and Favor: It's Not Law': Extra-legal Regulation of Foreign Foster Homes in China." *University of Pennsylvania Asian Law Review* 12 (2017): 357–405.

Hopkins, Terence K., and Immanuel Wallerstein. "Commodity Chains in the World-Economy Prior to 1800." *Review (Fernand Braudel Center)* 10, no. 1 (1986): 157–170.

Hsing You-tien. *Making Capitalism in China: The Taiwan Connection*. Oxford: Oxford University Press 1998.

Hsiung Ping-Chun. *Living Rooms as Factories: Class, Gender, and the Satellite Factory System in Taiwan*. Philadelphia, PA: Temple University Press, 1996.

Huang Chang-ling and Suk-jun Lim. *Globalization and the Corporate Strategies: South Korea and Taiwan's Footwear Industries in Transition*. Paper presented to the Annual Meeting of the American Political Science Association, Philadelphia, Pennsylvania, 2006.

Huang Yasheng. *Capitalism with Chinese Characteristics: Entrepreneurship and the State*. Cambridge: Cambridge University Press, 2008.

Ihara, Kensaku. "Taiwan Tech Companies' China Exit Fuels $25bn Investment Drive." *Nikkei Asia*. May 28, 2020. Accessed November 20, 2020. https://asia.nikkei.com/Business/Business-trends/Taiwan-tech-companies-China-exit-fuels-25bn-investment-drive.

Johnson, Ian. "Is a Buddhist Group Changing China? Or Is China Changing It?" *New York Times*. June 24, 2017.

Johnson, Joel. "1 Million Workers. 90 Million iPhones. 17 Suicides. Who's to Blame?" *Wired*. February 28, 2011. https://www.wired.com/2011/02/ff-joelinchina/.

Khan, Saif M., and Carrick Flynn. "Maintaining China's Dependence on Democracies for Advanced Computer Chips." *Global China: Assessing China's Growing Role in the World*. Brookings Institution. April 2020. Accessed December 15, 2020. https://www.brookings.edu/wp-content/uploads/2020/04/FP_20200427_computer_chips_khan_flynn.pdf.

Kirby, William C., Billy Chan, and Dawn H. Lau. "Taiwan Semiconductor Manufacturing Company Limited: A Global Company's China Strategy (B)." Harvard Business School Supplement 320-045, November 2019, revised January 2020.

Kynge, James, and Mure Dickie. "China Warns Taiwan Businessmen." *Financial Times*. April 10, 2000.

Lee Chun-Yi. "Green Taiwan vis-à-vis China's the Red Supply Chain." University of Nottingham Asia Research Institute Blog. January 22, 2016. Accessed December

15, 2020. https://theasiadialogue.com/2016/01/22/green-taiwan-vis-a-vis-chinas
-the-red-supply-chain/.

———. "Social Dimensions of the Changing Cross-Strait Relations in the Case of
Taishangs." In *New Dynamics in Cross-Taiwan Strait Relations: How Far Can the
Rapprochement Go?*, edited by Weixing Hu, 190–203. London: Routledge, 2013.

———. "Taiwan and China in a Global Value Chain: The Case of the Electronics
Industry." In *Taiwan's Impact on China: Why Soft Power Matters More than
Economic or Political Inputs*, edited by Steve Tsang. Cham, Switzerland: Palgrave
Macmillan, 2017.

———. *Taiwanese Business or Chinese Security Asset: A Changing Pattern of
Interaction between Taiwanese Businesses and Chinese Governments*. London:
Routledge, 2011.

Leng Tse-Kang. "Cross-Strait Economic Relations and China's Rise: The Case of
the IT Sector." In *Taiwan and China: Fitful Embrace*, edited by Lowell Dittmer.
Berkeley: University of California Press, 2017.

Li Lauly. "MOEA Eases China Investment Rule." *Taipei Times*. August 14, 2015.
https://www.taipeitimes.com/News/front/archives/2015/08/14/2003625310.

Liou Chih-hsian. "Varieties of State Capitalism across the Taiwan Strait: A
Comparison and Its Implications." In *Taiwan and China: Fitful Embrace*, edited
by Lowell Dittmer. Berkeley: University of California Press, 2017.

Loa Lok-sin. "Taiwan Buddhist Master: 'No Taiwanese.'" *Taipei Times*. March 31,
2009.

Osborne, Michael West. *China's Special Economic Zones*. Paris: Development Centre
of the Organisation for Economic Co-operation and Development, 1986.

Ping Deng. "Taiwan's Restriction of Investment in China in the 1990s: A Relative
Gains Approach." *Asian Survey* 40, no. 6 (2000): 958–980.

"A Policy of 'One Country, Two Systems' on Taiwan." Ministry of Foreign Affairs of
the People's Republic of China. Accessed November 24, 2020. https://www.fmprc
.gov.cn/mfa_eng/ziliao_665539/3602_665543/3604_665547/t18027.shtml.

Reardon, Lawrence. *The Reluctant Dragon: Crisis Cycles in Chinese Foreign
Economic Policy*. Seattle: University of Washington Press, 2002.

Reid, Toy, and Shelley Rigger. "Taiwanese Investors in Mainland China: Creating a Context for Peace?" in *Cross-Strait at the Turing Point: Institution, Identity and Democracy*, edited by I. Yuan. Taipei: Institute of International Relations, 2008.

Rubinstein, Murray. *The Revival of the Mazu Cult and Taiwanese Pilgrimage to Fujian*. Working Papers Issue 5. Cambridge, MA: Fairbank Center, 1994.

Sanger, David. "PC Powerhouse (Made in Taiwan)." *New York Times*. September 28, 1988.

Sun, Gordon. "Evaluating the 'Red Supply Chain.'" Taiwan Institute of Economic Research. 2015. Accessed December 15, 2020. http://english.tier.org.tw/V35/eng _analysis/pec3010.aspx?GUID=4f51831c-f5a2-4865-8c74-5a367e31ad79.

Tang Shui-yan. "Informal Credit Markets and Economic Development in Taiwan." *World Development* 23, no. 5 (1995): 845–855.

Tanner, Murray Scot. *Chinese Economic Coercion against Taiwan: A Tricky Weapon to Use*. Santa Monica, CA: RAND National Defense Research Institute, 2007.

Tian, John Q. *Government, Business, and the Politics of Interdependence and Conflict across the Taiwan Strait*. New York: Palgrave-Macmillan, 2006.

"Tourism Statistics." Ministry of Transportation and Communications, Tourism Bureau. Accessed November 25, 2020. https://admin.taiwan.net.tw/English /FileUploadCategoryListE003130.aspx?CategoryID=b54db814-c958-4618-9392 -03a00f709e7a&appname=FileUploadCategoryListE003130.

Tsai Chung-min. "The Nature and Trend of Taiwanese Investment in China (1991–2014): Business Orientation, Profit Seeking, and Depoliticization." In *Taiwan and China: Fitful Embrace*, edited by Lowell Dittmer. Berkeley: University of California Press, 2017.

Wang, Jenn-hwan, and Sheng-wen Tseng. "Managing Cross-Border Innovation Networks: Taiwan's IC Design Industry." In *Border Crossing in Greater China: Production, Community and Identity*, edited by Jenn-hwan Wang. London: Routledge, 2015.

Weller, Robert P. "Cosmologies in the Remaking: Variation and Time in Chinese Temple Religion." In *It Happens among People: Resonances and Extensions of the Work of Fredrik Barth*, edited by Keping Wu and Robert Weller. New York: Berghahn Books, 2019.

World Integrated Trade Solutions. "China 1994 Import Partner Share." World
Bank. https://wits.worldbank.org/CountryProfile/en/Country/CHN/Year/1994
/TradeFlow/Import/Partner/ALL/Product/manuf.

Wu, Debby. "China's Days as World's Factory Are Over, iPhone Maker Says."
Bloomberg. August 12, 2020. https://www.bloomberg.com/news
/articles/2020-08-12/hon-hai-beats-profit-estimates-after-pandemic-spurs
-apple-demand.

Wu Rwei-ren. "Fragment Of/f Empires: The Peripheral Formation of Taiwanese
Nationalism." *Social Science Japan*, no. 30 (December 2004): 16–18.

Yamashita Kazunari. "Taiwan IT Sector Battles Threat of 'Red Supply Chain.'"
Nikkei Asian Review. March 15, 2016. Accessed November 25, 2020. https://
asia.nikkei.com/Business/Taiwan-IT-sector-battles-threat-of-red-supply-chain.

Yang, Sophia. "China's Pro-Unification 31 Measures for Taiwan Have Failed:
Academia Sinica Scholar." *Taiwan News*. January 26, 2019. Accessed November
19, 2020. https://www.taiwannews.com.tw/en/news/3625988.

Yu Ying Lee. "Zhangban Xinniang: dangdai Taiwan hunshaye de xingqi yu fazhan
lishi" [Dressing up the bride: The historical rise and development of Taiwan's
bridal industry]. *Feng Chia Journal of Humanities and Social Sciences*, no. 8
(2004): 183–217.

Zhang, J. J. "Paying Homage to the 'Heavenly Mother': Cultural-Geopolitics of the
Mazu Pilgrimage and Its Implications on Rapprochement between China and
Taiwan." *Geoforum* 84 (2017).

Index

Made in the USA
Las Vegas, NV
05 October 2021